Globalization of Corporate R&D

In recent years, transnational corporations have begun to develop strategic research and development capabilities in developing countries in order to gain access to foreign science and technology resources as well as to benefit from cheaper wage and production costs. In this innovative study, Prasada Reddy addresses several fundamental questions:

- What are the driving forces behind this phenomenon?
- Why are these new trends mainly visible among companies dealing with new science-based technologies, such as electronics or new materials?
- What are the implications of this trend for 'host' countries?

The book presents important new research material, in the form of detailed case studies of India and Singapore, and offers an evolutionary theoretical basis for comprehending the processes at work. As a result, the book illuminates our understanding of both the behaviour of transnational corporations, and the broader processes of globalization.

Globalization of Corporate R&D will be of essential interest to those working in the fields of development studies, economics or international business.

Prasada Reddy is a faculty member at the Research Policy Institute, Lund University, Sweden, and has worked as a consultant to the UN. He has written widely on the issues of industrialization, foreign direct investment and technology transfer, and is currently working in the area of trade-related intellectual property rights.

Routledge Studies in International Business and the World Economy

Globalization of Corporate R&D

Implications for innovation systems
in host countries

Prasada Reddy

London and New York

First published 2000
by Routledge
11 New Fetter Lane, London EC4P 4EE

Simultaneously published in the USA and Canada
by Routledge
29 West 35th Street, New York, NY 10001

Routledge is an imprint of the Taylor & Francis Group

© 2000 Prasada Reddy

Typeset in Garamond by
Keystroke, Jacaranda Lodge, Wolverhampton
Printed and bound in Great Britain by
TJ International Ltd, Padstow, Cornwall

British Library Cataloguing in Publication Data
A catalogue record for this book is available from the British Library

Library of Congress Cataloging in Publication Data
Reddy, Prasada.
    Globalization of corporate R&D : implications for innovation systems in host
    countries / Prasada Reddy.
        p.   cm.
    Includes bibliographical references and index.
    1. International business enterprises—Developing countries. 2. Research,
    Industrial—Developing countries. 3. Competition, International. I. Title.

    HD2755.5 .R415 2000
    338'.064—dc21

                                                                    00–020720

ISBN 0–415–20435–6

For my parents
Chengal Reddy and Kamalamma

Contents

Figures

Tables

Preface

In the early 1990s I started working at the Research Policy Institute, Lund University, Sweden, where research work on internationalization of R&D was being led by Professor Jon Sigurdson. At about the same time, research on the globalization of corporate R&D started picking up momentum world-wide. I was soon bitten by the bug and a look at the literature showed that the main focus was on happenings within the industrialized world, while the developing countries were being regarded as totally marginalized. Having worked in India in the 1980s, I was well aware that a couple of transnational corporations (TNCs) had already located their strategic R&D units in India. This made me curious as to whether the location of such units in a developing country was an offshoot of the globalization of R&D. Questions that aroused my interest were: What were the driving forces? What type of technologies were being developed? What were the implications for the host country? A survey of the existing literature did not help much as there were few studies dealing specifically with these issues.

My research started with case studies of the TNCs' R&D units in India, and based on the results, a questionnaire survey was duly designed and administered. The results showed that TNCs that located strategic R&D in India were mainly in the new science-based technologies.

To validate my hypothesis that globalization of corporate R&D was evolving further to encompass more geographical areas outside the industrialized world, it was necessary for me to develop a database of TNCs' R&D activities in developing Asia and transition economies. Based on the research work over the years, I have developed an evolutionary framework of the globalization of corporate R&D dating back roughly to the 1960s. The phenomenon has been analysed in terms of waves and the driving forces in each of these waves, the type of R&D located abroad in each wave and the potential implications for the host country have been identified.

This book may well be deemed an extensive study of the globalization of R&D, but more emphasis has certainly been laid on the emerging patterns. I hope readers will find the book useful and interesting.

Acknowledgements

In carrying out this research, several individuals, institutions and companies have helped me immensely over the years. Acknowledging all individually would be impractical. I would therefore like to thank the people who have guided me in my research as well as those who have offered suggestions and comments on my earlier papers. The people with whom I have had the privilege of continuously interacting with include: Claes Brundenius, Andrew Jamison, Anders Granberg, Christer Gunnarsson, Bo Göransson, Jon Sigurdson, Arni Sverrisson and Rikard Stankiewicz.

The financial support received from the Swedish International Development Agency (SIDA/SAREC) and the Swedish Council for Planning and Co-ordination of Research (FRN) is gratefully acknowledged.

I would also like to thank Anna Alwerud and Catta Torhell for library support, Birgitta Dahl and Ulla Kockum for administrative support and Anders Lundström for secretarial assistance. A special debt of gratitude to Petter Ek and Jaya Reddy for their unstinting moral support.

I owe special thanks to the publishers Elsevier Science and Quorum Books, Greenwood Publishing Group Inc. who have kindly given permission to use copyright material.

Needless to say, all the usual disclaimers apply.

Abbreviations

ACP	AT&T Consumer Products Pte. Ltd.
ARCI	Astra Research Centre India
ASIC	application specific integrated circuits
BEPC	Beijing Electron Positron Collider
CAD	computer-aided design
CAM	computer-aided manufacturing
CAS	Chinese Academy of Sciences
CASE	computer-aided software engineering
CATI	co-operative agreements and technology indicators
C-DAC	Centre for Development of Advanced Computing
C-DOT	Centre for Development of Telematics
CEC	Commission of the European Communities
CII	current impact index
CMC	Computer Maintenance Corporation
CMM	capability maturity model
CSIR	Council for Scientific and Industrial Research
CTU	corporate technology unit
DBRCI	Daimler-Benz Research Centre India
DC	development centre
DCMDP	Delhi Cloth Merchants Data Processing
DRAMS	dynamic random access memories
DSIR	Department of Scientific and Industrial Research
DSP	digital signal processor
DST	Department of Science and Technology
EAE	emerging Asian economies
EDA	electronic design automation
EDB	Economic Development Board
FDI	foreign direct investment
FSL	Fujitsu Singapore Pte. Ltd.
GATT	General Agreement on Tariffs and Trade
GERD	gross expenditure on research and development
GENI	Gene India
GNP	gross national product

GTU	global technology unit
HCL	Hindustan Computers Ltd.
HKITC	Hong Kong Industrial Technology Centre
HKUST	Hong Kong University of Science and Technology
HP	Hewlett Packard
HSS	Hughes Software Systems
IC	integrated circuit
ICT	information and communication technologies
IDRC	International Development Research Centre
IIL	internationally interdependent laboratory
IISc	Indian Institute of Science
IIT	Indian Institute of Technology
IMCB	Institute of Molecular and Cell Biology
IME	Institute of Microelectronics
IPR	intellectual property right
IRI	Industrial Research Institute
ISDN	integrated services digital network
IT	information technology
ITRI	Industrial Technology Research Institute
ITSA	information technology strategic alliances
ITU	indigenous technology unit
KIST	Korean Institute of Science and Technology
KOSEF	Korean Science and Engineering Foundation
LAN	local area network
LIL	locally integrated laboratory
MERIT	Maastricht Economic Research Institute on Innovation and Technology
MIT	Massachusetts Institute of Technology
MITI	Ministry of International Trade and Industry
MNC	multinational corporation
MNE	multinational enterprise
MOST	Ministry of Science and Technology
NCL	National Chemical Laboratories
NEERI	National Environmental Engineering Research Institute
NIEs	newly industrializing economies
NIMHANS	National Institute of Mental Health and Neurosciences
NRDC	National Research and Development Corporation
NSB	National Science Board
NSF	National Science Foundation
NSFC	National Science Foundation of China
NSTB	National Science and Technology Board
NTP	National Technology Plan
OECD	Organisation for Economic Co-operation and Development
OEM	original equipment manufacturing
ORG	operations research group

R&D	Research and Development
REC	Regional Engineering College
RISC	reduced instruction set chip
RPI	Research Policy Institute
RSE	research scientists and engineers
RTU	regional technology unit
S&T	science and technology
SCI	science citation index
SEI	Software Engineering Institute
SL	support laboratory
SMEs	small and medium-sized enterprises
SONIS	Sony International (Singapore) Ltd.
SSEC	Sony Semiconductor Engineering Centre
TCS	Tata Consultancy Services
TDICI	Technology Development and Information Corporation of India
TFP	total factor productivity
TI	Texas Instruments Inc.
TIFR	Tata Institute of Fundamental Research
TNC	transnational corporation
TRIPs	trade-related intellectual property rights
TTU	technology transfer unit
UNCTAD	United Nations Conference on Trade and Development
UNDP	United Nations Development Programme
UNESCO	United Nations Educational, Social and Cultural Organisation
UNIDO	United Nations Industrial Development Organisation
VLSI	very large-scale integration
WAN	wide area network
WHO	World Health Organisation
WITL	Wipro Information Technologies Ltd.
WTO	World Trade Organisation

Introduction

Internationalization of corporate technology development activities is not as recent a phenomenon as it is thought to be. Since the 1960s, companies have been performing some sort of research and development (R&D) activities outside their home countries for one reason or the other. In a study, Cantwell (1998) found that even as early as in the 1930s, the largest European and American companies performed about 7 per cent of their total R&D outside their home countries. But, the magnitude, nature and scope of the overseas R&D performed in the past were limited. Much of such R&D was undertaken either to facilitate technology transfer by adapting the parent's technology to local operating conditions or to gain a greater share of the local markets by developing products that met the preferences of the local customers better.

In the 1990s, globalization of corporate R&D has attracted greater attention from economists and policy-makers mainly due to its changing characteristic features and its potential implications. The performance of overseas R&D by transnational corporations (TNCs) has not only increased substantially in quantitative terms, but the nature of such R&D has also undergone significant qualitative change. The scope of work in overseas R&D units of TNCs has gone beyond adaptation tasks to encompass innovation activities to develop products for the global markets or even performance of basic research to develop generic technologies.

Several studies have shown the increasing trend of globalization of corporate R&D. Among them, Zander's (1994) study showed that in 1980, 30 per cent of all technological activity of a sample of Swedish TNCs was carried out abroad. By 1990, this figure had gone up to 40 per cent. Kuemmerle's (1999) analysis of thirty-two TNCs showed that in 1965, these TNCs carried out 6.2 per cent of their R&D outside their home countries, whereas in 1995, this figure had risen to 25.8 per cent.

However, there are wide differences in the degree of globalization of corporate R&D between different industry groups. The pharmaceutical industry, followed by industries such as food and beverages, machinery and transportation equipment manufacturing show higher levels of internationalization of R&D (Niosi, 1999). For instance, in the case of Japanese TNCs, most of their R&D units abroad are in the electronic equipment, pharmaceutical and automotive industries (Odagiri and Yasuda, 1996). In general, it is observed that technology-intensive industries, such as electronics, biotechnology, chemicals and pharmaceuticals tend to internationalize their strategic R&D to a greater degree than other industries.

The significant increase in the overseas R&D activities of TNCs in recent years can be mainly attributed to the changes in TNCs' strategies to attain global competitiveness. According to Pearce (1999), the new strategic approach involves recasting of the roles of individual affiliates and their intra-group interdependencies. In the traditional approach, the scope of R&D performed by an affiliate had to fit within the framework of a bilateral relationship between the parent and the individual affiliate. However, the new approach involves the performance of distinctive operations in the framework of an interdependent network of mutually supportive facilities. 'Overseas R&D units now provide much more than an outlet for the effective application of centrally-created product technology. Instead they play increasingly powerful roles in the creative process themselves' (ibid., p. 160).

Over the years, various methods of exploiting internationally dispersed innovation activities have been evolving. Bartlett and Ghoshal (1991) suggested four different types of management structures:

1   Centre-for-global – developing new products and processes in the home country for the global markets;
2   Local-for-local – developing products and processes independently in each of the R&D units abroad for use in the local market of the affiliate;
3   Locally linked – developing novel products and processes in each location for global exploitation;
4   Globally linked – developing novelty through the collaboration of R&D units located in different countries for exploitation in the global markets.

Each type has specific advantages and disadvantages, but all the four types could be adopted at the same time for different projects within the same TNC.

Håkanson (1990) suggests that the organizational structure of TNCs for international R&D has undergone three evolutionary stages: the centralized hub, the decentralized federation and the integrated network. Now an emerging evolutionary framework considers the 'organizational learning' by TNCs as the core explanation for globalization of R&D. This is reflected in the TNCs locating their R&D units abroad closer to major centres of innovation, where reputable universities, public laboratories and R&D units of competitors exist. Learning takes place through closer interaction with major customers, suppliers and knowledge producers, such as universities (Niosi, 1999).

In the 1970s, the product life cycle model provided the basis for analysing the foreign direct investment (FDI). Based on this model, TNCs were viewed as developing new technologies at home and later transferring them to their affiliates abroad after the technologies reached the maturity phase. R&D was seen as having a certain 'stickiness', such as the need for closer co-ordination between R&D and other functions of the firm, and the scale intensity of R&D, binding it to the home countries. This model envisaged a centralized R&D structure, with one or more central laboratories in the home country and several miniature laboratories abroad in order to undertake adaptation of a parent's technology to the local conditions. However, later several empirical studies showed the product life cycle model to be inadequate to explain the internationalization process. TNCs have diffused new technologies abroad faster than the time frame suggested by the model. There were also several differences between the approaches of TNCs based in different industrialized countries. TNCs based in smaller countries, such as Sweden, Switzerland and The Netherlands, had internationalized a higher share of their R&D than the TNCs based in large countries. Sectoral differences have also emerged, with high-technology industries showing a greater propensity to globalize their R&D than the medium- and low-technology industries (Niosi, 1999).

The growing trend of international technological alliances is another important element in the globalization of R&D. The traditional approach, using transaction costs as the basis, considered that the TNCs tend to develop technology in-house and internalize within their corporate networks by transferring technology to their own affiliates rather than selling it to other companies. However, since the late 1980s, TNCs have been entering into technological alliances with foreign companies and research institutes in an effort to develop new technologies and products. This new strategy runs contrary to the strategy of internalization. In the evolutionary approach, such alliances are viewed as evolving strategies of the TNCs, designed to successfully compete in a turbulent business environment (Niosi, 1995).

According to Pearce (1999, p. 157) the growing importance of overseas R&D units in TNCs' strategies reflects:

> i) an increasing involvement in product development rather than adaptation, ii) an interdependent rather than dependent position in group technology programmes, iii) increased relevance of supply side influences (host country technology competencies, capacities and heritage), iv) decline of centralising forces on R&D (e.g. economies of scale, communication and co-ordination problems, concerns of knowledge security).

The scope and level of technological activities carried out abroad by TNCs are determined by the national capabilities of both home and host countries. Cantwell and Janne (1999) propose that when TNCs based in countries with more advanced technological capabilities in a given industry relocate to less advanced countries in the same industry, they tend to differentiate their technological activities. On the other hand, when TNCs based in less advanced countries relocate R&D abroad, they tend to specialize within the same areas of the parent company at home. They also suggest that the TNCs located in leading centres in a particular industry tend to build up specialization on the basis of the local technological capabilities in host countries. At the same time,

TNCs located in less advanced centres tend to draw more on their home-based capabilities, by replicating their home specialization abroad.

The globalization of corporate R&D has been mainly limited to location of R&D units within the industrialized countries, where much of the R&D is concentrated. However, globalization of corporate R&D continues to evolve as a phenomenon. In recent years, the globalization processes have been encompassing more industrial sectors, as well as more geographical areas. Hitherto uncommon locations are attracting R&D-related foreign direct investments by TNCs.

Since the mid-1980s, as an offshoot of the globalization of corporate R&D, TNCs have started performing some of their strategic R&D in some developing countries. TNCs involved in this new trend seem to be mostly those dealing with new technologies. This strategic move by TNCs is facilitated by the availability of large pools of scientifically and technically trained manpower, at substantially lower wages compared to their counterparts in industrialized countries, and an adequate infrastructure. This trend shows signs of emerging as a phenomenon similar to that of the establishment of off-shore production facilities in low-cost countries. However, this does not imply that a substantial proportion of corporate R&D is being relocated to developing countries. More than 90 per cent of the world's industrial R&D is still being carried out within the industrialized world.

The primary driving forces behind the new trends are:

1 technology-related, i.e. to gain access to foreign science and technology (S&T) resources;
2 cost-related, i.e. to exploit the cost differentials between different countries;
3 organization-related, i.e. rationalization of TNCs' internal operations, where an affiliate in a developing country is assigned a regional or a global product mandate.

The performance of strategic R&D, aimed at developing products for global/ regional markets or mission-oriented basic research by TNCs, has implications for the innovation capabilities in developing host countries.

Almost all the research carried out so far on globalization of corporate strategic R&D relates to happenings within the industrialized world. Based on new data, this study focuses on the aspects of integration of some developing countries into the phenomenon of globalization of corporate R&D. In that sense, this study adds to the current knowledge and contributes to a better understanding of the globalization process.

The aim of this study is to better understand the dynamics of the globalization process. The study develops a conceptual framework of the evolution of globalization of corporate R&D. The study also addresses the following issues: (1) R&D-related investments in developing countries by TNCs; (2) the driving forces behind the emerging phenomenon; and (3) its implications for the developing host countries, particularly for building up national innovation capability. While the study is carried out in a broader framework of developing countries in general, for in-depth analysis of the factors under-lying the phenomenon the study focuses on two host countries, India and Singapore.

Structure of the book

This book is organized into 8 chapters. Chapter 1 discusses the developments in global business environment to analyse the general background in which globalization of corporate R&D is taking place. The chapter also discusses the general conditions under which the new trends in globalization of corporate R&D are emerging, i.e. the context in which globalization of R&D has come to extend its scope to developing countries.

Chapter 2 seeks theoretical explanations to the background developments described in the Introduction. In the first part of the chapter, the theories of internationalization of production are reviewed to better understand the globalization phenomenon in a broader perspective and analyse the links between internationalization of production and R&D activities. In the second part, studies relating to the internationalization of R&D are discussed in a historical perspective to bring out the changes in the driving forces over a period of time. The review also includes an analysis relating to the emergence of a new techno-economic paradigm and opportunities for latecomers to catch up, since the majority of the companies carrying out higher-order R&D seems to be those dealing with new technologies. An analytical framework developed for better understanding of the evolutionary process of globalization of corporate R&D is set out in the last part.

Chapter 3 provides an analysis of the science and technology environment in selected developing host countries that facilitates the performance of higher-order R&D by TNCs. The first section presents a macro-level picture of developing countries in general and a comparative analysis of the S&T potential in selected developing countries. The second section offers a detailed analysis of the national systems of innovation in the case study country, India. The aim of this chapter is to highlight the aspects of the S&T environment in developing countries that have the potential to support performance of higher-order R&D, especially since previous studies describe the environment in developing countries as suitable only for low-tech activities.

Chapter 4 offers some empirical evidence of international corporate R&D activities in developing countries. With the help of a database developed at the Research Policy Institute, Lund University, by the author, an analysis of TNCs' R&D activities in developing Asian countries is presented. This chapter also includes some company-specific illustrations of higher-order R&D activities in some developing countries.

Chapter 5 presents the TNCs' R&D activities in India, through three in-depth case studies and a questionnaire survey. The survey brings out the differences in R&D in conventional and new technologies.

Chapter 6 presents TNCs' R&D activities in Singapore, through four in-depth case studies. These case studies carried out in India and Singapore help in analysing the driving forces and the global and local links established by these R&D units. Chapter 7 analyses the implications for innovation capability in the host countries and draws policy implications, while Chapter 8 presents the conclusions of the study.

1 The global business environment

The globalization of corporate R&D is taking place in a rapidly changing business environment. Some of these changes are external to the companies, but directly affect their internal operations, which in turn adds to the volatility of the business environment. This dynamic background is analysed under four sub-headings: global competition; corporate technology development strategies; rationalization of global corporate structures; and corporate R&D and the developing world.

Global competition

Since the 1980s, global competition, in several industries, has been intensifying rapidly, mounting pressure on the profitability and survival of the companies. The characteristic features of the historical pattern of internationalization have been considerably affected during this period, mainly due to two factors: the deregulation and thereby globalization of financial markets; and the emergence of new technologies which enabled as well as compelled moves towards increased globalization (OECD, 1992, p. 209).

This globalization process has brought about several changes in trade, investments and technologies. Historically trade has created economic ties between countries. However, today a substantial amount of cross-border trade takes place between the affiliates of the same firm (intra-firm) and between firms (inter-firm). This pattern of trade is integrating the industries in new ways at the global level. The pattern of direct and portfolio investments abroad is contributing to the spread of locations, assets and ownership of firms among nations. The link between financial centres in different countries is enabling private savings and corporate profits to be pooled globally and borrowers and lenders to be linked internationally (Brainard, 1990, p. 2).

As the OECD (1992) observes, the emergence of new technology, which is acting both as an enabling factor and at the same time a driving force towards further globalization, lies at the root of this process:

> As a result of telematics, substantial changes have taken place in the economics of location, both within countries and, increasingly, across

national boundaries. The convergence of computer, communication and control technology has opened up vast new opportunities for MNEs [multinational enterprises] to deploy resources and operations on a truly world-wide scale. It has now become technically feasible for MNEs, banks, industrial and service firms to install intra-corporate world-wide information networks, through which headquarters' management can link together production and marketing facilities around the world. Firms can adopt network forms, building a wide variety of inter-firm alliances and linkages and developing corporate strategies involving new kinds of interactions with suppliers, customers and competitors.

(OECD, 1992, p. 211)

In addition to the above two factors, as noted by Porter (1980, pp. 294–8; 1986a, pp. 2–3) the following broad forces are leading to growing international competition and widespread globalization of industry scope:

- *Growing similarity of countries.* Countries are becoming similar in terms of availability of infrastructure, distribution channels and marketing approaches. Similar products and brands are being marketed world-wide, reflecting the convergence of customer needs in different countries. The economic differences among developed countries and some advanced developing countries (such as the newly industrializing economies – NIEs) are narrowing in areas like income, factor costs, energy costs, etc. Part of the reason for this development is the aggressiveness of TNCs in diffusing technologies around the world.
- *Falling trade barriers.* Successive rounds of international agreements, resulting in the establishment of the World Trade Organisation, led to the lowering of tariff levels and other trade barriers. Regional economic groupings such as the European Union, North American Free Trade Area and Association of South East Asian Nations are also facilitating trade and other relations among different countries.
- *Emergence of new large-scale markets.* Traditionally the USA has been the strategic market for global competition because of its large size. However, with the liberalization of economies in countries such as China, India and Russia, they are emerging as huge markets with a number of implications. If these countries control access to their markets, their domestic firms may become major global players. Therefore, gaining access to these markets may become a crucial strategic factor in the future because of the scale economies it provides to the successful firm.
- *Technological restructuring.* Several industries have been significantly affected by some technological revolutions, such as microelectronics, information systems and advanced new materials that are reshaping competition. These technological developments are redefining industry structures and opening up unprecedented opportunities for shifts in industry leadership in international markets.

- *Emergence of new global competitors.* The forces leading to dramatic shifts in international competitive positions have resulted in some new firms, mainly from East Asia, establishing themselves as fully-fledged international competitors within the space of a decade. These new players have exploited the new competitive conditions and the cross-cutting technological changes to leapfrog even well established rivals. The intensity of competition has also risen, setting higher standards for success.

Corporate technology development strategies

TNCs, traditionally, tended to confine technology development activities to their home countries. The companies were expected to derive competitive advantage, especially technological knowledge, from their distinctive domestic environment, leading to exploitation of this advantage abroad (Hymer, 1976; Vernon, 1966). According to Terpstra (1977), technology development activities are kept close to home-base, not only for security reasons, but also because of economies of scale, better communication and co-ordination, 'and because intensive centralised R&D backs up profitable home country innovations' (ibid., p. 26).

However, the changing pattern of global competition, coupled with rapid technological changes leading to the shortening of product life cycles, placed innovation as a key source of competitive strength. Companies are adopting a variety of strategies to attain this technological edge and thus maintain their competitiveness. As a result, TNCs are increasingly transcending national boundaries, not just in marketing and production activities, but also in R&D activities. R&D, the cornerstone of technological and thereby the competitive strength of companies as well as nations, is becoming an international activity.

Terpstra (1977) gives several reasons for the increased internationalization of R&D. They are: to transfer technology from headquarters to subsidiaries abroad; in response to host country pressures; to encourage localization of development of technologies; to improve public relations; to access foreign talent and engineering resources; to reduce development costs by utilizing cheaper engineering resources abroad; to take advantage of local ideas and products; to speed up development through parallel efforts by several laboratories simultaneously; in response to greater sensitivity to the market; continuation of R&D facilities after acquisition of a company abroad; and to take advantage of some tax laws (ibid., pp. 24–32).

Technological and socio-economic developments over the last couple of decades are leading to a more unified market, in which consumer needs can be largely met through standardized products, e.g. watches, cameras, etc. This requires capturing global-scale economies to remain competitive (Levitt, 1983). However, at the same time, a growing segment of consumers in some markets are demanding differentiated products that meet their unique preferences.[1] The success of companies such as Amstrad of UK, that began by responding to such local demand, underlines the significance of such a trend (Bartlett and

Ghoshal, 1991, p. 27). These developments brought innovation into the domain
of global strategies.

> R&D must play its role in product development for worldwide markets,
> which requires that R&D function have an unusual knowledge of technical
> issues and buyer needs globally. Similarly, process R&D is often crucial
> in global industries to facilitate the development of global-scale economies
> and learning to achieve consistent quality. Not only must R&D develop
> new products and processes, but new process technology must often be
> transferred to facilities around the world that operate under different
> economic and cultural circumstances.
>
> (Porter, 1986a, p. 52)

The convergence of consumer preferences world-wide and the international
diffusion of technology have influenced the location of R&D. Companies can
no longer depend only on their domestic environment to provide them with
advanced technological capabilities and innovative environment. Today, new
needs or trends can arise in any advanced market and the latest technologies
may be located in some other country. TNCs attempt to gain competitive
advantage by sensing needs in one country, responding with capabilities located
in a second, and diffusing the resulting innovation to markets around the globe
(Bartlett and Ghoshal, 1991, p. 12).

The conventional concept of comparative advantage is viewed as arising from
differences in factor cost or quality among countries, leading to production in
locations with advantages in a specific industry and exporting the product to
other countries. Hence, the comparative advantage is expected to be derived
from the location where the firms perform their activities. TNCs can and do
attempt to locate activities wherever the comparative advantage lies. Moreover,
unlike the conventional views that confine comparative advantage issues
to production activities, the concept applies also to other activities in the value
chain, such as R&D, distribution and advertising. Comparative advantage
becomes specific to the activity and not the location of the entire value chain.
The manufacture of components may be located in Taiwan, software development may be located in India and basic R&D may be performed in the USA.
Such intra-firm international specialization and arbitrage of activities are made
possible by the growing ability to co-ordinate and configure globally (Porter,
1986a, pp. 37–8).

The technology dimension to global competition raises the complex issue
of location of R&D functions. The literature suggests that, in general, R&D
is located in proximity to large or potentially large markets, and advanced
markets with a leading edge of industry development.[2] TNCs have the option
of locating technology development activities in countries that offer better
comparative advantages. Increasingly, the best location for R&D is not necessarily the USA or the European countries. Moreover, the ideal location may
differ for sub-tasks within the R&D function and for different products in the

range. For instance, Xerox located R&D on small copiers in Japan, on medium-volume copiers in Europe and on high-volume copiers in USA. Apart from reflecting Xerox's global network of partners, such an allocation also suggests that each of these locations is the most advanced market for the respective type of copiers (Porter, 1986a, p. 51).

In a parallel development, the R&D activities in new technologies are increasingly becoming science-based. In the generation of new technologies there is now a greater need for inputs from different disciplines of science and technology. This requirement for innovation is compelling firms to source technologies, not only by geographically dispersing in-house R&D world-wide, but also externally from universities and other firms, both at home and abroad. As a consequence of the dynamic global business environment, involving increased competitive pressures and increasing the science base of new technologies, global sourcing of innovations has become a necessity in recent decades.[3]

According to Cantwell (1992, p. 77), TNCs adopt internationally integrated approach to technology development for two reasons: (1) to take advantage of the distinct features of innovations in different national innovation systems and thus gain access to complementary technologies; (2) to gain access to new lines of innovation. The blurring of boundaries between different disciplines is compelling firms to access a broader technology base through an international strategy.

Rationalization of global corporate structures

> [T]he modern corporation is mainly to be understood as the product of a series of organizational innovations that have had the purpose and effect of economizing on transaction costs.
>
> (Williamson, 1981, p. 1537)

In the face of changing currents in the global competition, companies have been rationalizing their activities, including those of production and R&D activities. Prominent among such rationalization efforts has been the alteration of the earlier multi-domestic approach, in which TNCs established subsidiaries that were more or less replicas of the parent but on a much smaller scale. These subsidiaries produced products mainly for the local markets in their respective host countries. Such subsidiaries mainly depended on the parent company for their technology requirements, which were in turn adapted to suit the local conditions (Porter, 1986a). These subsidiaries produced most, if not all, of the product range of the parent. However, subsidiaries, being small in size, often had difficulties in reaching the optimal scale of production (Pearce, 1989).

According to Porter (1986a, pp. 17–19), the pattern of global competition is different for different industries. In their competitive scope industries fall into a spectrum from multi-domestic to global. In multi-domestic industries, the competition occurs on a country-by-country basis. A TNC makes a one-time transfer of know-how, which is adapted to the local conditions. The competitive advantages of the firm then become largely specific to the conditions in the country. The multi-domestic industry is basically a collection of domestic industries. Industries in which this pattern of competition is prevalent include retailing, consumer packaged goods, distribution, insurance, consumer finance and caustic chemicals. In global industry, on the other hand, a company's competitive position in one country is significantly affected by its position in other countries or vice versa. The global industry is a series of linked domestic industries in which the rivals compete with each other on a world-wide basis. This type of competition is seen in industries that include commercial aircraft, TV sets, semiconductors, copiers, automobiles and watches. In multi-domestic industry, a company manages its international activities like a portfolio, because its strategy in a country is largely determined by the competitive conditions in that country. Therefore, each subsidiary is allowed substantial autonomy and control of all the important activities needed to do business in that industry. In global industry, a company must find ways to integrate its activities on a world-wide basis to capture the links among countries. In global competition a company has to perform some activities in each of the countries in which it competes.

Companies are increasingly moving away from the multi-domestic approach towards a new approach in which each subsidiary forms an integral part of the global strategy, where subsidiaries are assigned specialized tasks in the activities planned and organized from the centre (Porter, 1986a, 1986b).

Bartlett and Ghoshal (1991, pp. 48–53) also have similar categorization of TNCs' organizational approaches: multinational organization; international organization; and global organization. Companies are rapidly moving from all these approaches towards what they call a 'transnational' approach. The comparative organizational characteristics of these different approaches are given in Table 1.1

In a transnational approach the strength of the configuration comes from its fundamental characteristics: dispersion, specialization and interdependence. The ability to sense diverse market needs, technological trends and competitive actions remains crucial, however, because such stimuli represent an important source of innovation. A dispersed configuration allows TNCs to capitalize on factor cost differentials. They not only have access to low-cost labour and materials, but can tap into an international pool of increasingly scarce technological and managerial resources. By specializing operations and giving them a broader mandate, TNCs can capture minimum-scale efficiencies and yet retain a dispersed structure. The viability of this approach has been greatly enhanced by the latest generation of manufacturing technologies. In the past, specialization and dedicated assets tended to create a rigidity that was particularly risky in an environment of shortening product life cycles and rapid changes in costs, technologies and tastes. By using flexible manufacturing technologies, however, specialized operations can overcome the scale rigidities (Bartlett and Ghoshal, 1991).

Table 1.1 Organizational characteristics of different approaches

Organizational characteristics	Multinational	Global	International	Transnational
Configuration of assets and capabilities	Decentralized and nationally self-sufficient	Centralized and globally scaled	Sources of core competencies centralized, others decentralized	Dispersed, interdependent, and specialized
Role of overseas operations	Sensing and exploiting local opportunities	Implementing parent company strategies	Adapting and leveraging parent company competencies	Differentiated contributions by national units to integrated world-wide operations
Development and diffusion of knowledge	Knowledge developed and retained within each unit	Knowledge developed and retained at the centre	Knowledge developed at the centre and transferred to overseas units	Knowledge developed jointly and shared world-wide

Source: Bartlett and Ghoshal (1991, p. 65)

One version of a rationalized structure of a TNC is what Pearce (1989, pp. 119–21) calls 'rationalized product subsidiary'. In this type of structure, an individual subsidiary is assigned the task of producing only a part of the parent's product line, which perhaps is not even relevant to the host country's domestic market. Such output is mainly meant for export markets, while part of the local demand not catered to by the subsidiary's production will be met through imports from the company's global network. Such specialization allows achievement of a greater level of efficiency and optimal scale economies. A common form of such a rationalized structure involves subsidiaries specializing in the production of specific components or parts for final products or executing a specific stage in a vertically integrated production process. R&D in rationalized product subsidiaries relates to the range of specialized products produced by the subsidiary. Such R&D being part of the global strategy, the results will be shared with the other partners in the network through the centralized facility and thus contribute to the development of new products. A good example of a rationalized product subsidiary is Hewlett Packard's affiliate in Penang, Malaysia, which has become a global centre for many components used in the company's microwave products and is now being assigned the responsibility for computer hard-disk drives on transfer from Palo Alto, USA (*Business Week*, 19 December 1994, p. 45).

Another form of subsidiary that is emerging is what is termed 'world product mandate subsidiary' (Poynter and Rugman 1982; Bonin and Perron, 1986). In this form, the parent assigns exclusively to a subsidiary the entire responsibility for R&D and production activities for a particular product to be marketed world-wide, either by the affiliate itself or with the help of the parent's global network. In other words, the subsidiary becomes the international centre for that product. R&D performed by such a subsidiary, supporting the evolution of its product line, will be of a higher order. In its product development activities, the subsidiary may also draw from the basic research of the group (Pearce, 1989). A good example of such an affiliate is Hewlett Packard's plant in Singapore which was opened in 1970 originally to assemble keyboards, but has now become the global R&D and production centre for the company's line of portable ink-jet printers. It is also the centre for all handheld devices of the company such as personal digital assistants and calculators (*Business Week*, 19 December 1994, p. 45).

Corporate R&D and the developing world

Until the mid-1980s, the globalization of corporate R&D was confined to the industrialized world. In the few cases where some R&D activities were performed outside the industrialized countries, they were limited to adaptation, local technical services or in a very few cases to product development for the local market. However, in recent years, globalization of R&D has come to include efforts to exploit cost differentials. Since the mid-1980s, TNCs have started locating some of their strategic R&D in some developing countries. R&D activities being carried out in these countries relate not only to products required for the local markets, but also to those of strategic importance to the company's world-wide operations. This move by TNCs is facilitated by the availability of large cadres of research personnel at substantially lower wages and adequate infrastructure in these countries (Reddy, 1993). The total costs of carrying out R&D in countries like India, with researchers having qualifications corresponding to those of their counterparts in Western countries, are estimated to be only one-tenth of the costs in Western countries (Granstrand *et al.*, 1992, p. 10). Hence, this trend shows signs of emerging as a phenomenon similar to that of the establishment of off-shore production facilities in low-cost countries.

Apart from the high cost factor, there has also been a shortage of R&D personnel in industrialized countries. For instance, two Swedish companies, ASEA and Ericsson,[4] alone would require 150 per cent of all electronics engineering graduates in Sweden. The problems are similar in other emerging areas such as biotechnology (Håkanson, 1990, p. 261). Such shortages are also common in the rest of Europe, the USA, and Japan (OECD, 1988, p. 36). On the other hand, in some developing countries such talents have been lying dormant due to under-utilization by the indigenous industry. In most of these countries either industrialization did not take place at a corresponding level, or the existing industry, because of its low emphasis on R&D, has not been able to fully utilize the available trained manpower. For instance, the availability of specialized biotechnology researchers is many times greater in India, with its conglomeration of knowledge activities in biotechnology and software, than in Sweden (Granstrand *et al.*, 1992; Håkanson, 1990).

An evaluation of the patterns of scientific co-operation among countries and industries indicates the emergence of an international market for investments in research, education and scientific and engineering personnel. The existence of such a market and the necessity of scientific knowledge for competitiveness are leading the corporations to direct their investments to those geographical areas which can best meet their research and manpower needs. New and less common locations are being chosen for R&D activities as the TNCs recognize the talents available in countries like Israel, Brazil, India (which has the world's third largest pool of scientists), South Korea (which produces as many engineers each year as the UK, Germany and Sweden combined), Singapore and other Pacific rim countries (OECD, 1988, pp. 35–6). In an annual survey of R&D trends conducted by the Industrial Research Institute (IRI), USA, (1992) among senior R&D managers, out of 156 respondents, 97 (62 per cent) stated that the geographical scope of their search for external sourcing of technology is global and not confined to the USA, Europe and Japan only (Chatterji and Manuel, 1993, pp. 21–6).

In their efforts to rationalize their global activities, TNCs are locating even higher-order activities such as R&D in developing countries that have the required resources. Earlier location of such higher order activities was confined to the industrialized countries. A truly global approach may require the company to locate production or R&D facilities in other countries to take advantage of lower wage rates, to gain market access or to take advantage of foreign technology (Porter, 1990). Apart from upgrading the operations of their affiliates in developing countries, in industries where R&D activities can be geographically de-linked from production activities, TNCs are also establishing stand-alone R&D affiliates, subcontracting R&D to local firms or research institutes and sponsoring basic research in universities in developing countries (Reddy, 1994).

Moreover, the global economic factors are also tilting the balance more towards some developing countries. The economies of East Asia and Latin America are growing at a faster rate than the industrialized countries in terms of real GDP growth. Brazil, Taiwan and South Korea are growing at 7–8 per cent per annum compared to Europe, Japan and the USA at 2–2.5 per cent (Martin, 1994, p. 118). As a corollary to these growth patterns, the direction of the flow of FDI moved substantially towards the emerging economies. During 1975–80, developing countries received 23.4 per cent of the total US$ 32.1 billion annual average. During 1980–85 this went up to 24.8 per cent of a total of US$ 48.7 billion per annum (Vonortas, 1989). By 1992, developing countries received roughly 33 per cent of the total global FDI of US$ 150 billion (Martin, 1994, p. 118). Thus, the share of developing countries in global inward FDI increased from an annual average of US$ 7.5 billion during 1975–80, to US$ 12.1 billion during 1980–85 and to US$ 50 billion in 1992. This substantial increase of inward FDI within a decade reflects a dramatic increase in industrial activity in emerging economies (Fusfeld, 1995, p. 266).

The main factors providing economic justifications for enhanced R&D in developing economies today are: (1) the recognition that emerging economies are themselves growing markets for advanced products; and (2) the ability of emerging economies to produce advanced manufactured products for export in global markets. There are large reserves of scientists and engineers in the NIEs, Latin America and countries such as India and China. A number of technical personnel in developing countries already provide the necessary support for manufacturing activities, technology adaptation, product improvement, and customer technical services. With the extensive facilities created by TNCs through FDI over the last decade, a large segment of technical people is exposed to the requirements for competitiveness in world trade (Fusfeld, 1995, pp. 266–71).

2 Globalization of corporate R&D

A conceptual framework

Almost all the past studies on globalization of R&D relate to happenings within the industrialized world. This study, on the other hand, deals with the new trend of locating higher-order R&D activities in developing countries. Therefore it becomes relevant to begin by a brief review of some of the theories pertaining to the internationalization of production. The reasons for this are twofold: first, internationalization of production is temporally and logically expected to take place prior to internationalization of R&D;[1] second, the involvement of developing countries in international production activities is far greater than their involvement in international R&D activities. Hence, a few theories relating to internationalization of production are first analysed to see whether they could be integrated with the analysis of internationalization of R&D, to arrive at a broader framework of the process of globalization.

Theories of internationalization of production

In the 1960s several studies, beginning with Stephen Hymer's doctoral dissertation, analysing foreign direct investments (FDI) were carried out. These studies explained FDI as a natural growth and process of an oligopolistic firm that has some sort of superiority, to maximize profits. TNCs are able to successfully compete abroad because of some specific countervailing advantages that the local firms do not possess and which more than compensate for the disadvantages that a TNC faces in a foreign market (Hymer, 1972).

All firms are not equal in their ability to operate in an industry, some have considerable advantages in particular activities, and the possession of these advantages may cause these firms to have extensive international operations. These advantages are of many kinds as there are different functions in manufacturing and marketing a product. The advantage may be that a firm can acquire factors of production at a lower cost than others can, or it may have knowledge or control of a more efficient production function, or may have better distribution channels or a differentiated product. Of all these, the knowledge or technological advantage over local firms is the most important (Hymer, 1976).

Extending this argument further, other studies argued that imperfections in markets are important additional factors that ensure successful exploitation of their specific advantages through discriminatory pricing (Kindleberger, 1969; Caves, 1971; Horst, 1978). In Caves' (1971) model, firms expand abroad through horizontal and vertical extension or conglomerate diversification. In horizontal extension, the firm produces the same product in several countries. In vertical integration across nations, the firm gets directly involved in other stages of the production process, whether backward or forward stages or both, connected with the products it already produces. Other types of expansion abroad are called conglomerate diversification. Horizontal expansion takes place because of the possession of a special asset, which once acquired by the firm can be utilized in additional activities at little or no cost. However, the return that can be obtained through a firm's special asset (e.g. product differentiation) in a foreign market to a large extent depends on local production. Firms resort to FDI to exploit these oligopolistic characteristics. The investments involving vertical integration are motivated by the need to avoid oligopolistic uncertainty and the erection of barriers to the entry of new competitors. In situations where both buyers and sellers are few in number, uncertainty over long-term supplies and prices can be eliminated by backward integration.

In his later work, Caves (1982) favoured transactional costs as an explanation for FDI. Vertical integration means internalization of the market for inter-mediate products for reasons of contracting costs and uncertainties. He extended his analysis of vertical integration investments to include those that involve sub-dividing production processes and relocating the labour-intensive and footloose processes abroad. It is transactional costs that determine the decisions regarding the allocation of different production processes between internal facilities and facilities abroad. Vertical and horizontal extensions are often combined to involve subsidiaries in both producing components and marketing the final products to the local market.

Combining these oligopolistic characteristics with the theory of international trade, Vernon (1966) proposed his 'product life cycle' theory. In his product life cycle there are three stages – innovation, growth and maturity of the product. In the innovation stage, the design of the product often changes, technology is not stable and the market is not familiar with the product. The product will be price-inelastic. At this stage R&D is still important because of the necessity of changes in design. Countries with abundant skilled labour would have an advantage in the production of these products. During the growth stage, sales of the product increase and a mass production system is introduced. At this stage the industry attracts more entrants and the competition among producers increases. In the final maturity stage, technology and product parameters become standardized, while managerial skills and production costs become more important than innovative skills. Consequently, manufacturing usually shifts to countries with low costs of production.

Vernon (1974) further developed the link between location of production, multinationality and oligopolistic structures. There are three stages of oligopoly: first is 'innovation-based oligopoly', where the barriers to entry arise from new technologies. Hence, the first location of production of new products is likely to be the country where R&D takes place, usually the home country. The second stage is 'mature oligopoly', where the barriers to entry are erected not by innovation, but by scale of production, transportation or marketing. The search for equilibrium in the mature oligopolies leads to geographical concentration of investment, which cannot be explained on the basis of comparative costs. In situations where economies of scale are not a strong enough barrier, oligopolistic equilibrium is maintained through cartels or product differentiation. The third stage, 'senescent oligopoly', is a situation where such strategies are not successful and the equilibrium is fragile, making the firm look for cost advantages. A TNC operates world-wide, so when the factor costs are considered, it takes into account not only the factor costs prevailing in the location of the subsidiary, but also in other parts of the world.

The R&D implications that have been added on subsequently to the original product life cycle theory suggest extensive centralized R&D in home countries for technology development. However, later studies showed that in some industries at least, the changes in the attitude of TNCs, both as a result of internal pressures from the well-established subsidiaries and the external environment in the form of pressures from the host country government, have led to the product cycle becoming 'highly compressed' (Giddy, 1978, p. 92), leading to a programme of near simultaneous innovations in several major markets (Pearce, 1989, p. 7; Terpstra, 1977, p. 30).

In a later paper, Vernon (1979) himself analysed the applicability of the product cycle model to the scenario of the late 1970s and 1980s and admitted its shortcomings. He analysed two main factors to arrive at his conclusions: (1) the degree of internationalization and diffusion of new products; and (2) the changes in the European macro-environment. He observed that there was a considerable increase in the spread of the geographical network of TNCs' operations. As TNCs increasingly adopted a global approach, the spread of their operations increased, and the overall time lag between the introduction of a new product in the USA and its diffusion into other locations decreased dramatically. By the late 1970s, there were a number of changes in Europe's macro-environment, closing the gap between Europe and the USA. Moreover, the global standardization of a number of products, such as computers and pharmaceuticals, made the product cycle theory less applicable.

Dunning's (1977) eclectic paradigm attempts to synthesize different theories of international production in a general framework of analysis that accommodates both the trade and investment theories. There are three sets of factors, which enable the internationalization of production. First is 'ownership advantages' which are specific to a particular firm and enable it to exploit the investment opportunities abroad. There are three types of ownership advantages: (1) those that accrue from the ownership of proprietary or intangible assets and need not arise due to multinationality; (2) those that a subsidiary enjoys from belonging to an established large firm over the others producing in the same location; and (3) those that accrue from multinationality. Second is 'locational advantages', which are specific to a country and makes it attractive to foreign investors. Third, 'internalization advantages' are benefits that are derived from internal markets and allow firms to bypass external markets and the costs associated with them.

Three conditions are necessary for FDI to take place: (1) the firm concerned must possess net ownership advantages *vis-à-vis* other firms serving the same market; (2) the firm must perceive benefits from internalizing the use of its advantages rather than selling them in external markets, e.g. licensing; and (3) the host country must offer locational advantages to be used in conjunction with those deriving from ownership and internalization (Dunning, 1980).

A country's competitive position depends not only on its locational and ownership advantages, but also on the desire and ability of firms to internalize the resulting advantages. The motivation for internalizing comes from the existence of market imperfections that confer special advantages on internal markets as opposed to external ones. Such market imperfections may be 'structural' (e.g. barriers to competition) and 'cognitive' (lack of knowledge on the part of seller as well as buyer about products and processes). Differing policies between countries create incentives for internalization across national boundaries, and internalization further helps firms to acquire and enhance those assets that give them an ownership advantage (Dunning, 1977).

Dunning's concepts of locational and ownership advantages can be applied to partially explain how R&D is internationalized. A country's locational advantages, such as availability of large pools of scientific and technical personnel and existence of good universities, may attract R&D investments of a particular type into the country. TNCs may combine these with their ownership advantage of the ability to organize R&D through global networks. However, the model cannot be applied to explain other important factors such as why R&D needs to be internationalized, the changes in the driving forces and the emergence of the new techno-economic paradigm. Nor can it be applied to explain the differences in factors required and the driving forces for locating different types of R&D functions abroad.

A country may have locational advantage in one factor, such as availability of trained personnel, but it may lack other advantages such as communication and infrastructural facilities. Therefore, even if a firm wants to internalize the advantage it finds in a location, the lack or inadequacy of complementary assets required may prevent it from doing so. Moreover, the eclectic paradigm is also based on market imperfections providing the primary motivation for TNCs' operations abroad, whereas one of the major driving forces for internationalization of R&D seems to be the competition for accessing science and technology resources. The degree of market imperfections in the labour market for research personnel may be negligible. In internationalization of production a firm exploits an existing ownership advantage, whereas in internationalization of R&D a firm attempts to create or acquire an ownership advantage.

Some theories focus on the 'supply-side' requirements of R&D in order to fulfil its role as a factor in the competitive advantage of TNCs. The main issue of analysis has been the complexity of organizing R&D at the multinational level compared with the firms at the national level, rather than the broader issue of the globalization process itself (Howells, 1990). The ability to tap into pools of scientific and technical personnel and the attraction of low-cost research bases have been considered key elements in this process. The importance of international recruitment of scarce scientific and technological talent is not a new phenomenon (Liebenau, 1984). In the post-war period, major companies, instead of continuous reliance on international recruitment and migration, started locating R&D laboratories abroad in order to gain access to research talents that were in short supply at home (Dunning, 1988).

Such moves by TNCs to tap the scientific talent on a global basis may be seen as a reflection of the wider process of a new international division of labour (Frobel *et al.*, 1980). TNCs are seen as seeking to exploit valuable supplies of scarce skilled labour as well as the much larger supplies of low-skilled, low-cost, less militant workers in the more general production process (Schoenberger, 1988). An additional factor on the supply side is the attraction of TNCs to a low cost but competent research capacity abroad (Howells, 1990). For instance, the UK has been an attractive location for R&D by US-based TNCs because of its low cost and other factors such as scientific reputation, common language and similar cultural background (NEDO, 1973; Craemer, 1976).

Theories of the internationalization of production offer only a partial explanation for the location of R&D abroad, because of their narrow treatment of R&D as an exogenous factor that contributes to the oligopolistic advantages of the TNC. These theories are too weak to offer satisfactory explanations for the issues of globalization of R&D as a strategy in the organization of TNCs. However, the changes in the macro-environment, which Vernon (1979) discussed, may be taken as the starting point in analysing the driving forces behind the internationalization of R&D.

Internationalization of R&D – studies in the 1970s

The early recognition that TNCs might be performing some R&D abroad was highlighted in the pioneering surveys of TNCs' operations in some industrialized host countries. These survey studies include Dunning (1958) for the UK, Brash (1966) for Australia, Safarian (1966) for Canada and Stubenitsky (1970) for The Netherlands. Following the pattern of these surveys, most later studies relating to the role of FDI have also attempted to include an analysis of the performance of R&D by subsidiaries in host countries.

In addition to these host country studies, the benchmark survey of US direct investment abroad by the US Department of Commerce in 1966 and an analysis of these data by the US Tariff Commission (1973) also showed that US-based TNCs performed some R&D abroad. Further analysis of these data by Craemer

(1976, pp. 2–3) revealed that 86 per cent of the 500 largest US manufacturers in 1966 incurred foreign R&D expenditures, which accounted for 97 per cent of the total R&D expenditures abroad by US-based companies.

In the past, TNCs tended to confine R&D functions to their home countries and, when the necessity arose, they performed R&D abroad related to adaptation or in a few cases product development for the local market. Even these limited R&D activities were mostly confined to industrialized countries and a few large developing countries. Such R&D was considered an additional and inevitable cost of technology transfer; hence a reduction of R&D costs was not a motive for locating R&D abroad. Studies in the late 1970s (Craemer, 1976; Ronstadt, 1977; and Behrman and Fischer, 1980) confirmed these conventional practices.

Ronstadt's (1977) survey of R&D abroad by seven US-based TNCs, which in total had fifty-five R&D units abroad, distinguished between different types of R&D activities. This survey helped to draw some hypotheses regarding the evolution of each of these different overseas R&D facilities. He identified the following four types of foreign R&D units of US-based TNCs: (1) Technology Transfer Units (TTUs); (2) Indigenous Technology Units (ITUs); (3) Global Technology Units (GTUs); and (4) Corporate Technology Units (CTUs).

TTUs were closely linked to manufacturing units and were established when the product and process technologies need to be adapted to the local conditions, and when there was a need for continuous support of technical services. This was perhaps considered a cost-effective way of dealing with technical problems rather than sending R&D missions from headquarters. ITUs were R&D units set up to develop new and/or improved products for the local markets, and were established when the subsidiary was able to identify locally distinctive investment opportunities, and convince the parent company of its ability to implement such new product development. GTUs were established when a single product was envisaged for the global market. In such cases, the decision regarding the allocation of R&D tasks to foreign affiliates tended to depend on two factors: first, TNCs might allocate parts of the product range to particular manufacturing subsidiaries abroad; therefore, it might be beneficial to carry out R&D relevant to that part of the product range in the same place. Second, the immense resources needed to develop a globally competitive product range might necessitate utilization of the resources available in the subsidiaries abroad by organizing a decentralized but integrated R&D programme. The main function of CTU was to generate new technologies of a long-term or exploratory nature exclusively for the parent company in order to protect the firm's future competitive position. CTUs were often established abroad to recruit top scientists, who could not be relocated to the USA on a long-term basis. Although four distinctive kinds of R&D units, each serving a purpose, were established abroad by the US-based TNCs, over time, however, all four types tended to depart from their original character and followed a common pattern of evolution with overlapping functions.

Table 2.1 gives the locational distribution of R&D (TTUs) by the US-based TNCs studied by Ronstadt. The data show that almost all the TTUs were concentrated in the industrialized countries. Only India, among the developing countries, attracted two TTUs. In the few cases where TTUs were created outside the industrialized countries, the host country had the potential for a large market with unique characteristics. The affiliates in Latin America, Africa and Far East Asia did not require permanent R&D units to facilitate technology transfer, as the technology was standardized by the time investments were made in these countries. Whenever problems arose, temporary R&D teams from the USA or Europe solved the problems.

Behrman and Fischer (1980) surveyed thirty-one US, and seventeen European companies during 1977–78. They found that some TNCs located R&D facilities in the more advanced developing countries among whom the most important were Brazil, India and Mexico. However, TNCs' R&D activities in these countries were limited to adaptations, local technical services (TTU type), and, in a few cases, product development for the local markets (ITU type). Most of the R&D performed abroad by the TNCs was found to be applied R&D and this varied significantly depending on the market orientation. The most critical incentive to locate these limited R&D activities abroad was the presence of a profitable affiliate and a growing and sophisticated market with an adequate scientific and technical structure.

According to Behrman and Fischer (1980), the geographical market scope of the products that a firm produces is reflected in the type of R&D unit it locates abroad. Home market companies are those whose foreign subsidiaries mainly support the companies' home market operations, either by supplying raw materials to the parent or manufacturing a particular component for it, or performing a specialized stage in a vertically integrated production process. The nature of such activities prevents subsidiary level R&D or product adaptation, except for marginal process adaptations to suit local conditions. So, home market companies tend to establish only low-level technical support or test facilities. Host market companies are those whose subsidiaries abroad are

Table 2.1 Location of TTUs established by seven US-based TNCs

Country	No. of units	Percentage
Great Britain	7	23
Germany	6	19
France	6	19
Italy	2	7
Switzerland	1	3
Belgium	2	7
Netherlands	1	3
Canada	4	13
India	2	7
Total	31	100

Source: Ronstadt (1984, p. 246)

predominantly oriented to servicing the domestic markets of the countries in which they operate. Such subsidiaries often need to adapt the products and processes to suit the local demand and conditions or sometimes even create distinctively new products for the local market. Therefore these subsidiaries may be allowed to carry out the necessary R&D locally. World market companies integrate their subsidiaries abroad into a centrally co-ordinated programme to service standardized world markets. R&D in the subsidiaries of world market companies may similarly be assigned a specialized role in a centrally co-ordinated programme. Such R&D is often motivated by the availability of required scientific and technical skills in the host country. So, world market companies tend to establish global or corporate product units. World market companies can operate the whole range of research facilities globally, according to their market presence and research requirements.

Burstall *et al*. (1981) link the evolution of an R&D centre's capability from a limited unit to that with a comprehensive research capacity to the scientific and industrial capacity of the host economy. They in turn relate this to the technological capacity of a foreign affiliate moving from a 'first-order capacity' unit, which only receives and adapts research and technology to a 'second-order capacity' unit which can develop and transmit new technologies to other affiliates.

Another classification of R&D laboratories abroad, which is complementary to Ronstadt's classification, is made by Hood and Young (1982): support laboratory (SL); locally integrated laboratory (LIL); and international interdependent laboratory (IIL). The primary function of a SL is to assist the production and marketing facilities in the host country through technical services and adaptation of products and processes to suit local conditions. The LIL also caters to the local markets and production by developing products that are more than marginal adaptations of the existing product range of the parent company. Its work is likely to be oriented to original development work rather than a fully independent creative process. The IIL is primarily geared towards the global R&D activity of the parent rather than towards the other activities of the parent in the host country. IIL undertakes the centrally assigned tasks in an R&D programme, which may involve R&D units in several other locations.

With the relevance and the important characteristics of overseas R&D having been established by the pioneering studies discussed above, the later studies attempted to analyse the issue of the determinants of overseas R&D by using industry- or firm-level data. Among the determinants tested were economies of scale in R&D, the extent of overseas sales and production, and R&D intensity and product characteristics.

In his empirical study, Lall (1979) investigated the relationship between the US-based TNCs' propensity to perform R&D abroad and the overall R&D intensity of their industries. In his view, the extent to which R&D can be shifted abroad depends on the 'links' between R&D and other activities. Research of a basic nature is not likely to have close links with other functional areas of a firm's operations. On the other hand, the minor development work of applying given technologies and adapting them to specific material and marketing needs in each manufacturing unit is closely linked with production. But minor development work is not closely tied to the strategic planning decision of headquarters. The need for development work varies between industries, being most prevalent in engineering industries where detailed design is an integral part of the production process. Since such adaptive R&D is likely to be carried out in the majority of subsidiaries, it may result in a high absolute value of foreign R&D, as well as high R&D in relation to sales, but not in a high propensity to perform overseas R&D.

In his analysis of links, Lall (1979) observed differences between groups of industries and concluded that R&D functions can be more easily uncoupled in process industries than in engineering industries. The flexibility in location of R&D in the process industries arises from the relative weakness of certain links in these industries. In process industries, there is little need to adapt the product to individual markets, therefore R&D in these industries is not drawn for market-related reasons. Moreover, in these industries new product development can be uncoupled effectively from research into the new production process, once again creating scope for optimal diffusion of applied R&D. Therefore, in the process industries group, research intensity and the propensity to undertake foreign R&D are positively related. On the other hand, engineering industries require continuous interaction between all activities in the innovation process itself and between R&D and other functions such as procurement, production and marketing. This need for strong links between functions within the organization and the need for feedback from the users, make R&D in engineering industries difficult to internationalize.

Globalization of R&D since the 1980s

The above studies have provided valuable insights into the organization of overseas research activity. However, they were based on observations and trends of TNCs' R&D in the 1970s and earlier. At the time, TNCs tended to confine R&D to their home countries and when the necessity arose performed adaptation and in some cases local product development abroad. The firms derived their competitive advantage, especially knowledge (innovation) and technical advantage, from their domestic environment.

A number of major changes have been taking place since the 1980s in the nature and scope of R&D activities performed internationally by TNCs. The changing dynamics of R&D being performed abroad has given rise to concepts of 'internationalization' and 'globalization'. These concepts are used somewhat differently by different researchers. According to Petrella (1992, p. 6), internationalization involves joint R&D between two or more firms from different countries; multinationalization involves the establishment of R&D activities by a firm in countries other than its home country; and globalization involves development of a global R&D strategy by the corporation both at the internal level (in-house R&D) and the external level (R&D alliances, mergers, acquisitions, university contracts, etc.) in all R&D areas (basic, strategic, applied, etc.). Casson and Singh (1993, p. 31) consider internationalization as an approach in which overseas R&D units are given a small and usually subordinate role in corporate research activity, whereas globalization involves a greater commitment to overseas R&D, based on systematic division of labour between laboratories in different countries. Internationalization is usually motivated by the need to support overseas production and marketing, whereas globalization is independent of such motives.

These changes in the nature and patterns of globalization of R&D can be analysed at different levels: the global techno-economic environment; global intra-organizational networks; and global inter-organizational networks.

Global techno-economic environment

The changing business environment

According to Levitt (1983), technological developments over the last couple of decades have combined to create a unified market place in which companies must capture global-scale economies to remain competitive. He argues that the world's needs and preferences have become homogenized and that such commonality of preferences is leading to the standardization of products, manufacturing and trade. If the artificial trade barriers were removed, the global reach would be greater.[2]

> A powerful force drives the world toward a converging commonality, and that force is technology. It has proletarianized communication, transport and travel. It has made isolated places and impoverished peoples eager for modernity's allurements . . . The result is a new commercial reality – the emergence of global markets for standardized consumer products on a previously unimagined scale of magnitude.
>
> (Levitt, 1983, p. 92)

In many industries, radical technological innovations also brought changes in industry economics and allowed companies to develop and manufacture products on a global basis, e.g. quartz technology has transformed watch-making into a scale-intensive global industry. In some industries that were not affected by external forces of change, companies started attempting to achieve global economies, by rationalizing their product lines, standardizing parts, and specializing their manufacturing operations. Such internal rationalization of operations led to a second wave of globalization in a range of industries such as automobiles, office equipment, industrial bearings, construction equipment and machine tools (Bartlett and Ghoshal, 1991, p. 5).

However, the global competition became much more complex in the 1980s. According to Bartlett and Ghoshal (1991), in many industries, a growing segment of consumers started favouring differentiated products and services, thereby creating opportunities for competitors willing to meet such demand patterns. To cater for such groups of consumers, some companies began to develop differentiated products across markets, moving away from earlier standardized global designs. However, the most important force for localization has been the policies of national governments that define the necessary levels of local content, technology transfer and a variety of other conditions from re-export commitments to plant location requirements. 'Together, these forces have enhanced the need for national differentiation, requiring the major global competitors to become more responsive to local needs, while protecting their world-scale economies' (ibid., p. 27).

Thus the forces for localization, which should logically be in converse relationship to the forces of global integration, are also contributing significantly in an indirect manner to the globalization process. The globalized basis of competition has created a need for the generation of new products and improvement of existing product lines on the basis of distinctive characteristics of national markets and production environments that may require local adaptive work (Pearce, 1991, p. 13).

Over the past decade, such forces have also been increasing the need for world-wide learning and innovation. In a period of rapidly changing technology and shortening product life cycles, a company's ability to develop and diffuse successful innovations has become a key competitive strength. As major global competitors achieve parity in the scale of their operations and their international market positions, the ability to link and leverage knowledge globally is increasingly the factor that differentiates the winners from the losers and the survivors (Bartlett and Ghoshal, 1991). Companies are also increasingly recognizing the importance of internationally diversified inputs into the research process (Pearce, 1991, p. 13).

> Coupled with the convergence of consumer preferences worldwide, the diffusion of technology has significantly influenced both the pace and the locus of innovation. No longer can US-based companies assume, as they often did in the decades just after World War II, that their domestic environment provides them with the most sophisticated consumers and the most advanced technological capabilities, and thus the most innovative environment in the world. Today, the newest consumer trend or market need can emerge in Australia or Italy, and the latest technologies may be located in Japan or Sweden. Companies see that they can gain competitive advantage by sensing needs in one country, responding with capabilities located in a second, and diffusing the resulting innovation to markets around the globe.
>
> (Bartlett and Ghoshal, 1991, p. 12)

To acquire a co-ordinated access to a wide range of innovative stimuli and sources of scientific creativity has become the primary reason for the globalization of R&D by TNCs. The assimilation of dispersed heterogeneous inputs into coherent creative programs may be a major facet of a competitive global strategy of the leading companies (Pearce, 1989).

The changing science and technology dynamics

In recent decades, a number of far-reaching changes have occurred in the macro techno-economic environment that are in turn influencing the growth of global R&D systems. One such driving force has been the emergence of new pervasive technologies, in particular microelectronics, information and communication technologies (ICT), biotechnology and advanced materials, which are diffusing rapidly through creation of new products, processes and services leading to productivity improvements and new work practices.[3] Development of these technologies requires a broad and diverse range of scientific disciplines and technological inputs, crossing the traditional boundaries between scientific and technological disciplines and categorization such as basic research and applied and development (Howells, 1990). For instance, in the field of high-temperature superconductors, basic research is being done with a view to commercial applications in the future. Similarly, in some areas of biotechnology, significant progress in applications will not be possible without breakthroughs in the understanding of basic biology and biochemistry (CEC, 1989).

R&D functions, especially in the high-tech industries, such as pharmaceuticals, chemicals, microelectronics, biotechnology and new materials, have become more science-based and research-intensive (Freeman, 1982). The need to improve the interface between basic research, on the one hand, and development work, on the other, arises from the increasing complexity, cost and time taken to generate new innovations. Increasing R&D costs, coupled with shortening product life cycles, have compelled firms to recoup their costs as rapidly as possible, while still retaining their monopolistic positions. Therefore, firms have started launching their new products in as large a geographical market area as possible, increasingly on a global market basis (Howells, 1990). The emergence of new generic technologies is also affecting the operations of TNCs, first, by increasing the need for global sourcing of technologies, and second, by facilitating such globalization of technology development activities.

According to Chesnais (1988a), there are two series of major driving forces explaining why present trends of international sourcing of technology, reflecting a qualitative change, will not be easily reversed. The first series of factors relate to the 'global competition'. In all R&D-intensive industries, and in industries where scale economies are critical, competition now takes place: (1) between a relatively small number of large firms (e.g. oligopolistic); (2) in a geographical area which includes the respective home and host markets of rival TNCs, as well as third markets, within and outside OECD; and (3) through a wide range of means by which firms can gain access to technology and markets. 'Such rivalry implies "mutual recognition" and a variety of combinations between competition and cooperation' (ibid., p. 509).

The second series of factors relate to contemporary developments in science and technology (S&T), which explain why access to a broader S&T base that was an 'advantage' in earlier phases is now a 'necessity'. The general trend has been that: (1) basic scientific knowledge is playing an increasingly crucial role in major technological advance, i.e. the knowledge base of corporate technology is increasingly founded in basic science; (2) many recent major innovations have occurred through cross-fertilization of different scientific disciplines; and (3) technology has acquired stronger systemic features. The ongoing paradigmatic changes in S&T are increasing the pressure on firms. Companies attempt to relieve these pressures partly by increasing in-house R&D, both at home and abroad or by the establishment of joint venture R&D firms or through the external acquisition of knowledge from other organizations, such as universities (when the knowledge is close to basic research) or firms (Chesnais, 1988a, pp. 509–10).

To meet these pressures, TNCs increased their spending on research during the 1980s, mainly in two ways: (1) expansion of own R&D activities; and (2) sponsoring research in academic institutions. As a result, the corporate sector now accounts for a substantial and rapidly growing part of total national expenditure on R&D in most OECD countries. The corporate sector is increasingly performing basic research. In Japan, such expenditures now account for 35 per cent of the country's total spending on basic research. In the USA, the corporate sector spent 17 per cent of the total national expenditure for basic research in 1986. Each of the fourteen OECD countries, for which trend data are available, has also reported substantial increases in corporate sponsorship of research in academic institutions (OECD, 1988, p. 12). In the USA, industry-financed R&D in the higher education sector increased from 2.7 per cent in 1981 to 3.8 per cent in 1985 and to 4.9 per cent in 1991. The figures for Japan also show an increase from 1.5 per cent in 1981 to 2.4 per cent in 1985 and to 3.7 per cent in 1991 (OECD, 1994).

In their efforts to expand their own R&D activities, TNCs, especially those dealing with new technologies, are assigning new tasks to their subsidiaries abroad. In conventional terms, technology flow is perceived as unidirectional from the parent company to the affiliate abroad. R&D abroad has dealt primarily with the adaptation of transferred technologies and, in some cases, additional innovation needed to serve the local markets. However, a study of German companies by Wortmann (1990) indicated that in recent years there has been a qualitative change in the R&D performed abroad by the German companies, especially in the high-tech sectors. Companies have started considering foreign R&D as a source of knowledge and technology.

Most of the R&D activities carried out abroad in new technologies have a global or at least regional orientation. New technologies have a higher level of standardization compared to conventional technologies and therefore their products have global/regional market scope. The adaptations required for local environments are marginal or nil compared to conventional technologies, which required either extensive adaptation or special design and development for each market. Hence, there seem to be very few TTU and ITU types of R&D centres in new technologies (Reddy, 1993). That is perhaps why, among the companies studied by Ronstadt (1977), only IBM (a new technology firm) had GTU and CTU types of R&D centres abroad. Wortmann (1990) also mentions the special case of IBM's research in Germany, where almost all products are designed not for a specific region but for the world markets. Product manufacturing need not take place in the same country where R&D took place.

Michalet and Delapierre (1978) also discussed the case of IBM. By the mid-1970s, IBM had set up a world-based set of R&D activities organized independently of its manufacturing affiliates. The tasks assigned to the laboratories did not necessarily match those of the subsidiary's production units to which the given laboratories formally belonged. The development tasks were distributed on a world-wide basis among all the other laboratories. IBM successfully carried out sourcing and centralization of scientific and technical knowledge and resources on an international scale. To facilitate such a geographically dispersed operations and to pool the corporate technological resources, IBM established a vast telecommunications network. Computers in the laboratories were inter-connected on a world-wide basis and a central databank was operated at the corporate R&D headquarters.

The centralization of external scientific and technological knowledge is not limited to 'science-based' or R&D-intensive industries, but has been equally important in industries such as food processing, where innovation relies heavily on inter-industry transfers of technology (Chesnais, 1988a). What this implies is that in new technologies the R&D need not necessarily be located in proximity to the manufacturing site or the market. This flexibility of new technologies (uncoupling from manufacturing) allows the R&D to be performed in locations of proximity to pools of research personnel and knowledge centres.

Prior to the mid-1970s, one of the reasons stated by TNCs for not internationalizing R&D was the difficulties involved with supervision and control (Mansfield, 1974). However, the introduction of telematics and improvement of information and communication technologies has significantly increased the scope for global sourcing of technologies by TNCs. ICT helps in R&D activities in two ways: first, in processing the data and experiments, such as simulation, leading to increased productivity and lowering of costs by eliminating the need to build expensive proto-types; second, in transmission of the data and results not only within the laboratory, but also across geographical distances.

> For obvious reasons, the telecommunications and computer and data-processing industries were leaders in using the new methods of control, and they have probably seen the greatest development in world-wide organisation of corporate R&D and in international sourcing of scientific and technical resources. As early as the mid-1970s, several large firms in these industries had a kind of international technical system with a foot

in several national systems which allowed them to ensure the flow of technology within international group structures.

(OECD, 1992, p. 224)

In the context of R&D activities, the geographical location assumes importance, because it affects the volume of communication and its quality (e.g. the frequency of face-to-face contact). Companies have recognized the importance of good communication, especially in a highly creative knowledge- and information-intensive activity such as R&D, with its inherent high levels of uncertainty and risk. Hence, in the 1960s and 1970s, companies confined R&D activities to a few locations within the home country (Howells, 1995). Distance can affect the pattern of communication between R&D staff, due to the distance-decay pattern of contact links (Allen, 1977). However, the introduction of ICT in corporate networks after the late 1970s enabled R&D staff in different geographical locations world-wide to exchange data and interact, almost with the same effect as face-to-face contact.

A survey of forty US and European TNCs indicated that among seven main reasons for firms adopting ICT networks in their operations, was the possibility for internationalizing the R&D capacities and thus achieve a greater division of labour in accordance with the technical requirements of the tasks and the scientific capability of countries and affiliates (Antonelli, 1984, p. 15).

Global intra-organizational networks

The changing R&D conditions

Prior to the Second World War very few firms performed R&D abroad. Even by 1965, the overseas R&D expenditure of US-based TNCs amounted to only 6.5 per cent of their total R&D expenditure (US Tariff Commission, 1973). Craemer (1976) estimated it to be even lower at 4.6 per cent for 1966. By 1972, this figure had risen to 7.9 per cent. However, it is only since the mid-1970s that firms have started performing R&D abroad in a significant way (Howells, 1990). This increase in international R&D activities has been the result of firms' general move towards a global operating environment. This is reflected in the fact that a large proportion of firms with R&D establishments abroad have gained them through acquisitions of foreign companies (Behrman and Fischer, 1980). However, as companies' approach shifted from catering for a local market abroad towards a global market approach, the role of R&D has increased from that of a support function to a more integrated activity. Hence, the need to tap into the scientific and technological resources and expertise abroad has become vital.

A survey of US-based TNCs showed that the desire to 'have a window on foreign science' was a major motive for establishing R&D facilities abroad. Other major motives include access to special skills not easily available at home, developing new sources of technology or simply establishing corporate activities related to S&T on an international scale (Fusfeld, 1986). In conjunction with the changes in macro techno-economic conditions, the conditions in the labour market for R&D personnel are also changing, which means it also has cost implications. These factors have necessitated expansion of global intra-organizational networks.

The key driving force for globalization of R&D in recent years has been the increasing demand and competition for skilled scientists. In the USA alone it has been estimated that there will be a potential shortfall of 500,00 scientists and engineers in 2010 as a result of demographic trends and the pattern of university admissions (CEC, 1989). The Science and Technology Agency in Japan estimates that by 2050 there will be a shortage of some 480,000 researchers in Japan. This will be about half of the estimated requirement for R&D personnel by that year (Swinbanks, 1992, pp. 3–4). In The Netherlands, to prevent the shortages of research personnel in the future, the enrolment in exact sciences is projected to need an increase of 35 per cent during 1996–2000, 44 per cent in 2001–5 and 59 per cent in 2006–10, as compared to the present position. This means the proportion of students in higher education opting for exact and natural sciences would have to increase from the present 42 per cent to over 56 per cent during 1996–2000 and 69 per cent during 2006–10 (Berendsen *et al.*, 1995, p. 306).

The demand for scientists and engineers, and national disparities in the incentives offered to them, have led to reported shortages in several OECD countries. The mismatch between the outputs of higher education and the needs of the industry is giving rise to shortages of research personnel throughout the OECD. In recent years, firms in the USA, Japan, the UK, Germany, Finland, The Netherlands, Sweden and other countries have reported difficulties in recruiting research personnel in certain categories, especially in engineering fields related to electronics, automation and CAD/CAM. In OECD countries, there has also been a decline in the intake of students in some fields of science and technology. This decline is likely to be sharper in the future as a result of demographic changes in several countries (OECD, 1988).

Shortages in research personnel are compelling companies to widen their research networks in order to tap more geographically dispersed scientific talent (Doz, 1987). The patterns of scientific co-operation between countries and industries indicate the emergence of an international market for investments in research, education and scientific and engineering personnel. The existence of such a market and the necessity of scientific knowledge for competitiveness are leading corporations to direct their investments to those geographical areas which can best meet their research and manpower needs. New and uncommon locations for research are now becoming locations for international corporate R&D, as the TNCs recognize the talent available in countries like Israel (where the US company National Semiconductor carried out much of its work on the new 32 bit microprocessor), Brazil, and India, which has the world's third largest pool of scientists (OECD, 1988, pp. 35–6). In their search for ideal R&D locations, TNCs have crossed the conventional boundaries and started tapping scientific resources wherever they are accessible, including those in developing countries.

TNCs locate more advanced R&D activities abroad to exploit the resources that are more expensive or not readily available at home. Such resources include university-based research and specific know-how in production engineering and the skills and sophistication of users (Håkanson and Zander, 1986). TNCs are also sensitive to variations in the cost of R&D inputs from country to country (Mansfield *et al.*, 1979). Conditions for research and access to resources for carrying out research vary around the world and therefore, subject to costs involved, relocation of R&D may in the long run improve the competitive position of the company (Sigurdson, 1990). These observations of TNCs' behaviour are also reflected in the trends of locating R&D in some developing countries, which offer access to resources with required knowledge, at substantially lower costs *vis-à-vis* the industrialized countries.

From the operational perspective of TNCs, the nature of demand and the increasing science base of new technologies are leading to homogenization of certain international markets and standardization of technologies for the global markets. At the same time, they are also generating wider variety and fragmentation in other markets (Granstrand *et al.*, 1992). This necessitates changing the traditional headquarters–subsidiary relationships into a global intra-organizational network-based management structure. The creation, exploitation and dissemination of new technology in a global organization require simultaneous achievement of efficiency, local responsiveness, and world-wide learning and know-how transfer. These management tasks will be the critical ones in the management of modern global corporations (Bartlett and Ghoshal, 1991).

According to Porter (1986a and b), the TNCs have been compelled to shift from a multi-domestic approach, where each subsidiary was confined to servicing a local market, to a global strategy, where subsidiaries are assigned a specialized role to play in the developments planned and organized from the centre. This new role of subsidiaries may involve an increased emphasis on deriving distinctive new product variants as part of a regional or world product mandate, or if a unique 'global product' is envisaged, providing research input into its creation.

Selection of the location of R&D by TNCs depends on several criteria. These include: proximity to a manufacturing site; availability of local universities and professionals; ability to build up a critical mass of local researchers (most important for global technological research); attractiveness of sources of tech-nical excellence, e.g. universities, customers or suppliers, etc.; and availability of excellent communication systems (de Meyer and Mizushima, 1989). The choice of location of R&D also depends on the type of technology to be developed and the advantages of national scientific capacity. For instance, the UK has been attracting significant foreign R&D investments in the pharma-ceutical industry, because of the high quality British science in the life sciences and in chemistry. Similarly, Germany has been a centre for foreign R&D

activities in the electrical engineering and electronics industries, reflecting German excellence in these areas (Wortmann, 1990). Even in the selection of low-cost locations, it is observed that TNCs have followed the same criteria. Although developing countries are lagging behind the developed countries in industrialization, some of them have internationally famous academic institutions. TNCs consider them to be almost on a par with the academic establishments in the industrialized world. Therefore, when the R&D is close to basic science research, it becomes cheaper to perform in developing countries (Reddy, 1993).

The changing motivations for globalization of R&D

Behrman and Fischer (1980) in their survey of US and European companies found that overseas R&D by companies, especially in developing countries, was mostly limited to adaptations, local technical services and, at the most, product development for the local market. Location of these R&D activities was considered an additional and inevitable cost of technology transfer, and therefore, reducing R&D costs was not a motive for overseas R&D. The most critical incentive to locate R&D in a particular foreign country was the presence of a profitable affiliate and a growing and sophisticated market with an adequate scientific and technical structure. In other words, the main motive for the location of R&D abroad was to be close to the market. TNCs' perceptions of the economies of centralized R&D and the perceived difficulties of assembling an adequate R&D staff in other countries seem to have been the main obstacles to locating R&D abroad. This means that the TNCs did not consider foreign countries as sources of technological knowledge and tapping into foreign science and technology resources was not a motive for locating R&D abroad. Government inducements and pressures appeared to be effective in the location of R&D. However, these conclusions were based on a survey in the late 1970s, when the type of R&D performed abroad was mostly technology transfer activities (TTU functions).

Dörrenbächer and Wortmann (1991) analyse the motives for internationalization of R&D on two different levels: First, if the R&D is performed at the location which is most efficient within the framework of the corporate R&D system, then it is regarded as a 'R&D-related motive'. Second, if the overseas R&D serves purposes not related to an improvement of the company's R&D system, then it is considered an 'R&D-unrelated motive'. There are basically two kinds of R&D-related motives: first is the R&D abroad, which supports the local production. In such centres, technology transferred from the parent company to the subsidiary is adapted to the local market and production requirements. The second type of R&D abroad is aimed at the generation of new technologies that will be used by the entire company. In the context of R&D-unrelated motives, there could be requirements of national governments aiming at the preservation of R&D potential in their countries. Such motives also include improving the image of the company not only *vis-à-vis* the government or other customers, but attracting qualified personnel who want to work for 'interesting' companies that provide career opportunities.

According to Håkanson (1992), based on the dominant motive for their establishment, foreign R&D units can be grouped into five categories: (1) political factors; (2) production support; (3) market proximity; (4) monitor research; and (5) multimotive units. Except for the last one, each category of an R&D unit is predominantly associated with a specific type of establishment process: (a) acquisitions; (b) evolution of activities in greenfield subsidiaries; and (c) 'direct placement' of R&D units.

Ronstadt (1977), in his study of the US companies found that almost all the R&D units abroad were established for reasons directly related to the performance of R&D functions. Non-R&D goals – such as monitoring foreign R&D activities, exploiting 'cheap R&D labour' or using 'trapped or blocked' funds – played no role in the majority of cases and were of secondary importance in only a few cases.

According to Granstrand, Håkanson and Sjölander (1992), the reasons for internationalization of R&D can be divided into two groups: (1) 'demand-oriented' factors, i.e. circumstances leading to establishment of R&D abroad to better serve the foreign national markets; and (2) 'supply-oriented' factors, referring to characteristics in the local foreign environment that enhance the efficiency of R&D by providing, for instance, access to technical expertise, perhaps at a lower cost than elsewhere or access to universities and other research establishments.

While the globalization of R&D has become a necessity, the primary motives for such moves differ among companies. From the literature survey,[4] the motives for location of R&D abroad can be summarized as follows: market-related (size, proximity and importance); technology-related (to tap into foreign S&T resources); cost-related (to exploit cost differentials); technology monitoring (to monitor new developments in science and technology, competitors' analysis, etc.); and non-R&D-related (pressures by national governments, improving the company's image, etc.). However, these motives are not mutually exclusive and a TNC may locate R&D abroad for more than one motive.

In the context of the changing dynamics of global R&D, analysis of these motives assumes greater importance. The type of R&D performed abroad is closely linked to the motives for globalization of R&D. The past research studies have neglected to take this key relationship into account. This study analyses the relationship between the type of R&D performed abroad and the primary motives for globalization of corporate R&D.

Market-related motives are observed to lead mostly to the TTU, ITU and RTU types of R&D functions, whereas technology-related and cost-related motives are important for GTU and CTU functions. The RTU type of R&D function is uniquely placed in the sense that it is linked to both market-related and technology-related motives. However, depending on the growth of the market and the change in the orientation of the company, R&D units abroad are graduated to perform increasingly higher order R&D functions.

Over time, technology-related motives are observed to have become more important than market-related motives (Cantwell, 1992). The impetus for the globalization of R&D is increasingly being provided by the need for 'know-how' rather than 'know-what' to develop (Dunning, 1992). In recent years, supply-related factors, i.e. the availability of highly skilled scientists and engineers, and a dynamic scientific infrastructure, etc., have become more important for globalization of R&D than demand-related factors, i.e. the need for customer contact and market proximity to adapt products and processes (Håkanson, 1992).

Tapping foreign S&T resources is the primary motive for establishing GTU and CTU types of R&D abroad. However, faced with the increasing R&D intensity of technologies and decreasing profits, TNCs are increasingly concerned about reducing R&D costs. This has to be achieved without compromising the primary objective of generating new technologies and improving the innovativeness of the company. One way of achieving these twin objectives is to carry out R&D, at least some parts of it, in low-cost locations that have the required S&T capacity (Reddy and Sigurdson, 1994). In the generation of new technologies, the innovative potential in the foreign country does not necessarily have to be more advanced than the potential in the TNC's home country, i.e. industrialized countries. Technology expertise can be complementary (Dörrenbächer and Wortmann, 1991).

The emergence of global inter-organizational networks

As part of the phenomenon of globalization of corporate R&D, inter-organizational technology co-operation is becoming an important element world-wide. Such co-operation exists not only between the firms, but also between the firms and academic establishments. Inter-firm co-operation as such is not a new phenomenon. Joint ventures between firms have been around for many decades. However, since the 1980s the number and the variety of forms of inter-firm alliances have grown significantly.

Teece (1992, pp. 19–20) defines a strategic alliance as a web of agreements whereby two or more partners share the commitment to reach a common goal by pooling their resources together and co-ordinating their activities. A strategic alliance denotes some degree of strategic and operational co-ordination. Such agreements take a variety of forms ranging from non-equity agreements associated with one-way or two-way licensing, through to joint venture agreements, equity participation or a consortium. The activities range from pre-competitive, basic research agreements to competitive R&D and technology co-operation and manufacturing and marketing, i.e. covering the whole range of R&D to the commercialization process (Chesnais, 1988b).

Increased global competitive pressures, shortage of knowledge resources, the growing complexity of technological systems, world-wide market entry strategies and simultaneous product introduction are seen as the reasons for spurt in international inter-firm alliances (Mytelka, 1991; Hagedoorn and

Schakenraad, 1993). These inter-firm co-operative agreements in R&D are distinct from traditional modes of joint venture and licensing because:

1 These new forms of agreement focus on knowledge production and sharing in contrast with one-way transfer of technology. Knowledge in this context includes R&D, design, engineering, marketing and management capabilities.
2 There is little or no equity involvement by participants.
3 Such partnerships are a part of the long-term strategy of the firms rather than an opportunistic response to short-term financial gains.

(Mytelka, 1990)

Broadly speaking, there are two schools of thought that analyse firm behaviour, competitive strategy and the inter-firm collaboration, first, the 'competitive forces' (Porter, 1980) analysis of firm strategy in which a firm's performance is mainly dependent on the structure of the industry within which it operates, such as the forces of entry barriers, substitutes, bargaining power of suppliers and buyers, and intra-industry rivalry. The key determinants of a firm's behaviour, including its decision to form alliances with other firms are moulded by the external forces rather than by the firm's internal managerial, technical, marketing, and other resources. On the other hand, the 'resource-based' analysis of the firm treats the firm as a collection of sticky and difficult-to-imitate resources and capabilities. These resources may be physical, such as product designs and production processes, or intangible, such as brand equity. They include knowledge of specific markets or user needs, decision-making process or management systems, and complex networks for marketing and distribution of products (Mowery *et al.*, 1998, p. 508). The sale or acquisition of such resources through arm's-length market transactions are difficult to organize and are vulnerable to high risks of failure (Teece, 1982). In the resource-based framework inter-firm alliances are seen as mechanisms designed to combine the features of both markets and intra-firm organization and thus facilitate firms' access to these capabilities (Kogut, 1988; Hamel, 1991).

Forrest and Martin (1992, pp. 41–2) categorize inter-firm alliances into three groups. These groups need not be mutually exclusive:

1 Technology development alliances – to enhance the R&D capability of the firm to ensure its competitiveness in the rapidly evolving field of knowledge relevant to its focus.
2 Commercialization alliances – to provide the firm with and expanded manufacturing and marketing capabilities.
3 Financial alliances – to help provide the firm with the capital needed to support its technology acquisition and commercialization strategies.

Mowery (1992, p. 211) defines international collaborative venture as 'interfirm collaboration in product development, manufacture, or marketing that spans national boundaries, is not based on arm's-length market transactions and includes substantial and continual contributions by partners of capital, technology, or other assets'. He distinguishes between four types of technology-focused collaborative agreements: (a) those involving collaboration among firms in research alone; (b) those relating to the exchange of 'proven' technologies within a single product line or across multiple products, e.g. most widely in practice as cross-licensing in global microelectronics industry; (c) joint development of one or more products, e.g. common in commercial aircraft and engines, telecommunications, microelectronics and biotechnology; and (d) collaboration across different functions, with one firm providing a new product or process for marketing, manufacture or application in a foreign market by another.

These inter-organizational alliances or technology co-operation agreements have largely been ignored in the past studies on internationalization of R&D, even though for some TNCs, it was the only form of their international research and technical activities (Howells, 1990). However, it was mostly in the 1980s that such agreements became more common. For instance, Hladik (1985, p. 64), in her study of 420 overseas joint ventures of US-based TNCs in the manufacturing sector during 1974–82, found that only 15 per cent of the joint ventures were engaged in R&D of any sort, including minor product adaptations as well as higher-order R&D activities.

However, in the 1980s, such agreements grew dramatically. The LAREA/CEREM (1988b) conducted a study of 500 agreements between firms in which at least one European company was a partner. The agreements covering four sectors – information technology, biotechnology, materials technology and aerospace technology – were analysed by activities into knowledge production, goods production, commercialization and global agreements. Over a five-year period 1980–85, the number of agreements involving either knowledge production or knowledge sharing component increased from 11 per cent in 1980 to 47 per cent per year in 1985.

According to Hagedoorn and Schakenraad (1989), the reasons for technology co-operation agreements between firms include: the extremely high costs and risks of R&D in high-tech industries; quick pre-emption strategies on a world scale, even at the cost of loss of potential monopoly profits; technology transfer and complementarity; exploration of new markets and market niches; reducing the time lag between discovery and market introduction; and monitoring the evolution of technologies and opportunities.

A database of inter-firm alliances available is the Co-operative Agreements and Technology Indicators (CATI) developed in the late 1980s at MERIT. During 1980–96, the database recorded a total of 8,254 inter-firm technology agreements. Their numbers grew from an average of less than 300 a year in the early 1980s to more than 600 a year in the mid-1990s. The figure in 1996 was 650 (UNCTAD, 1998, p. 23).

Table 2.2 gives some data on global trends in technology alliances in new technologies. International strategic technology alliances increased sharply in

Table 2.2 Distribution of technology alliances in new technologies, 1980–96

Year	Total	Biotechnology	Information technologies	New material
1980–84	998	293	601	104
1985–89	1952	571	1097	284
1990	287	34	222	31
1991	264	34	212	18
1992	355	82	240	33
1993	399	117	226	56
1994	489	174	277	38
1995	587	199	340	48
1996	483	168	280	35
Total	5814	1672	3495	647

Source: MERIT-CATI database, as given in NSB, 1998, pp. A–182, table 4–48

the early 1980s and accelerated as the decade continued. Although the growth of inter-firm alliances tapered off in the early 1990s, they started increasing again during the middle part of this decade. The establishment of strategic technology alliances has been particularly extensive in high-tech firms in such core areas as information technologies, biotechnology, and new materials (NSB, 1998).

The increase in such technology co-operation agreements was not confined only to core technologies such as information technology, biotechnology and new materials. Even non-core technologies, such as chemicals, aviation/defence, automotive and heavy electrical equipment have registered a spurt in such agreements. Such agreements in non-core technologies account for about 25 per cent of the total strategic alliances made in the 1980s (Hagedoorn, 1995).

The database shows two types of agreements: first, one-way flow of technologies from licensor to licensee or in the case of joint ventures, from one partner to the other; second, two-ways flows of technologies involving joint R&D ventures and programmes. During 1988–91, a yearly average of 223 one-way and 279 two-way agreements were entered into. However, during 1992–95, the average figure for one-way agreements fell to 158, while that of the two-way agreements rose to 468. This pattern continued in 1996, when one-way and two-way agreements registered were 109 and 541, respectively (UNCTAD, 1998, p. 25).

While the global trends indicate a spurt in the growth of inter-firm alliances, they are geographically evenly distributed. The Triad (the USA, Western Europe and Japan) accounts for more than 90 per cent of the total technology co-operation agreements reached world-wide. The majority segment of the agreements involving non-Triad countries covers projects between firms from the newly industrializing economies (NIEs) and the Triad (Hagedoorn and Schakenraad, 1990). Using the MERIT-CATI databank, Freeman and

Hagedoorn (1994) concluded that there are severe limitations to the possibilities for developing countries and NIEs to catch up with the industrialized countries. The data indicate only marginal involvement of firms from the NIEs and almost no involvement of firms from developing countries in the inter-firm strategic technology partnering.

The database registered only 455 agreements involving firms from developing countries. However, their number has been increasing from an annual average of ten agreements in the early 1980s to about forty in the mid-1990s. The share of firms from developing countries has also increased from 4.9 per cent of the 4,270 agreements registered in the 1980s to 6.2 per cent of the 3,984 agreements in the 1990s (UNCTAD, 1998, p. 27). The agreements between the firms from developing countries have also been significant, accounting for about 7 per cent of the 455 agreements that involved a developing country firm. The largest proportion of the agreements involving a developing country has been in the information technology, which accounted for 27 per cent of the total. The agreements in chemical and automotive industries accounted for 19 per cent and 9 per cent of the total, respectively. A reflection of the capability of the developing country firms to become a viable technology partner is reflected in the increasing proportion of the two-way agreements. In the 1980s, 78 per cent of the information technology agreements involving a developing country firm were of the one-way type, but in the 1990s, the proportion of two-way agreements increased to 55 per cent (UNCTAD, 1998, pp. 28–9).

Impact on host countries

A few studies have been done on the impact of TNCs' R&D activities on the host country. Whatever the implications suggested by the few studies, they tend to be postulated hypotheses. Whether the performance of R&D by TNCs contributes to the enhancement or retardation of independent technological capability of the host country is a complicated issue.

According to Dunning (1992), there are now two opposing views regarding the impact of TNCs' R&D on the host countries. One view considers inward R&D investments to be, in general, beneficial to economic growth, by providing technology and managerial skills, which in turn create indirect positive effects for the host country at a lower-cost. These positive effects include technical support to local suppliers and customers, contract jobs from foreign R&D units to local R&D organizations, etc. The counter-view argues that R&D activities by foreign firms tend to tap into unique local R&D resources with little or no benefit to the host country. Concentrating on problems of little relevance to the local economy, they may be a little more than disguised 'brain-drain', diverting scarce technical resources from more useful purposes.

However, in the context of developing countries, where the scientific and technical resources are under-utilized, the counter-view may not hold much strength. The benefits are greater, while the costs involved may be marginal.

In the case of developing host countries, the cost factor may be that such R&D activities may create islands of 'high-tech enclaves' with little diffusion of knowledge into the economy. However, knowledge and skills cannot be isolated in the long term. The mobility of researchers, the need for local procurement of staff and materials, etc. are bound to diffuse technologies throughout the economy. One of the most important benefits is that international corporate R&D activities are infusing the scientific community in developing countries with a commercial culture (Reddy, 1993).

In general, an R&D affiliate is expected to benefit the host country in three ways: first, by adapting products and processes to local conditions, it improves the efficiency of the local manufacturing facilities. This, in turn, may benefit the host country by increasing the size of output, employment and tax revenue, and the consumers would have access to products better suited to their requirements, at perhaps a lower price. Second, by assisting the local production affiliate to introduce a new product, R&D may help improve the export performance of the affiliate; and finally, through its links with the local S&T community an R&D unit derives benefit as well as contributes to the widening of the scope of capabilities of local S&T resources (Pearce, 1989).

According to Behrman and Fischer (1980) the benefits are 'non-specific' and 'tied mostly to whatever upgrading of local institutions the firm feels is necessary in order to improve the efficiency of its production and marketing operations'. There appeared to be little diffusion of trained manpower into the local communities. However, the authors feel that considerably more data are needed before any conclusions can be drawn. Their studies included only TTU and some ITU type of R&D.

When analysing the implications for the host countries, it is important to consider the type of R&D being performed and its direct and indirect effects. Depending on the type of R&D being carried out, the impact on the host country varies. Each type of R&D unit displays distinctive links with the local affiliate, the corporate headquarters and with the local science and technology system. The ties are virtually non-existent for a TTU, whose main technology links are with the parent; somewhat strong for an ITU, which may (but not always) to some extent draw on the local science and technology system to develop products particularly designed for the local market. In this type of R&D unit, its links with the local marketing function assume greater importance than links with the local S&T system; stronger for a GTU and strongest for a CTU. In these two types of R&D units, the primary motive being that of exploiting local sources of S&T that cannot be accessed easily from outside the country, strong local links are established (Westney, 1988).

Following Hood and Young's (1982) classification, the benefits of a support laboratory (SL) tend to be of a short-term and static nature. Its operations may benefit consumers by providing products of appropriate quality and price, which would not have been possible without it. Being basically dependent on the parent for technologies, it is unlikely to provide opportunities for learning wider types of expertise needed to develop a more broadly based innovative capability. The locally integrated laboratory may benefit local consumers by making available distinctive new products and may also open up export opportunities. Since it draws on the parent's knowledge-base for its activities, the contact with the parent may help its personnel to enhance their knowledge of the entire innovation process. The international interdependent laboratory performs more basic scientific research, but may not provide substantial benefits to the host country. Because its operations are linked to a centrally co-ordinated programme, its innovations may not benefit manufacturing or marketing operations in the host country, except that its personnel would be more prestigious and creative (Pearce, 1989).

Location of R&D facilities by TNCs would increase the size of the technology-base of the host country, through employment of local research personnel. However, the recruitment of these resources by TNCs, on the other hand, may pre-empt their availability to domestic firms. The final impact, however, depends on the type of R&D performed by the TNCs, the type of local resources used by them and the supply conditions for such resources in the host economy (UNCTAD, 1995).

Debates on the impact of the entry of TNCs on the host economy are mainly concerned about the potential 'spillovers' or 'external' effects. The technological spillovers may help the local firms to enhance their efficiency, but while some spillovers do occur, the scope for copying technologies free of charge are almost nil. The data search, reverse engineering and training of staff in the use of new production methods, etc., make learning an expensive and time-consuming exercise. However, there are several other ways in which spillovers can help. One of the most important ways is through competition. The inefficient local firms may be compelled by the competition from foreign firms to enhance their productivity by investing in import of new technologies and training of personnel. Another positive spillover effect is TNC training of workers and managers, who would then be available to the entire economy. The magnitude of another potential positive effect will depend on the extent to which TNCs transfer the product or process know-how to the local supplier industry. TNCs' enforcement of quality, delivery and price conditions may lead to transfer of technology and the upgrading of the domestic supplier industry (Menzler-Hokkanen, 1995).

However, such transfer of technology is not an established practice in the relations between TNCs and their developing host countries. Transfer of substantial knowledge takes place mainly if the TNC establishes or develops its own supplier, possibly with restrictions to supply only to that TNC (Jansson, 1982, p. 30). But, Reuber *et al.*, (1973, pp. 203–5) found that some TNCs are active in establishing a supplier network in the host country. In their survey of foreign projects in developing countries, they found that sixteen out of seventy respondents were engaged in training local suppliers and this was more common in investments made in catering for the domestic market in the host country, rather than in export-oriented projects.

Depending on the situation, globalization of R&D may result in three kinds of scenarios. First, situations which create positive-sum games for the TNCs, the home countries and the host countries. Second, situations of zero-sum games, and finally, situations of negative-sum games. If the national innovation systems of both home and host countries are well developed and capable of reaping positive allocative effects, foreign R&D will result in positive externalities. If the host country's system lacks such a capability in a particular industry, it could be built up by providing 'infant innovation system protection'. However, such a policy may not be effective in cases where foreign direct investments in that industry have already reached a significant level. If a foreign firm acquires R&D resources in another country for less than their local opportunity cost and uses these resources to out-compete the local industry, there will be negative effects on the local economy. This happens when the host country's stock of research personnel is scarce and local competitors are small but growing (Granstrand *et al.*, 1993).

In order to increase the positive host country effects of international corporate R&D activities, their interaction with local industry and the S&T infrastructure through related production or marketing must be ensured. To be able to reap positive benefits of such R&D, the national S&T infrastructure and the whole national system of innovation must have sufficient strength. The task for national policy-making bodies involves building up local S&T capabilities to exploit foreign R&D and technology, sustaining frontier national research capabilities in some areas and providing an environment conducive to technology based innovation and entrepreneurship (Granstrand *et al.*, 1993).

New technologies and catching-up opportunities

In the analysis of development, what was interesting had been the extraordinary success of Japan, followed by South Korea in technological and economic catch-up. Initially, the Japanese success was attributed to copying, imitating and importing foreign technologies and data on the technology balance of payments were often cited to support this view. They showed a large deficit for Japan and a correspondingly large surplus for the USA. However, as Japanese products and processes began to out-perform those of the USA and Europe, it became clear that this explanation was no longer sufficient. Japanese industrial R&D expenditures as a proportion of civil industrial net output surpassed those of the USA in the 1970s and total civil R&D as a fraction of GNP surpassed the USA in the 1980s. The Japanese success began to be explained more in terms of R&D-intensity, especially as Japanese R&D was highly concentrated in the fastest-growing industries, such as electronics (Freeman, 1994).

Conventional wisdom states that the most viable point of entry into the industrialization process for developing countries to be mature technologies because of low production costs and low skill requirements. But, according to Perez and Soete (1988) these are industries that have already exhausted their technological dynamism. Countries adopting this strategy may face the risk of getting caught in a low wage and low growth pattern. The catching-up process, on the other hand, involves acquiring the capacity to improve upon the old and generate new technologies rather than simply being able to use them. This implies that countries that begin their industrialization process as early imitators or innovators will be more successful in catching up. Conventional theories perceived technology to be cumulative uni-directional process, and development was seen as a race along a fixed track, where catching up depends on the relative speed. While speed is an important and relevant aspect, history is full of examples of how successful overtaking has been mainly based on running in a new direction. In other words, a change in the techno-economic paradigm opens up new windows of opportunity for the latecomers to industrialization.

One of the main weaknesses of the product life cycle theory is that it assumes that products are independent of one another. Every new product is regarded as a radical innovation and the successive improvements to it and to its production process are the incremental changes, which bring it to maturity. The next product is again a radical innovation following a similar evolutionary path. In practice, however, each product cycle develops within a broader family, which in turn is part of an even broader technological system. Successive products within a technological system are equivalent to incremental innovations to a product (Freeman and Perez, 1988; Perez, 1988). In other words, each new product benefits from the knowledge and experience developed for its predecessors. However, the pattern is not the same in the case of bio-technology today which, as a system, is in its very early stages of development, just as some of the technology systems presently growing in microelectronics and its applications. A new technology system, on the other hand, emerges from radical innovations in a complete departure from the previous systems (Perez and Soete, 1988).

The life cycles of the technology systems approach are more relevant for development strategies than that of the product life cycle approach, because the former facilitates the identification of those families of products and processes which will provide better opportunities for learning and catching up. There are four development phases of a new technology system as proposed by Perez and Soete (1988):

- Phase I (introduction), involves original design and engineering, with the product in focus. Therefore, the science and technology knowledge required will be high, whereas relevant skills and investment required will be low. The level of locational advantages required may be high for successful introduction.
- Phase II (rapid market growth), with the product development completed, the focus shifts to the production process and improvements to the product. Since the technological solution is already embodied in both product and production equipment, the science and technology knowledge required will be low, but the skills and investment required will be high. Locational

and infrastructural economies generated by the innovation itself would also grow, making them more easily available to the late entrants.

- Phase III (productivity and firm's growth), the focus will be on managing the firm's growth and capturing market share. Scaling up the plant and incremental innovations to improve productivity become important. The capital costs and management skills required can be very high. Entry at this stage for new entrants will be extremely difficult. By then the science and technology knowledge required will have become low. The importance of locational advantages will also be low.
- Phase IV (maturity), the whole system is by now standardized and further investments in technological improvements result in diminishing returns. Firms would be willing to sell the technologies to others. Firms and locations with low costs of production will become competitive, but fixed investment costs will be high. The threshold of entry at this point is low, even though costs of entry could be high.

Phases I and IV are potential entry points for entrants, but with vastly different costs and requirements. Save for the need for a high level of externalities and of science and technology knowledge, entry into the new technologies is easier for developing countries during Phase I, because of low capital and experience requirements. This partially explains the cases of some innovations in electronics and biotechnology occurring outside the industrialized countries. However, as the system evolves, it may require not only constant technological effort, but also a growing flow of investment to generate synergies for self-sustained growth processes.

This implies that, if a developing country has adequate reserves of well-qualified university graduates, a window of opportunity opens for relatively independent entry into new products in a new technology system in its early phases. This partly explains the innovations in electronics that have occurred outside the main industrialized countries. The critical issue would be whether such endogenous generation of knowledge and skills will be sufficient to sustain the growth as the system evolves. The sustained growth requires constant technological effort as well as increasing investments. Development involves acquiring the capacity to establish inter-related technology systems in evolution, which generates synergies for self-sustained growth processes (Perez and Soete, 1988).

The technology systems are in turn the elements of a techno-economic paradigm which also evolves through different phases, and is composed of a series of inter-related technology systems. Each new techno-economic paradigm requires, generates and diffuses new types of knowledge and skills and creates an environment for easy entry into more products within these systems. Mature industries and products get redefined, new products and industries appear, giving rise to new technology systems based on new types of knowledge, skills and new locational and infrastructural advantages. The firms and nations that are well-established leaders in old technology systems will find it expensive to get rid of their experience and acquire new skills. However, the new firms and latecomer countries, for whatever reason, acquire the new knowledge and skills more quickly. 'That is why these periods of paradigm change have historically allowed some countries to catch up and even surpass the previous leaders' (Perez and Soete, 1988, p. 477).

Soete (1983), when analysing the international diffusion of technologies, argues that each crisis in a long wave results in a restructuring of the relative positions of countries. This is partly because the new technologies open up opportunities of 'leapfrogging' to some of the countries that are not locked, for various reasons, into the previous industrial structure. The emergence of new techno-economic paradigm provides technological leapfrogging opportunities to the latecomers. The main reason for this will be the slower diffusion of new technologies in the countries that are leaders in the old techno-economic paradigm, even though the new technologies originate from within them.

> [T]he possible previous investment outlays in the existing technology, the commitment to the latter from both management, the skilled labor force and even the development research geared towards improving upon the existing technology, might well hamper the diffusion of the major new technology to such an extent that it will diffuse more quickly elsewhere, in a country uncommitted, both in terms of actual production and investment, to the old technological paradigm.
>
> (Soete, 1985, p. 414)

According to Soete (ibid., pp. 416–18), the scope for technological leapfrogging by the latecomers to industrialization is at its greatest now, because of the emergence of the new microelectronics paradigm. He lists several reasons for it: first, in the international technology market, the magnitude of competition is increasing, the pressures of which are leading to faster and greater international diffusion of technologies, especially to the NIEs. Second, while other technologies are of the labour-saving type, with labour productivity growth taking place mainly at the expense of capital productivity, microelectronics is characterized by rapid growth in both labour and capital productivity, i.e. capital-saving nature of technical change (Soete and Dosi, 1983). Third, the new electronics paradigm has 'deskilling' effects on a wide variety of highly specialized technical (mechanical and electrical) skills, leading to more social resistance to its diffusion in advanced countries than in semi- or newly-industrializing countries, where such skills are in short supply.

Moreover, as Teubal (1982) points out, new technologies, such as electronics, differ fundamentally from technical changes in the process industries, such as materials and chemicals, as well as in the mechanical and electrical industries because of their greater dependence on scientific knowledge and technical education. In the latter group of industries technical change is based on 'learning by doing' and 'learning by using'. On the other hand, skills in the electronics industry can more easily be acquired through 'learning by training'. This opens up entry opportunities for developing countries that have capacity in scientific and technical education.

While new technologies open up new opportunities, they also pose several challenges to the latecomers. As pointed out by Ernst and O'Connor (1989), the new manufacturing technologies are expected to lead to flexibility in the scale of production, but, while they have improved the scope for factor cost reduction and product differentiation, the investment thresholds due to economies of scale still remain high in many areas. Moreover, unlike the mass production systems, the existence of a variety of approaches to factory automation through new technologies make the choice of appropriate entry strategies for latecomers more complex. The systemic nature of new technologies also poses new forms of competitive challenges to the latecomers, and the mastery of production technologies is often not enough to gain leverage in the system. Design capability, systems engineering and marketing networks have become the core activities and their integration with manufacturing depends on management information and control systems. Moreover, the increasing science base of new technologies makes access to basic research crucial for technological advancement.

The simultaneous development and interaction of several new generic technologies are also complicating the environment for latecomers. Multi-sourcing of scientific and technical inputs, through a combination of joint ventures, contract R&D, licensing, collaboration with universities, etc., has become essential for corporate success. However, the effectiveness, cost and speed of this external sourcing of technologies, to a large extent, depend on the firm's in-house technological capability and on the S&T infrastructure support available to it. Therefore, expanding the internal capacity for knowledge accumulation has become crucial for success. This in turn increases the investment thresholds substantially (Ernst and O'Connor, 1989).

However, while resource requirements are high for the generation of new generic technologies, they open up several areas of application and product development that have lower resource requirements. It is often not necessary to be able to generate new technologies. The experience of the NIEs shows that application and effective utilization of new technologies can help firms to compete successfully in the global markets. Traditionally the literature focused on three aspects of technology development: invention, innovation and diffusion. The first refers to the initial discovery, the second to the commercialization of the discovery and the third deals with the spread and application of the innovation throughout the economy. Although the literature presents it in a simplistic schematic view, there are feedback effects from diffusion to innovation and from both to invention. The NIEs, who are latecomers to industrialization, in the initial stages of their industrialization, focused on the accelerated diffusion of new technologies throughout the economy. NIEs had put limited efforts into invention and innovation, as their main objective had been to catch up with the technology leaders, i.e. industrialized countries. The new product or process technologies that were first introduced in the industrialized countries lost little time in finding their way into the NIEs (O'Connor, 1995).

The advances in new technologies, such as ICT, are also facilitating latecomers' access to basic science. Scientific knowledge is increasingly being stored and transmitted across nations in digital forms, giving greater access to basic science. For instance, through the Internet, scientists in Taiwan today can run the same computational models as the scientists in the USA (*Business Week*, 19 December 1994).

The emergence of new technologies has changed the rules of the game in global competition by transforming the industrial production system. Because of this change in the technological paradigm, no country or firm, however well entrenched in the global markets, is certain of maintaining its competitive lead. The threats posed to the TNCs by the newly-emerged high-tech firms in the electronics and biotechnology sectors are evidence of this phenomenon. For instance, Nokia of Finland has today emerged as the second largest supplier of mobile telephones world-wide. Similarly, in the semiconductor business, the US firms dominated the market for dynamic random access memories (DRAMS) between 1975 and 1985. Then the Japanese companies gained the market and hoped to retain their lead long into the twenty-first century. However, in the meantime, the Samsung group of South Korea snatched the lead through phenomenal growth in a very short period. From being in ninth place in memory chips in 1989, it reached the number one position in the world in 1993. Recently, Samsung became the first company in the world to develop a working proto-type of the 256 megabit chips that will dominate the market by the year 2000 (*Business Week*, 19 December 1994, p. 23).

The NIEs started their industrialization process in the 1960s, producing labour-intensive products under joint ventures or sub-contracting arrangements with firms from industrialized countries. In the 1970s the NIEs entered a new technology system by manufacturing simple consumer electronics and by assembling and testing semiconductors. Prior to that, most of the firms in NIEs were involved in the electrical goods sector, clothing and other industries. At the time when NIEs made their entry into the electronics industry, a new technology system, very few other developing countries had entered the new field. Within a decade in the 1980s electronics surpassed clothing and other sectors as the largest export industry. To meet more complex export demands, latecomer firms acquired advanced technological know-how and skills to design products independently of the foreign buyers. However, most of them continued to manufacture for the TNCs under original equipment manufacturing (OEM) arrangements. Others, such as Acer of Taiwan, entered as engineering-intensive, small start-ups with advanced capabilities. NIEs' entry into a new technology system was facilitated by the new communications and transport infrastructures and the availability of well-educated human resources (Hobday, 1995).

During the latter half of the 1980s, these countries made the transition from consumer electronics and simple assembly activities to complex industrial systems, including computers, semiconductors, disk drives and peripherals. By the late 1980s industrial electronics had become the largest electronics export item from the NIEs. By the early 1990s, the leading NIE firms, such as Samsung of South Korea, had narrowed the technology gap with the market leaders and were able to enter into more equal strategic partnership with the TNCs. The latecomers pursued bold strategies towards technological acquisition and global competitiveness. Through constant learning, firms transformed their initial low-cost labour advantages into highly competitive low-cost precision engineering and management. Some acquired foreign firms in Silicon Valley and other locations to gain technological skills and access to markets. Others formed long-term R&D partnerships with foreign market leaders. In some cases experimental design and R&D began fairly early on and there was feedback between the early and later stages (Hobday, 1995).

The breakthrough for NIEs came when the industrialization pattern shifted from conventional technologies to the new technology system. Entry into electronics opened up vast opportunities for their application and development of new electronics-based products. Electronics also opened up new niche-areas of business, where the NIE firms are not in direct competition with TNCs from industrialized countries. The earlier conventional industries such as textiles, garments, etc., only offered limited opportunities in terms of product range and application potential, and thereby for economic growth, and almost no opportunities for catching up. Being one of the few early developing-country entrants into the new technology system, NIEs reaped the full benefits.

In the early stages of industrialization ICT was not an important factor in NIEs' rapid growth, but it became increasingly important in the 1970s and 1980s. A process of structural and technical change of this magnitude in a short period of time is difficult to achieve without a well-functioning national system of innovation. The national systems of innovation of NIEs reveal many features similar to those of Japan. For instance, like Japan, South Korea has been a heavy importer of foreign technology, but also like Japan has been making intense efforts to upgrade its own technology through indigenous R&D (Freeman, 1994).

From the mid-1980s, studies on catching-up and convergence emphasized technological spillovers as leading to convergence. However, such convergence did not happen to all countries. NIEs have been quite effective in catching up. A study by Dollar (1991) showed that between 1966 and 1978, the total factor productivity (TFP) converged between South Korea and Germany, particularly more rapidly in those industries in which the former's relative TFP was initially very low. A study by Dowrick and Gemmell (1991) concluded that convergence is occurring between the two clubs of high income and middle income countries, whereas the low income countries are falling behind.

The systemic nature of new technologies implies that random technological spillovers even of radical technological advances may have only limited ability to bring about economic convergence. While the technologies and thereby catching up opportunities are in principle available to all countries, the more successful are differentiated by the major indigenous efforts to develop through such a technological revolution (Freeman, 1994).

Evolution of globalization of R&D: a conceptual framework

Most of the research studies that have been carried out on internationalization of R&D tended to focus on the internal organization of research laboratories within major, mainly US-based TNCs. These studies did not consider several important aspects of globalization of R&D such as – international inter-organizational collaborations; the supply and mobility of scientific and technical personnel within and between organizations and countries; the links between R&D laboratories and other corporate functions, and associated with this, the role of communication and information flows in the research process.[5]

Studies that have been carried out since the late 1980s[6] have contributed to the better understanding of the determinants of overseas R&D by TNCs. However, they also tended to analyse the subject from the perspective of the firm and the management of geographically dispersed R&D, rather than an integrated analysis of the process of globalization as a macro concept, the changing dynamics of the driving forces behind it and its implications.

Moreover, all the research related to globalization of corporate R&D that has been carried out so far pertains to the happenings within the industrialized world. Developing countries were not considered as potential locations for carrying out high-tech R&D activities. The academic research relating to globalization of R&D failed to recognize the changes in science and technology environment in some of the developing countries, which are attempting to catch up with the industrialized world. This study is an attempt to develop a conceptual framework in an integrated manner, for better understanding of the globalization process.

Figure 2.1 shows the relationship between the actors involved in the phenomenon of globalization of corporate R&D, i.e. TNCs, home countries and host countries. The quantity and quality of R&D performed abroad by a TNC, i.e. the degree of globalization depend on the type and cost of knowledge available abroad that is complementary to the TNC's operations, i.e. the degree of complementarity. The greater the degree of complementarity available abroad, the greater would be the degree of globalization. Similarly, the degree of integration of TNC's activities in a host country depends on the degree of complementarity provided by that country. The greater the degree of com-plementary knowledge or skills available in a host country, the greater would be the degree of integration. TNCs tend to locate R&D in countries that offer a knowledge base that is complementary to their home country's knowledge base. This is mainly because the home country still remains the base for the largest proportion of R&D activities and a TNC by globalizing R&D either seeks to overcome shortages of specific inputs in the home country or expand its knowledge base into related activities. So, the greater the degree of

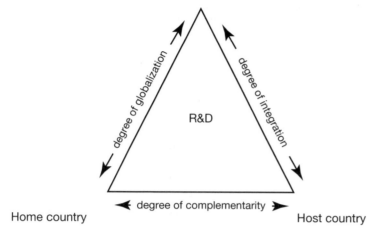

Figure 2.1 Globalization of corporate R&D–actor network

complementarity between the home country and host country, the greater would be the degree of globalization from home country and the greater would be the degree of integration with the host country.

With the emergence of a new techno-economic paradigm discussed earlier, TNCs are finding that some countries outside the industrialized world can provide complementary knowledge at competitive cost. So, such countries are now being integrated into the global corporate R&D networks. This is also reflected in the technology fields in which TNCs are performing some of their strategic R&D in developing countries. They are mainly in the technology areas belonging to the new techno-economic paradigm, i.e. microelectronics, biotechnology, software, etc.

Ronstadt (1977) classified international corporate R&D activities into four distinct units:

1   Technology Transfer Units (TTUs) – to facilitate the transfer of parent's technology to subsidiary, and to provide local technical services;
2   Indigenous Technology Units (ITUs) – to develop new products for the local market, drawing on local technology;
3   Global Technology Units (GTUs) – to develop new products and processes for major world markets;
4   Corporate Technology Units (CTUs) – to generate basic technology of a long-term or exploratory nature for use by the corporate parent.

According to Reddy and Sigurdson (1994), in recent years, corporate R&D structure has also undertaken an additional function: Regional Technology Units (RTUs) – to develop products for the regional markets.

While markets world-wide are integrating in terms of standards and technologies, some regional clusters are also emerging. National markets in these regional clusters share some common features and needs for specialized products. Examples of this can be found in biotechnology – food processing (special types of food, taste, etc.), pharmaceuticals (drugs for regional diseases), or in microelectronics (special software). To cater for such regional markets, TNCs have been establishing RTUs.

Waves of globalization of R&D

This study builds the analytical framework for globalization of R&D in terms of waves (phases). Such a framework helps a comprehensive understanding of globalization as a broader process, by analysing the driving forces in each time period, the type of R&D located abroad and the potential impact on the host countries. Each wave represents a set of distinctive characteristic features, yet reveals the continuation from one wave to the other.

The beginnings of internationalization of R&D – *first wave* prior to the 1970s:[7] the number of firms performing R&D abroad in the 1960s and earlier was extremely small. Most of the R&D performed abroad prior to the 1970s, was that of TTUs. The driving force for internationalization of R&D during this first wave was to gain entry into a market abroad and this required adaptation of the product and process technologies to local conditions and the need for continuous support of technical services. The establishment of TTUs was considered a more cost-effective way of dealing with technical problems than sending R&D missions from the headquarters. The categories of industries involved in this process were mostly mechanical, electrical and engineering, including automobile industries.

The growth of international corporate R&D – *second wave* in the 1970s: by the 1970s, firms had started performing R&D abroad in a significant way. The main driving force was to increase the local market share abroad. This required increased sensitivity to local market differences to enhance competitiveness and the firms' general move towards world market orientation. This was reflected in the fact that a large proportion of firms with R&D units abroad have gained them through acquisitions of companies abroad.[8] Moreover, the host country governments started pressurizing the TNCs for more technology transfer by means of industrial policies defining the local content requirements, re-export commitments, plant location requirements, etc. These driving forces triggered what can be considered the second wave of internationalization of R&D, with a characteristic difference from the earlier wave. ITU types of laboratories were set up to develop new and improved products for the local markets. This type of activity was predominant in branded packaged consumer goods, chemicals and allied products, etc.

From internationalization to globalization of R&D – *third wave* in the 1980s: a number of major changes have been taking place since the 1980s in the nature and scope of R&D undertaken abroad by TNCs. Increasingly, higher-order

R&D, such as RTU, GTU and CTU types, had been located abroad in what can be regarded as the third wave of globalization of R&D. Such R&D abroad is carried out as a part of long-term corporate strategy and is often carried out through inter-organizational collaboration. Hence, the change in the term from internationalization to globalization, reflecting the characteristic differences from the earlier waves. The main driving forces for this phenomenon were: first, the increasingly globalised basis of competition, aided by the convergence of consumer preferences world-wide, creating a need for world-wide learning; second, the increasing science base of new technologies, necessitating multi-sourcing of technologies. Third, the rationalization of TNCs' operations, assigning specific global roles to their affiliates abroad. These trends are visible mainly in the industries relating to microelectronics, pharmaceuticals, biotechnology and new materials. The improvement of information and communication technologies and the flexibility of new science-based technologies, that allow de-linking of R&D and manufacturing activities, have vastly facilitated this globalization process.

The evolving patterns of globalization of R&D – *fourth wave* in the 1990s: the key driving forces for globalization of R&D in the 1990s have been the increasing demand for skilled scientists and the rising R&D costs. These forces are triggering the fourth wave of globalization of R&D, encompassing non-OECD countries (some developing countries and transition economies) as well. The mismatch between the outputs of universities and the needs of the industry is giving rise to shortages of research personnel throughout the industrialized world, especially in engineering fields related to electronics, automation and CAD/CAM,[9] forcing companies to widen their research networks in order to tap more geographically dispersed scientific talent. The existence of an international market for investments in research, education and scientific and engineering personnel and the necessity of scientific knowledge for competitiveness are leading the corporations to direct their investments to those geographical areas which can best meet their research needs, including developing countries. TNCs are also sensitive to variations in the cost of R&D inputs from country to country.[10] This move by TNCs is facilitated by the availability of large pools of scientifically and technically trained manpower in these countries at substantially lower wages *vis-à-vis* the industrialized countries. The category of industries involved are microelectronics, biotechnology, pharmaceuticals, chemicals and software.

Figure 2.2 conceptualises the evolutionary process of the globalization of corporate R&D in the 1960s and 1970s. In each of the phases the driving forces acting on are categorized as supply-side and demand-side forces. As a response to these driving forces, the type of R&D performed abroad by TNCs and corollary implications for the host country are indicated.

In the 1960s, corporate R&D was mainly concentrated in the home countries. This was mainly because of the 'stickiness' of the R&D activities, such as the need for co-ordination of different functions and scale economies. These factors are categorized as the demand-side forces in Figure 2.2. These forces, coupled

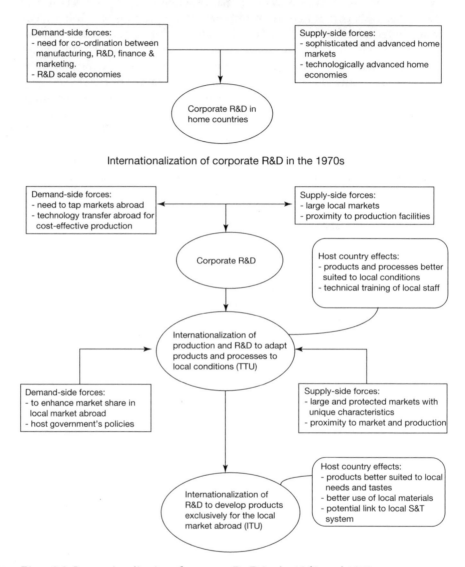

Corporate R&D in the 1960s

Demand-side forces:
- need for co-ordination between manufacturing, R&D, finance & marketing.
- R&D scale economies

Supply-side forces:
- sophisticated and advanced home markets
- technologically advanced home economies

Corporate R&D in home countries

Internationalization of corporate R&D in the 1970s

Demand-side forces:
- need to tap markets abroad
- technology transfer abroad for cost-effective production

Supply-side forces:
- large local markets
- proximity to production facilities

Corporate R&D

Host country effects:
- products and processes better suited to local conditions
- technical training of local staff

Internationalization of production and R&D to adapt products and processes to local conditions (TTU)

Demand-side forces:
- to enhance market share in local market abroad
- host government's policies

Supply-side forces:
- large and protected markets with unique characteristics
- proximity to market and production

Host country effects:
- products better suited to local needs and tastes
- better use of local materials
- potential link to local S&T system

Internationalization of R&D to develop products exclusively for the local market abroad (ITU)

Figure 2.2 Internationalization of corporate R&D in the 1960s and 1970s

with the supply-side forces such as technologically advanced and sophisticated home markets, ensured that R&D activities remained in the home countries.

By the late 1960s, the situation had changed, as can be noticed from the new demand-side and supply-side forces. TNCs responded by locating TTU type of R&D abroad. By the early 1970s, TNCs felt the need for expansion of their overseas markets and added to it the host country's policies influenced

Globalization of Corporate R&D: Since the 1980s

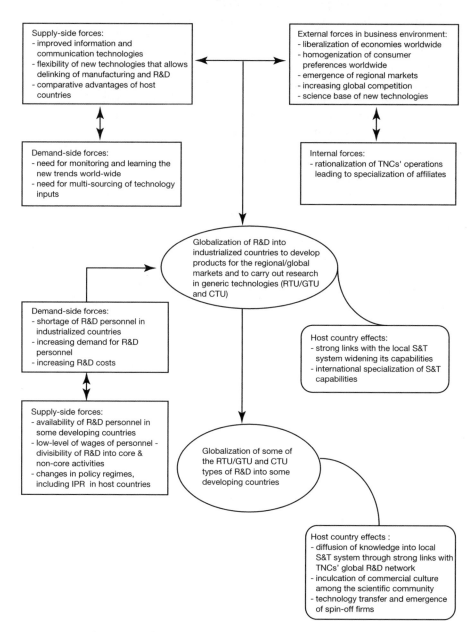

Figure 2.3 Globalization of corporate R&D in the 1980s and 1990s

TNCs to locate ITU type of R&D abroad. As could be seen from Figure 2.2 the host country benefits are greater in ITU type of R&D than the TTU type.

Figure 2.3 (see p. 55) suggests that by the time the 1980s arrived, the phenomenon had been transformed from internationalization to globalization of corporate R&D. This is also the period when the pervasive effects of new technologies (i.e. information and communication technologies, micro-electronics, biotechnology, etc.) began to be felt. So a new set of supply-side and demand-side forces started influencing TNCs' operations. In addition, the changes in the general business environment started exerting external pressures, which necessitated rationalization of TNCs' internal operations. In combination, all these driving forces influenced globalization of corporate R&D. TNCs started performing their strategic R&D outside their home countries, but mainly within the industrialized world.

By the mid-1980s, TNCs started feeling the need to expand their R&D-intensive activities and thereby the need to tap into larger pools of research personnel. Simultaneously the R&D costs started increasing significantly. These forces made TNCs look for suitable R&D locations outside the industrialized world. Such a move was aided by the supply-side forces emanating from some developing countries. As Figure 2.3 shows, the host country benefits of inward investments in RTU, GTU and CTU types of R&D are significantly more substantial than the other types and affect the innovation capability in host countries.

3   The innovation environment in the developing world

This chapter provides a general discussion on innovation environment in developing countries, with a more focused discussion on science and technology (S&T) in developing Asia. The discussion here does not deal with organizational structures as such, but more on characteristic features, links, strengths, weaknesses and ongoing changes that provide a conducive environment for R&D, with suitable illustrations. Rather than discussing the innovation environment in the whole developing world as a group, which would present a dismal picture obscuring the progress achieved in some of the more advanced developing countries, the discussion is focused only on countries that are emerging as host countries for international corporate R&D investments.

Many developing countries have an innovation environment characterized by dualism. In these countries, the industrial and education policies of the 1960s and 1970s have led to the emergence of an advanced segment that is small, but in terms of features and quality is comparable to the innovation systems of some of the industrialized countries. The larger part of the S&T environment in these countries, however, remains highly underdeveloped in comparison to the industrialized world. Transnational corporations (TNCs) are attempting to utilize this advanced segment for their R&D purposes. The question that arises is whether such R&D investments will bring benefits to the whole S&T system of the host countries, by forging strong links with the rest of the local S&T system, or only create islands of high-tech enclaves.

Innovation potential in developing countries: a comparative analysis

There has been a noticeable increase in the technological capacity of developing countries. Their share in the world R&D expenditure rose from 2.5 per cent in 1970 to 6.2 per cent in 1987, but came down to 4.0 per cent in 1990, perhaps, mainly because of increased R&D spending by the firms from industrialized countries. The developing countries' share of R&D scientists and engineers increased from 8.5 per cent in 1970 to 12.0 per cent in 1980 to 12.9 per cent in 1985 to 14.5 per cent in 1990[1] (UNESCO, 1987 and 1990 as given in Dunning, 1992; UNESCO, 1992). Developing countries have also more than doubled their share of world patenting between 1963–70 and 1974–84. Among the developing countries, Taiwan, South Korea, Brazil, Mexico, Hong Kong and India are currently among the leading patent filers in the USA. R&D activities of TNCs are often relatively important not only in industrialized countries, but also in some developing countries. The data are fragmentary, but in Australia, Belgium, Canada, the United Kingdom, Germany, South Korea, Singapore and India, in the 1980s, the share of national R&D expenditure accounted for by foreign-owned firms exceeded 15 per cent (Dunning, 1992).

However, the percentage of GNP spent on R&D by developing countries is still marginal, compared to what the industrialized countries spent. The proportion of GNP spent by developing countries on R&D grew only from 0.52 per cent in 1980 to 0.54 per cent in 1985 to 0.64 per cent in 1990. However, there are wide differences among developing countries, with some countries like South Korea, Taiwan, Singapore and India spending more than or about 1 per cent of their GNP on R&D. The data indicate that more rapid growth in R&D expenditures of developing countries took place during the late 1980s. The expenditure rose from US$ 12,571 million in 1980 to 13,016 million in 1985 to 18,325 million in 1990. The number of R&D scientists and engineers per million population in developing countries rose from 144 in 1980 to 158 in 1985 to 189 in 1990 (UNESCO, 1992, p. 5–12).

The data in Table 3.1 reflect the R&D capacity in selected countries. The data show that industrialized countries account for the largest proportion of R&D expenditures. However, some developing Asian countries, such as South Korea and Taiwan also spend nearly the same proportion of their GNP on R&D as the industrialized countries. The numbers of R&D scientists and engineers per million population in South Korea, Singapore and Taiwan are also matching the figures for the leading countries in the industrialized world. In terms of total number of scientists and engineers engaged in R&D, China, India and South Korea employ nearly as many people as in the more advanced industrialized countries. In large countries, such as China and India, even though the R&D scientists and engineers per million population are lower, because of their huge population base, the total number of scientists and engineers engaged in R&D tends to be high. This also indicates that even if the proportion of S&T personnel in total population seems lower, the supply of trained manpower in absolute numbers will be large.

During the course of their developmental efforts, many developing countries have considered science and technology education as a priority area and built up large cadres of scientific personnel. Some among them, including the large countries like Brazil, China and India took to building up competencies in basic science as the starting point, from which they expected downstream activities of applied research, product design and development, and manufacturing to flow smoothly. To their dismay, they have come to realize that the path from basic research to downstream activities is not an easy one, and they failed to establish proper links between different stages of the science

Table 3.1 R&D indicators for selected countries

Country	Year	Total R&D as % of GNP	No. of scientists and engineers in R&D	R&D scientists and engineers per million population
USA	1995	2.5	962,700	3,732
Japan	1994	2.9	787,402	6,309
Germany	1993	2.4	229,839	2,843
France	1994	2.4	149,193	2,584
UK	1993	2.2	140,000	2,417
Sweden	1993	3.4	32,288	3,714
South Korea	1994	2.8	117,486	2,636
Taiwan	1994	1.8	63,457	3,022
Singapore	1995	1.1	7,695	2,728
Brazil	1995	0.6	26,754	168
Malaysia	1992	0.4	1,633	87
India	1994	0.8	136,503	149
Argentina	1995	0.4	22,927	671
Mexico	1993	0.3	14,103	157
China	1995	0.5	422,700	350

Source: UNESCO *Statistical Yearbook* (1997) and national sources for Taiwan

and technology system. As a result, these countries now have large pools of highly qualified scientists and engineers in theoretical sciences, whose knowledge and skills are not fully exploited for economic growth. These cadres of scientific personnel are available for R&D work at substantially lower wages.

On the other hand, a few other developing countries, especially the newly industrialising economies (NIEs) attempted to build up science and technology capabilities by concentrating on downstream activities first. As a result, they have built up strong competencies in product design and manufacturing, and have now started moving toward upstream activities of basic and applied research. To enable them to do so, these countries took up science and technology education as a priority and built up large pools of trained manpower.

Some of the developing countries have also built up world-famous universities and research institutes, which have not only been producing well-trained graduates, but have also made some notable innovations in science and technology. For instance, the National Institute of Immunology in India has developed the world's first vaccine for birth control, which has successfully undergone field trials in Brazil, Chile, Finland, India and Sweden and is expected to be available in the global markets in a few years (IDRC, 1995, pp. 75–81). Researchers at the University of Chile in Santiago have successfully developed a method to bring fresh water to isolated villages, using 'fog-catching nets'. This technology is now being used in Chile, Ecuador, Peru and the Arabian Desert and is to spread to other parts of the world where there are water shortages (IDRC, 1995, pp. 115–25). TNCs' R&D activities in the developing world are observed to be concentrated in countries that have such centres of excellence, a good education system and an adequate supply of professionals. Often, R&D is conducted in collaboration with such research centres.

Among the developing countries that have been pursuing conscious policies to build up S&T capabilities, countries in the Asian region have been at the forefront. Asian country investments in science and technology have been increasing faster than economic growth rates in the region. According to the data compiled by the US National Science Foundation, since 1980, R&D expenditure has grown at annual rates of 15.8 per cent in Taiwan and 23 per cent in South Korea (*Science*, 15 October 1993, p. 348) and at 15 to 20 per cent across the region (Simon, 1995, p. xiv).

The growth in S&T systems is being fuelled by the huge investment in education, research institutions and infrastructure, especially telecommunications. This concerted effort of the governments in the region is reflected in the creation of new sources of national competitive advantage. The region's S&T systems are also deriving benefits also from the large inflows of FDI, both in manufacturing and R&D. TNCs' activities in the region, while utilizing the S&T resources, are in turn generating beneficial externalities. The change in the techno-economic paradigm and the emergence of microelectronics have led to the strengthening of S&T systems. Small and medium-size enterprises in the region have applied microelectronics technologies to exploit the niche markets for value added products. One of the greatest assets of the S&T systems in Asia has turned out to be the large pools of scientists and engineers educated in Western universities. Many of them, after working for TNCs and Western research institutes are returning home to carry out high-tech activities in their home countries, because of the new opportunities that have opened up in their home countries in the 1990s.

Table 3.2 shows the number of doctoral degrees awarded to Asian students in science and engineering (S&E) subjects by the universities in the USA. The number of doctoral degrees awarded to foreign students by US universities in S&E fields increased from about 5,000 in 1986 to 10,000 in 1995, accounting for 8.2 per cent average annual increase. This increase has been mainly due to the students from China, India, South Korea and Taiwan, who together accounted for 59 per cent of all S&E doctoral degrees earned by foreign students (NSF, 1996).

The number of foreign doctoral recipients returning to their home countries has also increased. A study (Finn, 1997) showed that about 47 per cent of the foreign students who were awarded doctorates S&E fields in 1990 and 1991 were working in the USA in 1995. The figures were higher for doctorates in physical sciences and engineering, and lower in the case of doctorates in life sciences and social sciences. The rates of stay were higher for students from India (79 per cent) and China (88 per cent), and was lower for South Korea with 10 per cent. In 1996, lower proportion of doctoral awardees, 59 per cent in

Table 3.2 Doctoral degrees in science and engineering (S&E) subjects awarded to Asian students by US universities

Country of origin	1986–95 (cumulative)
Total Asia	44,931
China	14,088
Hong Kong	952
India	7,554
Japan	1,276
South Korea	8,821
Taiwan	10,276
Thailand	956
Other Asia	1,008

Source: NSB (1998), pp. 2–31

the case of Indian students and 57 per cent in the case of Chinese students, accepted employment in the USA (NSB, 1998, pp. 2–28).

Table 3.3 gives data on the foreign-born faculty members in the S&E faculties in US universities. The data suggest that people from developing Asia are occupying important positions in the science and technology fields in the USA. While it may be interpreted as a brain drain from the developing countries, it can also be viewed more positively. It is groups of such people who reflect the S&T potential of developing countries. In many cases, they become conduits to TNCs' for location of value-added activities in their home countries.

Several developing countries have realized that building up indigenous technology capability is an essential for sustaining the industrialization process in the long run and have made efforts towards achieving this, even though all of them have not attained the same success. For a long time India and China have been pursuing basic and applied research and have been almost at the frontier in some fields, mainly military-related. In spite of such scientific expertise, the S&T systems of these countries have not been equally successful in acquiring proficiency in commercial applications as the developed country systems. As a result, there has been little diffusion of their scientific knowledge into the economy. For the diffusion process to be successful, it requires efficient intermediate links or bridging institutions. The imperfectly formed link in India and China has been their inefficient engineering and capital goods sectors. Another weakness of the S&T systems in India, China and Brazil has been the high degree of concentration of R&D activities in government-owned research institutes and enterprises, with a relatively narrow focus on military-related applications. Such a policy has led to achieving an advanced state of aeronautics, space and nuclear research in these large economies, but the spillover of this advanced knowledge to the civilian sector has been very limited (OECD, 1992).

In the NIEs, on the other hand, a greater percentage of R&D is oriented towards commercial applications. For instance, in Taiwan, the R&D system

Table 3.3 Major countries of origin of foreign-born science and engineering faculty
members in US universities, 1993

Country of origin	Number	Percentage
Total S&E faculty	242,812	100.0
US-born	193,606	79.7
Foreign-born	49,206	20.3
S&E faculty from major countries of origin	23,762	9.8
India	5,696	2.3
China	4,263	1.8
United Kingdom	3,149	1.3
Taiwan	2,491	1.0
Canada	2,206	0.9
South Korea	2,163	0.9
Germany	1,604	0.7
Iran	1,369	0.6
Greece	821	0.3
Other	25,446	10.5

Source: NSB (1998), pp. 2–30

includes a number of semi-public research institutes with close links to the
private sector and the researchers are given support in setting up their own
firms to commercialize their research results. In South Korea, the government
is inducing the private sector to establish research institutes to facilitate
technological development and industrial restructuring. The government
research institutes are increasingly focusing on improving the manufacturing
technologies to assist the private sector firms. The NIEs have better educated
populations, with access to education more evenly distributed. The educational
system has also been able to quickly adapt itself to the demands generated by
the restructuring of the economy and the required changes in the skill
composition of the labour force. In contrast, in India and Brazil, the
opportunities for education are more unevenly distributed and the average
educational level of their populations has been below that of the NIEs (OECD,
1992).

Table 3.4 gives data on the number of scientific and technical articles
published in journals in the Science Citation Index (SCI) in 1995, and their
distribution among different disciplines for different countries and the share
of these countries in the total number of articles. Five countries accounted for
more than 60 per cent of all articles in 1995: the USA (33 per cent), Japan (9
per cent), the UK (8 per cent), Germany (7 per cent) and France (5 per cent).
No other country's share reached 5 per cent of the total articles published (NSB,
1998, pp. 5–40).

However, the Asian developing countries have also contributed significantly.
Their publications have been growing rapidly over the years, since 1981: China
from 1,100 to 6,200 articles in 1995, Taiwan from 370 to 3,900, South Korea

Table 3.4 Scientific and technical articles by country and field and country's share in total articles, 1995 (number and %)

Fields	USA	UK	Italy	Argentina	Brazil	China	Taiwan	S. Korea	Singapore	India
All	142,792 (32.5)	32,980 (7.5)	14,117 (3.2)	1,581 (0.4)	2,760 (0.6)	6,200 (1.4)	3,884 (0.9)	2,964 (0.7)	891 (0.2)	7,851 (1.8)
clinical medicine	48,072 (37.4)	12,624 (9.4)	4,957 (3.7)	381 (0.3)	632 (0.5)	495 (0.4)	871 (0.6)	337 (0.3)	204 (0.2)	955 (0.7)
biomedical	28,081 (39.0)	5,758 (8.0)	2,039 (2.8)	264 (0.4)	497 (0.7)	464 (0.6)	341 (0.5)	238 (0.3)	93 (0.1)	1,043 (1.4)
biology	12,062 (31.9)	2,672 (7.6)	666 (1.9)	226 (0.6)	264 (0.8)	223 (0.6)	253 (0.7)	87 (0.2)	39 (0.1)	574 (1.6)
chemistry	10,880 (21.1)	3,573 (5.8)	1,931 (3.2)	232 (0.4)	333 (0.5)	1,463 (2.4)	694 (1.1)	829 (1.4)	118 (0.2)	2,376 (3.9)
physics	17,882 (24.1)	3,955 (5.3)	2,746 (3.7)	309 (0.4)	700 (0.9)	2,350 (3.2)	750 (1.0)	859 (1.2)	160 (0.2)	1,665 (2.2)
earth, space sciences	7,257 (40.4)	1,850 (8.0)	661 (2.9)	70 (0.3)	141 (0.6)	196 (0.8)	122 (0.5)	60 (0.3)	15 (0.1)	380 (1.6)
engineering, technology	10,229 (33.4)	2,087 (6.8)	831 (2.7)	83 (0.3)	125 (0.4)	757 (2.5)	796 (2.6)	515 (1.7)	222 (0.7)	779 (2.5)
mathematics	2,811 (35.2)	461 (5.8)	286 (3.6)	16 (0.2)	68 (0.9)	252 (3.2)	57 (0.7)	39 (0.5)	40 (0.5)	79 (1.0)

Source: SB (1998, pp. A-283–304)

from 170 to 3,000, Singapore from 120 to 900 and Hong Kong from 500 in 1987 to 1,100 in 1995. Their combined world share rose from 0.5 per cent in 1981 to 3.4 per cent in 1995. On the other hand, India's output of articles declined by 33 per cent since 1981, decreasing from 11,700 articles to 7,900 in 1995 (NSB, 1998, pp. 5–41).

The data suggest that among the Asian developing countries China's relative competitive advantage lies in physics, where it contributed 2,350 articles, accounting for 3.2 per cent of the world's total, and in chemistry, with 1,463 articles and a share of 2.4 per cent of the total. On the other hand, India has contributed relatively more in chemistry, with 2,376 articles and a world share of 2.2 per cent. South Korea, Taiwan and Singapore have the largest number of articles in physics, followed by chemistry. India's S&T base seems to be broader and relatively even across all the disciplines compared to other Asian developing countries. Except for India and Taiwan, the data for all the other Asian developing countries reflect low priority for research in clinical medicine.

One of the important indicators of the innovativeness of a country is the patenting activity of that country. Domestic patenting activity provides the following information about a country's technological development: patenting trends help identify countries that are loci of inventive activity; patenting activity of residents provides a measure of productivity of a country's science and technology manpower; and patenting by foreign inventors shows a country's attractiveness as a market for new technologies. Between 1985 and 1990, the number of patents granted in the Asian region increased by 44 per cent, rising from 65,000 new patents in 1985 to 93,000 in 1990. The increase in patenting activity was more pronounced in China, South Korea and Taiwan. About one-third more patents were granted to resident inventors in 1990, compared to 1985. The foreign inventors have been patenting in Asia at a more rapid pace than the region's residents (NSF, 1995).

In the 1970s, the number of US patents granted to the Asians nearly doubled and in the 1980s it tripled, largely due to the patents granted to the Japanese. The NIEs registered the most rapid growth in US patenting, with Taiwan and South Korea in the lead. NIEs' patenting activity in the USA quadrupled during the 1970s and increased tenfold during the 1980s, particularly after 1987. US patenting by the emerging Asian economies (EAE), which consist of China, India, Indonesia and Malaysia, shows no clear trend, as it declined during the 1970s, but increased during the 1980s and 1990s. Since 1986, China has been in the lead in patenting in the USA (NSF, 1995).

Table 3.5 gives data on the US patents granted to selected developing countries. The US patents granted are concentrated among a small group of advanced industrialized countries. For instance, two countries, Japan and Germany, obtained over 60 per cent of US patents granted to foreign inventors. The leading five countries, Japan, Germany, France, the UK and Canada, were granted about 80 per cent of the US patents granted to foreign inventors in 1995. Between 1982 and 1992, US patents granted to inventors from these five countries nearly doubled, reaching the highest in 1992 at 37,000 US

Table 3.5 Number of US patents granted to selected developing countries

Country	Total 1963–95	1991	1992	1993	1994	1995
Argentina	698	16	20	24	32	31
Brazil	874	61	40	57	60	63
China	545	52	41	53	48	62
Hong Kong	843	50	60	60	57	86
India	492	22	24	30	27	37
Mexico	1,614	28	39	45	44	40
South Korea	4,649	404	538	779	943	1,161
Taiwan	9,229	904	1,000	1,189	1,443	1,620

Source: NSB (1998, pp. A-373)

patents. Since then, the number of patents awarded to the leading industrialized countries has remained constant and in some cases has even begun to decline. On the other hand, Asian developing countries have stepped up their patenting activity in the United States, which is a reflection of their growing strength as inventors of new technologies. Prior to 1982, Taiwan was granted only 316 US patents, but during 1982–95, the figure shot up to nearly 9,000 US patents. US patenting by inventors from South Korea reflects similar growth pattern. Prior to 1982, South Korea had only 102 US patents, but since then more than 4,500 new patents have been added. Since 1982, China and Hong Kong have also rapidly increased their patenting in the United States (NSB, 1998, pp. 6–21). The data trends for the 1990s in Table 3.5 shows that all developing countries have been increasing their patenting activity in the USA. With realization of the importance of trade-related intellectual property rights (TRIPs) under the World Trade Organisation (WTO) growing among developing countries, this trend is likely to strengthen.

In a study, NSF (1995) measured the technological importance of the Asian and the US patents obtained in the USA in three ways:

1   *The Current Impact Index (CII)*: this captures the impact of a country's patents on the international technological development and the degree to which its patents contain important technological advances by calculating how frequently a country's recent patents are cited by all of the current year's patents.[2] This normalized indicator has an expected value of 1.0.
2   *Technology cycle time*: this identifies those countries that are inventing (patenting) in rapidly changing technology fields. This indicator identifies fast-changing technologies by measuring the median age of the patents cited as prior art.
3   *Science linkage*: this measures the degree to which a country's technology is linked to science by calculating the number of references to the scientific literature indicated on the front pages of the patent. This indicator attempts

to measure a country's activity in leading-edge technology and how close its new technology is to the scientific frontier.

The NIE patents scored lower than those of the USA and Japan in all three indicators, but in fields related to electronics and computer technologies, the NIEs appear to be following the Japanese model, i.e. rapidly advancing the state of the art in consumer-oriented technologies. The technology cycle time score in the patent classes covering computer hardware, radio and television, and electronics held by the NIEs improved upon more recent technologies than the US patenting in those categories. In the commercially important industry in which the EAEs were granted the most patents, the electronics industry, patents by China tended to show a strong science linkage, while patents by India had garnered more citations to their patents (a CII above 1.0) (NSF, 1995).

The market competitiveness of the region's technological advances when embodied in new products and processes provides an important evaluation of the economic productivity of a nation's S&T system. The Asian region, an important supplier of high-tech products to the USA, has become the source of more than half of all such products imported. Such success in selling high-tech products to a demanding market such as the USA indicates a highly productive S&T system. Asian sales of high-tech products to the USA averaged nearly US$ 34 billion annually, and exceeded Asian purchases of like-classified products from the USA each year between 1989 and 1991. The data in Table 3.6 indicate that computers, telecommunication equipment, and electronics account for 80 per cent of the region's high-tech sales in the USA and approximately 95 per cent of the NIEs' high-tech sales (NSF, 1995).

The fastest-growing product area for the region and also for Japan over this period was optoelectronic products. Japan's biotech products, although a very small share of Japan's technology sales in the USA, also found an increasingly receptive US market. Among the other Asian economies, the technology products that experienced the most growth in US sales varied. Two of the NIEs, Singapore and Taiwan, showed high US sales growth in advanced materials products. Aerospace was a key growth technology area for two EAEs, India and Malaysia, as well as for South Korea. For China and Indonesia, growth in US sales of computers and telecommunication products led all other technology product areas, while for Hong Kong, electronics experienced the fastest growing sales in the USA over the period (NSF, 1995).

In the analysis of innovation environments of different countries, it is also important to consider the cost of accessing the S&T resources, which becomes particularly relevant when accessing resources for corporate R&D. Table 3.7 gives the annual earnings of technical and managerial personnel for selected countries. The data clearly show that the cost of these personnel is several times lower in developing countries. It is this cost differential that TNCs are attempting to exploit by performing R&D activities in developing countries that have the required innovation environment.

Table 3.6 Composition of Asian high-tech sales in the USA, by product field, 1991 (percentages)

Product	Japan	Hong Kong	Singapore	South Korea	Taiwan	China	India	Indonesia	Malaysia
All fields (US$m)	19,793.4	1,047.6	5,952.8	3,357.4	3,441.2	355.5	15.2	89.4	2,332.0
Biotechnology	0.0	0.0	0.0	0.0	0.0	0.0	1.2	0.0	0.0
Life science	4.5	1.8	1.3	0.2	0.5	4.1	7.6	0.3	0.0
Optoelectronics	8.1	0.9	0.8	1.1	1.8	4.9	0.6	0.0	1.2
Computers, telecom	58.6	69.4	76.4	41.0	74.8	82.4	39.2	63.1	32.4
Electronics	17.0	27.1	19.2	52.8	19.4	0.6	14.2	29.2	65.6
Comp. integ. mfg.	6.4	0.1	0.2	0.3	0.9	0.3	2.7	0.0	0.0
Material design	2.3	0.8	0.7	1.0	2.3	0.2	15.1	0.1	0.7
Aerospace	3.1	0.1	1.4	3.5	0.3	7.2	19.3	7.3	0.0
Weapons	0.0	0.0	0.0	0.1	0.1	0.2	0.0	0.0	0.0

Source: Bureau of The Census, Foreign Trade Division, special tabulations, as given in NSF (1995, p. 25)

Table 3.7 Annual net income of personnel (US$)

Country/City	Engineers	Department manager
Japan (Tokyo)	51,400	76,800
USA (Chicago)	34,600	55,900
Germany (Frankfurt)	41,900	52,400
Italy (Milan)	23,100	20,400
South Korea (Seoul)	20,100	23,600
Brazil (São Paulo)	11,600	16,800
Thailand (Bangkok)	17,900	27,300
Hungary (Budapest)	4,200	6,400
India (Bombay)	2,100	4,300
Nigeria (Lagos)	1,600	1,500

Source: Union Bank of Switzerland, as given in *Business Week*, 19 December, 1994a. p. 42

South Korea

The South Korean government recognized, fairly early on, the importance of S&T for economic growth, especially for a country that has poor endowments of natural resources. Indigenous technology capability building through the establishment of research institutions for technology absorption, adaptation and innovation has been the core of S&T policies. This domestic technology capability was seen as complementing imported technologies to generate synergetic effects (Yu, 1995). At the time of independence in 1945, only a quarter of the 25 million population was literate and there were severe shortages of skilled workers, technicians, engineers and managers (Kim, 1989; Vogel, 1991). After independence, the government increased investment in education from 2.5 per cent of its budget in 1951 to more than 22 per cent in 1987 (Amsden, 1989, pp. 238–9; Kim, 1989, p. 18). In 1987, about 98.8 per cent of the population up to the age of 14 received education and the proportion pursuing university education rose from 10 per cent in 1970 to more than 25 per cent in 1987. In 1988, apart from the 1.4 million students enrolled in higher education at home, there were 50,000 more studying abroad (*Korea Business World*, December 1989, p. 8).

The Korean Institute of Science and Technology (KIST) was established in 1966 and several other institutes were added subsequently, with government funding, to carry out applied R&D and engineering and to train engineers and researchers in a range of fields such as machinery, electronics, telecommunications and energy. By 1990, the total number of people engaged in R&D activities had increased to 70,503, of which 55 per cent worked in private R&D laboratories, 30 per cent in educational institutes and 15 per cent in government research institutes (MOST, 1993, p. 23). An analysis of the S&T indicators shows a pattern of development with 'a slow start-up in the 1960s, a take-off in the 1970s, followed by rapid growth through the 1980s and into the 1990s' (Hobday, 1995).

Government spending on S&T-related activities increased more than sevenfold, in current prices, from US$ 702 million in 1981 to 5,259 million in 1990 and about fivefold in real terms, rising from 0.89 per cent of the GNP to 2.2 per cent (MOST, 1993, p. 21). However, the government's share in total national R&D effort was reduced steadily, due to increased efforts by the private corporate sector. By 1993, private firms accounted for over 80 per cent of total R&D expenditure, increasing from 48 per cent in 1980 and 10 per cent in 1965 (Swinbanks, 1993, p. 377; Lim, 1992, p. 14).

To enable it to catch up with the industrialized countries in high science and technology areas, South Korea is building science parks along the lines of Japan's Tsukuba Science City, with companies and research laboratories clustered together in one location. South Korea also initiated a US$ 12 billion Highly Advanced National Project, targeting fields ranging from pharmaceuticals to high-definition television. Funding for science is also rising rapidly, with the total R&D budget going up from US$ 620 million in 1980 to US$ 5 billion in 1990 in constant 1987 prices. Although South Korea has made advances in applied research, its university system and academic research are weak, so to strengthen this area support for basic research is also increasing. The budget of the Korean Science and Engineering Foundation (KOSEF), the main agency for distributing basic research grants, has gone up from US$ 1 million in 1977 to US$ 140 million in 1992 and is expected to go up to US$ 625 million by 2001 (*Science*, 15 October 1993, p. 355).

Although the design and R&D capabilities have improved over time, South Korea's S&T system is still weak in innovation and basic science research aspects, compared to the industrialized countries. In 1990, the number of research scientists and engineers per 10,000 workers in South Korea was only 33, whereas the figure for Japan was 87, the USA 77, Germany 56 and Switzerland 44. South Korea was better than Singapore with 28, but less than Taiwan with 44. (NSTB, 1991, pp. 12–17). The weakness of South Korea's science base is also reflected in the low quantity and quality of the papers published in the international journals. The Science Citation Index (SCI)'s data for 1990 showed that South Korea was ranked thirty-second in the world with only 1,800 publications and even the citation rate of these publications was very low (Swinbanks, 1993, p. 379). A partial explanation for this could be that the government and industrial efforts have been aiming at short-term and medium-term research projects that have a direct bearing on the economy rather than on long-term basic research (*Science*, 15 October 1993).

However, the in-house R&D strength and capabilities enabled the large South Korean companies to enter into strategic partnerships with the world's leading companies on a more equal footing, rather than as a junior partner. Such partnerships facilitate access to leading-edge technologies as well as markets (Freeman, 1994; Hobday, 1995). Some South Korean companies have also started establishing basic research institutes. For instance, Hanhyo Institute of Technology, a 40-person laboratory with an annual budget of US$ 7 million, established by the synthetic fibre-maker Hanil, is not geared towards producing a commercial product. Its long-term objective is to establish itself in bio-pharmaceuticals. The institute's strategy is to focus on advanced niche areas, such as basic research on angiogenesis, where there is relatively little global competition and there is a possibility for developing innovative products (*Science*, 15 October 1993).

China

China's S&T system is undergoing major changes. The Chinese Government considers science and technology to be twin engines of economic growth. The changes that are underway in the S&T system are the result of recent trends in S&T internationally as well as the reconstruction of the domestic economy. Among the changes are: (a) emphasis on the co-ordinated development of S&T; (b) increased efforts on R&D in applied science and technology; (c) establishment of horizontal links between scientific research institutes, industries and local governments; (d) acceleration of the commercialization of scientific research results; and (e) restructuring of the funding system to encourage research institutes to undertake R&D oriented towards economic development (Yuan, 1995).

As a result of these changes, the S&T system is moving from bureaucratically controlled resource allocation to competitive research grants. In an effort to persuade scientists to make direct contributions to the economy, the government has reduced the operating budgets of the institutes of the Chinese Academy of Sciences (CAS) by 70 per cent. At the same time, the government through the Natural Science Foundation of China (NSFC), founded in 1985, is attempting to foster a competitive environment through an investigator-initiated grant system for research projects. NSFC is organized into six departments: maths and physical sciences, chemical science, life science, earth science, materials and engineering science, and information science (*Science*, 15 October 1993; *Science*, 17 November 1995).

According to the Science and Technology Commission's figures, in 1993 China had 640,000 people engaged in R&D activities full-time, including 418,000 scientists and engineers. About 50 per cent of them work in government R&D institutions, a third in the universities and the rest in the corporate sector. In 1993, China incurred an expenditure of US$ 7.5 billion on science and technology-related activities, one-third of which was classified as R&D and the rest covered various activities including primary and secondary school teachers. About 7 per cent of the R&D funds are devoted to basic research, 30 per cent to applied research and the rest is classified as development. The Chinese Academy of Sciences (CAS) is the biggest scientific agency with an annual budget of US$ 300 million. It operates 123 institutes and employs 80,000 people across all fields of science. Apart from CAS and other organizations focused on research, most ministries also carry out mission-oriented R&D (*Science*, 17 November 1995, p. 1135).

In 1984, the Chinese Government initiated a programme called 'State Key Laboratories', supported by the State Planning Commission. The objective of this programme is to strengthen a few laboratories for a breakthrough into the forefront of global science. There are eighty such laboratories managed by several ministries and they are achieving successes. For instance, the Beijing Electron Positron Collider (BEPC), a 5.8-Ge V ring, China's first high-energy particle accelerator, was built in just four years at a cost of only US\$ 350 million. The laboratory gave a jump-start to China in many advanced technologies such as superconducting magnets, klystrons and electronics, and has recorded the world's best measurement of the tau lepton mass. As spin-off benefits, BEPC has also developed several commercial products such as superconducting magnets for medical magnetic-resonance imaging machines and high-vacuum technology for integrated circuit manufacturing (*Science*, 15 October 1993; *Science*, 17 November, 1995).

With the general budget situation for research institutes getting worse, many institutes have established spin-off companies or established links with industry. For instance, the Shanghai Institute of Biochemistry, known for synthesizing insulin in the 1960s, now owns a scientific equipment-making company and has converted its reagent factory into a joint venture with a Hong Kong company. Another institute in Chengdu manufactures an anti-hypertension drug, which it developed. China's military research establishment is also developing civilian products to earn profits. Apart from the regular products such as automobiles, refrigerators and washing machines, the military factories are also producing products incorporating their advanced technologies. Such products include satellites, nuclear reactors and computer-controlled tele-communications networks (*Science*, 15 October 1993).

However, the Chinese S&T system still has several structural and organizational weaknesses before it can catch up with the S&T systems in industrialized countries. Some of these weaknesses are lack of innovation, refusal to co-operate with other national laboratories, disregard for intellectual property rights and unfamiliarity with the cultural norms of international science and weakness of English language abilities among scientists. The Chinese S&T system is also dominated by secrecy. This lack of openness leads to organizational rivalries draining the strength of the scientific system. It is also difficult to understand the way individual programmes are undertaken and to obtain accurate and comprehensive pictures of many aspects of Chinese R&D activities (*Science*, 17 November 1995).

According to Yuan (1995) the Chinese S&T system has weaknesses in three aspects: first is the operating mechanism. The government management and central planning system insulated the research institutes from economic or market relevance or competition. As a result, the institutes lacked the capability and the initiative to serve the economic objectives. Second is the personnel management prior to 1978. The distribution of scientists and technicians was skewed, with most of them concentrated in institutions of higher learning and research centres, rather than in industry. The number of scientists and technicians working in industry and agriculture was less than the number of them employed in the administrative services. Consequently, when China needed to urgently develop energy sources, communication and transport, building materials, textiles and other industries, it was faced with an acute shortage of scientists and technicians in these areas. Third is the organizational structure. As there were no links between the research institutes and industry, the research, design, education and production systems lacked co-ordination and connection. The military and civilian sectors and the different government departments and the administrative regions of the country also did not work with one another.

Taiwan and Hong Kong

The other countries in Asia have also built up scientific and technological research institutes to assimilate and develop technologies. Taiwan' s Industrial Technology Research Institute (ITRI) was founded to develop a range of industrial technologies, including metals, chemicals, electronics, energy and aerospace. It assists Taiwan's small-scale industries by transferring production-ready technologies to them. Taiwan's domestic integrated circuit industry is mainly a spin-off of R&D activities at ITRI. ITRI also spun off two laboratories as private companies, United Microelectronics Corporation in 1979 and Taiwan Semiconductor Manufacturing Co. in 1986. Hong Kong established a new University of Science and Technology (HKUST) in 1991, with large funding and world-wide recruitment to foster regional development.

Hong Kong has also established a series of separate institutions for technology development and its integration with the industry. These institutes co-ordinate through a network of cross-board memberships to address the following issues:

- incubation and technology transfer for high-tech start-up companies, especially in information and materials technologies (Hong Kong Industrial Technology Centre – HKITC);
- providing multidisciplinary consultation and professional and technical education to companies (Hong Kong Productivity Council and HKITC);
- providing industry-specific technical centres for applied research (several design centres under the Vocational Training Council), such as Management Development Centre (research and training, especially for small owner-managed companies), ASIC design centre, Electronic Data Processing Centre, and Precision Sheet Metal Processing Centre.

(Liang and Denny, 1995)

The drive for new initiatives to build up S&T in Asian countries comes mainly from the talented and well-trained scientists and engineers returning home from the West. They are helping to link Asian science with the international mainstream. Such a reversal of the earlier brain drain trends is occurring because the scientists are attracted by the new opportunities and challenges and improved living conditions in their home countries. These returnees are also becoming instrumental in forging links between institutes in the region. Asian countries, realizing that as individual nations they do not possess the resources to develop S&T in all fields, are forming strategic alliances. For instance, the electrical engineering laboratory at Fudan University in Shanghai, China, is designing very large-scale integrated circuits to be fabricated by companies like United Microelectronics Corp. of Taiwan and Samsung of South Korea. Shanghai's Institute of Organic Chemistry is synthesising potential anti-cancer molecules for Singapore's IMCB (*Science*, 15 October 1993).

The innovation system in India

India was one of the few developing countries that adopted a scientific policy as early as in 1958. Since independence in 1947, through its five-year development plans, India has built up capabilities in a range of S&T fields. In recent years, the policy focus has been on health-related technologies, biotechnology, electronics, computers, education, oceanography and the environment.

S&T planning is now integrated with socio-economic planning. The financial allocation for scientific and technological activities in the five year plans increased from Rs. 2000 million in 1951–56 to Rs. 48 billion in 1985–90. The percentage of GNP spent on R&D rose significantly from 0.23 per cent in 1958–59 to 1.1 per cent in 1986–87, but went down to 0.83 per cent in 1992–93. The number of scientifically and technically trained manpower has gone up from 190,000 in 1950 to 3.4 million in 1992–93. In terms of S&T infrastructure, India has established a chain of national laboratories and institutions, apart from over 1,200 in-house R&D units set up by various public and private enterprises. By 1992–93, there were 2,519 R&D laboratories in the country (DST, 1994; Sikka, 1990).

The S&T manpower engaged in R&D activities has increased significantly over the last two decades. The figure went up from 109,766 in 1974 to 184,096 in 1980 to 244,049 in 1984 to 289,716 in 1988 (UNESCO, 1992, pp. 5–87). In terms of sources of funding for R&D activities, about 85 per cent of the expenditure comes from government agencies, with four areas, defence, agriculture, atomic energy and space accounting for over 50 per cent of the national R&D expenditure. The industrial sector, both public and private enterprises, accounts for 30 per cent of the R&D (Long, 1988, p. 395). The figures remained almost the same in 1994 (UNESCO, 1997).

India devotes approximately 14 per cent of the nation's R&D expenditure to basic research, 28 per cent for applied research, 32 per cent for development and 26 per cent for other activities, including administrative functions (DST, 1984–85). If this 26 per cent of R&D overheads is spread among R&D categories with equal weight, the figures would rise to 19 per cent for basic research, 38 per cent for applied research and 43 per cent for development.

The proportion spent on basic research appears to be quite high, more so because the data do not include the research conducted in the universities. Even in the USA, the allocation of R&D funds is 12 per cent for basic research, 22 per cent for applied research and 66 per cent for development, and nearly 60 per cent of the US expenditure for basic research is accounted for by the universities (Long, 1988, p. 407).

With this background information, individual components of the innovation system in India can be analysed. India's national system of innovation consists of (a) universities and 'institutes deemed to be universities'; (b) research institutes and laboratories managed by the central and state governments; and (c) the industrial sector, both public and private enterprises. Each of the components has built up remarkable capabilities and successes since independence. However, the scientific potential has remained confined within the individual components, without strong links and flows of information between them. The university system has been primarily concerned with education to supply theoretically trained manpower, whereas most of the national research efforts are concentrated in the national research institutes, without links to the industry and economy. Industry, on the other hand, has been mostly dependent on imported technologies, with little inclination for development of proprietary technologies. As a result, all three components, though performing their sphere of functions creditably, have failed to appreciate their inter-dependence. The functioning and structure have been somewhat similar to that of the national systems of innovation in the former Soviet Union and East European countries.

The university system in India

At the time of independence, India had only twenty universities, modelled on the British universities, whose main orientation was that of supervising affiliated teaching colleges, setting the curricula and administering examinations. Presently there are 183 universities[3] and 7,513 colleges affiliated to the universities (DST, 1994). The orientation of universities has changed from that of administrative supervision to direct involvement in research and graduate training activities. Except for a few national universities, the university system is under the jurisdiction of the state governments. Within the system the notables are the Indian Institutes of Technology (IITs), with a curriculum focused on science and engineering. These institutes are funded by the central government, with sufficiently large budgets to buy modern equipment and recruit talented staff. As a result, they have attained high standards comparable to the technical universities in the industrialized countries (Long, 1988). The nationwide stiff competition among students to enrol in the IITs enables the institutes to recruit the best talent.

University education in India is a mammoth activity, given the number of students (3.5 million in 1984–85) spread across the nation in thousands of colleges. In 1990, 750,000 bachelor degrees were awarded in all subjects, of which 23.4 per cent (175,774) were in the natural sciences and engineering fields (NSF, 1995, p. 39). In 1992–93, 4,579 doctoral degrees were awarded in S&T fields and 64.4 per cent of them were in pure science fields (DST, 1994). With the population growth, there is constant demand for more universities and colleges, while the concern for inadequate funding of existing units, and thereby the compromises made in quality, is also increasing. Among the important units within the university system for education and research, especially for S&T faculties, are the IITs, the Indian Institute of Science (IISc), the regional engineering colleges (RECs) and the central universities located in different regions of the country.

> The quality of India's colleges and universities proper is exceedingly variable. The several major universities in large cities, most of which have a few nearby colleges directly associated with them, are of relatively high quality, and all are extensively involved in research and in graduate training of scientists and engineers. Their nearby associated colleges also tend to be of much above average quality. In stark contrast, the isolated colleges in small towns far from the urban areas can be virtually incapable of giving adequate training in science or engineering. Often they have only the bare bones of laboratories and minimal scientific equipment and library facilities.
>
> (Long, 1988, p. 400)

In the evaluation of India's R&D programmes, the research activities of universities are generally not taken into account. This situation is similar to that of the US universities before the 1950s, i.e. before government support for research in the universities became significant. Even though the research activities of the US universities in science and engineering were substantial, they were not recognized explicitly in the budgetary provisions. The university research was categorized under training of graduate students and this has several disadvantages: first, by not recognizing the research contributions that universities make, the university groups are less likely to be brought into collaboration with other research organizations; second, this makes it difficult to raise adequate funding for Indian universities, especially for library and research equipment; third, 'it implicitly lends support to the feeling of many bright graduates of Indian colleges that they must go abroad to get a first class training in science and engineering' (Long, 1988).

The wide differences in the quality of education across the university system, the inadequate facilities in all except the important institutions and the high level of production of graduates tend to lead to high levels of unemployment of the educated. The problem of excess supply over demand for personnel is especially serious for science graduates and this may continue for a long time. There are about three million scientists and engineers (excluding medical doctors) and an annual entry of an additional 175,000 new graduates. An approximate estimation of scientific and technical positions requiring a graduate or higher degree will be about 100,000 college and university teachers, 125,000

R&D personnel, and 100,000 scientific and technical administrators, and with an upward adjustment there will be an estimated 350,000 scientific and technical jobs. Even if this number is likely to increase, it may not match the present 6 per cent growth in university enrolment (Long, 1988, pp. 401–2).

Indian Institutes of Technology (IIT)

IITs have a special place in the university system of India. Presently there are six IITs located in Bombay, Delhi, Kanpur, Kharagpur, Madras and Guwahati. These institutes were established on the lines of the Massachusetts Institute of Technology (MIT), USA, and IIT graduates are trained to become engineer-scientists, in contrast to the engineer-manager training style of other engineering colleges. IIT graduates receive substantial inputs of basic sciences, as an important component of their curricula. For instance, in IIT Bombay, basic sciences receive 30 per cent of the attention, engineering sciences 25 per cent, professional courses 30 per cent and the humanities and social sciences 15 per cent. The corresponding figures for MIT are 25.4 per cent for basic sciences, 20.5 per cent for engineering sciences, 32.1 per cent for professional courses and 21 per cent for the humanities and social sciences (Singh, 1995, p. 2392).

With the desire to be on par with the best institutes in the West and to remain abreast of the latest in the field of technology, the IITs devised their syllabi at a high level of sophistication. The faculty also comprises mainly people who were educated in the American universities and this led to a situation of graduates getting acquainted with the kind of technology that was not well diffused in the country, since Indian industry had been operating with obsolete pre-Second World War technologies. However, IITs earned a good national and international reputation for education. So, when the IIT graduates applied for higher education, the universities abroad, especially in the USA, offered them places and after completion of their education they were offered jobs in universities and industry. Thus, most of them stayed on abroad. Those who returned found themselves unsuited to Indian conditions, because they were trained to do advanced technological work including designing, whereas the Indian industry required only maintenance personnel (Singh, 1995).

Surveys conducted from time to time showed that over the years, about 30 per cent of the IIT graduates settled down abroad. The proportion was much higher for certain fields such as computers, electronics, etc. and less for civil engineering. Some graduates have become successful entrepreneurs themselves, while others have turned to managerial or civil service jobs (Singh, 1995). However, with the changes in the Indian economy since 1990, Indian industry is realizing the importance of developing modern technologies themselves and IIT graduates are finding better opportunities within the country. They are the most sought after R&D personnel by the TNCs, who are setting up global R&D facilities in India. These new opportunities are to some extent arresting the brain drain from the IITs, and in a reversal of the earlier brain drain, many

IIT graduates who settled abroad for many years are also returning to India either as entrepreneurs or as representatives of the TNCs.

Research institutes and laboratories

In 1994, in India 83.6 per cent of the national expenditure on S&T-related activities was incurred by the central and state governments and 15.4 per cent by the private sector (UNESCO, 1997). The central government supports the largest proportion of national R&D efforts through its scientific agencies. Each of these agencies supports a number of R&D units. Most of them are primarily focused on development, but several of them are mainly involved in basic research. For instance, four of the twelve R&D units under the Department of Atomic Energy are primarily institutes for basic research: Saha Institute of Nuclear Physics, Tata Institute of Fundamental Research, Variable Energy Cyclotron, and the Institute of Mathematical Sciences. In total, the central government supports about 500 R&D laboratories and the state governments support another 100 (Long, 1988).

The Council for Scientific and Industrial Research (CSIR) was established in 1942 as an autonomous body with responsibility for scientific and industrial research and development in India. It maintains a network of forty national laboratories, two co-operative industrial research associations, and eighty extension or field centres, in total accounting for about 10 per cent of the central government's expenditure on R&D. To facilitate the transfer of R&D results from the national R&D laboratories to industry, the National Research and Development Corporation (NRDC) was established in 1953, as a public sector corporation. Its main objectives are:

1   transferring technology and licensing know-how developed in the R&D institutions;
2   filling technological gaps in the country by promoting developmental projects in collaboration with industry;
3   participation in the equity capital of companies exclusively set up for the utilization of NRDC technologies for the first time;
4   encouraging inventive talent in the country;
5   development and transfer of technologies appropriate to the rural areas;
6   promoting utilization of Indian technology abroad;
7   promoting horizontal technology from industry to industry.

Although NRDC was seen as a vital link in the innovation chain, its success so far has been limited. Its comparative lack of success can be partly explained by the attitudes of Indian industry towards indigenous technologies and their preference for imported technologies.

India's tradition of national planning for socio-economic planning has also extended to research and development programmes. The government policies from time to time make a special case for increased emphasis on particular areas of S&T called 'thrust areas', two of which in recent years have been biotechnology and telecommunications.

Biotechnology research programme

In 1979–80, India decided to treat biotechnology as a new thrust area for research and development and to facilitate implementation of this decision, the National Biotechnology Board was set up within the Department of Science and Technology (DST). After monitoring and assessing the field, the Board issued a report on a long-term plan for biotechnology emphasizing the great potential of the field and its likely importance to major problem areas of India.

The Board identified manpower development as being crucial for bio-technology development in the country and recommended increased education and training programmes in the field, and devising of a scheme of incentives to speed up the development of industrial applications. Accordingly, several steps have been taken to accelerate the implementation of the new biotech-nology programmes. To carry out basic research in the field, CSIR established the Centre for Cellular and Molecular Biology and government support for R&D in genetic engineering has increased. To supervise and co-ordinate the multiple programmes, a new Department of Biotechnology was established within the Ministry of Science and Technology. India's capabilities in this new field were recognized in international circles, when UNIDO established its International Centre for Genetic Engineering and Biotechnology in India.

Centre for Development of Telematics (C-DOT)

India was well known for its poor telecommunications infrastructure until recently. Telecommunications was earlier considered a luxury by a developing country and was assigned a low priority in the national plans. However, in the 1980s, the government realized the importance of a reliable and well-spread telecommunications infrastructure for modernization and development. Until then the telecom industry in India depended entirely on imported technology and the manufacturing and marketing of telecommunication equipment and products were exclusively reserved for the public sector enterprises. Realizing the importance of telecom technology, the government of India has decided to develop capabilities in this technology and in August 1984, the Centre for Development of Telematics (C-DOT) was established with the following objectives: (a) to develop sophisticated telematics technology and products indigenously; (b) to digitize India's telephone network to improve the overall service; and (c) to prepare for an integrated services digital network (ISDN) in the future.

The plan at C-DOT was to use Indian-made components as far as possible, i.e. Indian-made micro-processors, even if they were not technologically sophis-ticated. This was to encourage the development of the indigenous component industry. The idea behind it was to have a system that might not be sophisticated, but one that was adequate and better suited to Indian conditions, and at the same time more advanced than the existing systems in India (Göransson, 1993).

With the cost of imported technologies in mind and the urgency of improving the telecommunications infrastructure, C-DOT was given a tight schedule of three years and about US$ 30 million to come up with usable products. C-DOT had to come up with products that suited Indian conditions, such as managing the heavy traffic due to low density of telephones among the population and operating conditions that need to cope with the power failures, etc. C-DOT successfully met the challenges and displayed its digital switching systems at the Telecom 87 exhibition in Geneva, Switzerland. By 1987, C-DOT had designed the following family of four digital switching systems: the Private Automatic Branch Exchange (PABX), the Rural Automatic Exchange (RAX), the Main Automatic Exchange (MAX) and the Trunk Automatic Exchange (TAX) and these systems had been licensed to several companies for manufacture. Several other developing countries had evinced interest in C-DOT technologies (*Communications International*, February 1988).

In the process of developing this product line, C-DOT built up a 500-strong manpower force trained in digital switching technology and about 100 different vendors in the country for capacitors, diodes, transistors, PCB connectors, mechanical backplanes and similar components. A quality control programme was set up with several laboratories as part of the programme. The C-DOT programme also enforced standardization of systems in the Indian telecom industry that was previously lacking (ibid.).

C-DOT was involved in co-ordinating with other telecom R&D organizations in India, including those involved in fibre-optics technology and also maintained close links with universities to encourage research in this area, through fellowships and research grants. Therefore, education and other competence-building efforts were one of the important elements of C-DOT's strategy, the idea being to have a buffer or surplus personnel to transfer to the industry. Such a strategy might also have led to companies sponsoring their engineers to join the design teams at C-DOT for a specified period, leading to a flow of personnel between R&D organizations and industry (Göransson, 1993).

New efforts at building links with the industry

In recent years S&T institutions in India have been strongly criticized for pursuing research that is of little relevance to the industries and the economy. Consequently, the Indian government through various measures is now encouraging scientists to work closely with industry. These measures include incentives such as bonuses and a share of royalties from products created through their research. While offering such incentives, the government is also reducing its budgetary support to the research programmes, compelling institutions to find alternative sources of funding.

In response to the changing national and international economic, trade and intellectual property environment, the CSIR is also reorienting itself to become more user-responsive and market-driven. Although it has obtained 470 patents so far, it has earned very little income from them. CSIR laboratories have not been successful in either developing relevant processes or marketing them. Technologies developed by them have not attracted the attention of industries because the processes have been unrelated, inappropriate or have been at the infancy stage, requiring the industry to take up further development work on them. At the same time, Indian industry also generally lacked the inclination or the ability to utilize these technologies, because of their preference for proven foreign technologies. However, the government directive now compels CSIR laboratories to earn at least 33 per cent of their budget from external sources. Presently only 11 per cent of CSIR's budget comes from private industry. In an effort to get closer to industry, CSIR is reconstituting the Research Advisory Councils of its laboratories. These powerful councils, which oversee each laboratory, are now required to draw two-thirds of their members from industry. The old councils comprised mostly eminent scientists with a few industrialists occasionally. This reconstitution of the councils is expected to lead the laboratories to incorporate research programmes that are relevant to the problems facing local industry (*Science*, 10 March 1995, pp. 1419–20; *EPW*, 1 July 1995, p. 1539).

However, there have already been several cases of universities and research institutes having strong links with the industry. For instance, the Department of Chemical Technology in Bombay University has received about US$ 600,000 over the last five years since 1990 from industry, most of it from the domestic Reliance Industries. Its faculty members have also been providing consultancy services to the industry. A third of such consultancy earnings by its faculty go to the department and in 1994 it amounted to US$ 133,000. One of the faculty members of the department designed a novel gas-liquid reactor for catalytic hydrogenation, a process used to produce industrial chemicals. The demand for this reactor is booming because the savings from the catalyst it uses cover the cost of the entire system in only three months (*Science*, 10 March 1995).

The National Environmental Engineering Research Institute (NEERI), a part of the CSIR network, is earning 65 per cent of its US$ 1.7 million annual budget by selling its products and services. There are about 146 externally funded projects at the institute ranging from developing biosurfactants from industrial waste to developing lead-resistant catalytic converters. Similarly, the Indian Institute of Science (IISc), through its collaboration with Metur Chemicals, helped India become self-sufficient in silicon manufacture. Although IISc gets about half of its budget from external sources, only 10 per cent comes from industry (*Science*, 10 March 1995).

R&D *in the industrial sector in India*

Indian industry's contribution to the nation's R&D efforts has not reached the desired level for an economy that wants to grow rapidly. Industry's share of national R&D expenditure increased from 24.3 per cent in 1990–91 to 26.4 per cent in 1992–93 (*Science*, 10 March 1995, p. 1419). This is in contrast to the industrialized countries where corporate R&D accounts for the largest portion of national R&D efforts. Hence, in recent years, the government has taken the initiative to increase R&D efforts by private industries and to facilitate collaboration between Indian and foreign companies.

At the time of independence in 1947, there were only eight R&D programmes within industry and now there are more than 1,000. Three independent factors led to this growth: first, the public sector industries established R&D units, partly to reduce the dependence on foreign technologies, and partly because some industries, with rapidly changing technologies (telecommunications and nuclear power), necessitated indigenous R&D; second, the affiliates of TNCs, for whom research was a normal component, established small but growing R&D programmes; and finally, the large private sector industries established increasingly developed R&D units, partly to overcome the constraints of importing technology, in larger measure to develop new processes and to adapt imported technologies to the local conditions (Long, 1988).

R&D is increasingly encouraged by the government for various reasons. The government realized the need for indigenous R&D in industries not only to develop proprietary technologies, but also to absorb the imported ones. The success of NIEs, who in the past had imported technologies from India, pointed out the weaknesses of Indian industry as well as the policies. The government's earlier restrictions on imports, including materials and equipment for R&D, permitted only the performance of limited industrial R&D in India. The government R&D programmes in CSIR laboratories had not been successful, for a variety of reasons, in enhancing the capability of Indian industry. Therefore, in 1985, the government, through the Department of Scientific and Industrial Research (DSIR), launched a comprehensive 'Promotion of Industrial Research' programme. The programme includes recognition of in-house R&D units; import facilities for research and development activities; import duty exemption; preferential treatment in licensing; and fiscal incentives for scientific research.

In 1992–93, the industrial sector accounted for 26.4 per cent of the total national expenditure on R&D activities, of which the private sector accounted for 56.8 per cent. However, industry as a whole spent only a marginal proportion of their sales on R&D. Industry invested only 0.57 per cent of their sales on R&D, with the private sector faring relatively better, with 0.64 per cent, than the public sector with 0.51 per cent. As on 1 April 1992, there were 37,182 personnel directly engaged in R&D activities in industry, of which 62 per cent were employed in the private sector companies. By level of qualification of industrial sector R&D personnel, 7.8 per cent were PhDs (9.2 per cent in private sector), 22.9 per cent post-graduates (25.9 per cent in private sector), 39.8 per cent graduates and 29.5 per cent diploma and other qualifications. In the private sector, the industrial groups transportation, electrical and electronics, drugs and pharmaceuticals, chemicals (other than fertilizers), industrial machinery and metallurgical industries accounted for 65.3 per cent of total R&D expenditures in 1992–93 (DST, 1994, pp. vii–viii).

The Indian patent system

India is not a signatory to the Paris and Berne Conventions, but offered intellectual property protection under its own Patents Act of 1970, some of the provisions of which are not in accordance with international practices. Indian law attempts to strike a balance between the interests of the property holder and the social interest as defined by the government. This Act differs from international practices with respect to drugs, medicines and food prepared or produced by chemical processes (NSF, 1995). Apart from the patent protection period being less than in international practice with respect to these industries, the Act also provides for the issue of compulsory licensing by the patent holders to others after a certain period of time. The unique feature of this Act, to which many foreign companies take objection, is that, in these two industries, the Indian Act does not provide patent protection to the product but only to the process. In other words, this permits imitators to arrive at the same product through a slight variation in the process. The Act also provides for compulsory production of the patented product within the country, within a specified period of time, to prevent loss of benefits due to dormant patents as occurs in many other developing countries. Nevertheless, an analysis of the patent data in India shows that many foreign firms have registered their patents in India.

During the period 1972–73 to 1991–92, a total of 40,944 patents were published in India, of which foreigners held 75 per cent. During the decade 1972–81, the average annual patent filing in India was of the order of 3,136 applications, with Indians accounting for 1,202 and foreigners 1,934. During the decade 1982–91, the average annual filing increased by about 300 applications to an average of 3,459, of which Indians accounted for 1,072 and foreigners 2,387. During this period the contribution of Indians decreased, while that of foreigners increased by nearly 23 per cent (CSIR, 1994, p. 32).

With 1972–73 as the base, between 1974–75 and 1984–85, the patent filing declined considerably. During this period, filing by Indians remained constant, but filing by foreigners declined in all these years. This decline is attributed to the fall in filing of food and drug patent applications by foreigners after the enforcement of the Patent Act, 1970. During the period 1974–75 to 1991–92, a total of 27,704 patents published in India originated abroad. The USA alone accounts for about one-third (34 per cent) of the patents held in India by foreigners, followed by West Germany (13.6 per cent) and the UK (11.2 per cent). Others include France (6.9 per cent), Japan (5.6 per cent), Switzerland

(4.7 per cent), Italy (3.6 per cent), the USSR (3.1 per cent) and The Netherlands (2.8 per cent). Countries registering a proportion of 1–2 per cent include Sweden, Australia, Hungary, former East Germany and Canada. About 21 other countries register a level of less than 1 per cent each. An analysis of patents held by seventeen major countries reveals that many of them substantially increased their patenting activity in India only recently, i.e. during the five-year period 1987–88 to 1991–92 (CSIR, 1994, pp. 10–14).

The top twelve patent holders along with the number of patents they hold in India are CSIR (1,409), Hoechst AG (543), Siemens AG (396), Hindustan Lever Ltd. (324), Union Carbide Corp. (292), Bayer AG (281), ICI (267), Westinghouse Brake and Signal Co. Ltd. (247), Lucas India (219), Shell International (198), Pfizer Inc. (188), Westinghouse Electric Corp. (180) (CSIR, 1994, p. 27). Among these, except for CSIR, all the others are transnational corporations.

At the beginning of 1999, India was preparing to amend its Patent and Copyrights Acts, in accordance with the regulations of the World Trade Organisation (WTO). The bill had been approved by the Indian parliament. India also decided to become a signatory to the Paris and Berne Conventions. Under the new Act, the food and drug industries are accorded the same treatment as in international practice, with the recognition of product patenting. As a result, the patent filing activity, both by Indian firms and transnational corporations, is expected to go up considerably in the near future.

The electronics industry in India

International corporate R&D activities in developing countries, in recent years, have been mainly dealing with new technologies, i.e. microelectronics (including ICT), biotechnology and new materials. Therefore, it is important to analyse the status of industries based on new technologies in a discussion on the R&D environment in the host country. Among new technologies, microelectronics is by far the most advanced in its industrial applications. Hence, in this section, the strengths and weaknesses of the Indian electronics industry, particularly the computer hardware and software industry, are analysed.

The Indian electronics industry has shown significant progress since its reliance on imports from TNCs in the 1960s. The first computer was introduced into India in 1956 for use at the Indian Statistical Institute. The growth and capability of the Indian computer industry are today the results of several policy changes that swung between being liberal and restrictive. Through these policy swings, the Indian computer industry managed to increase its growth rapidly.

Until liberalization in 1991, Indian manufacturers, due to the high tariff protection, were able to compete with the imports and achieve increasing import substitution. However, the import content in the computers produced in India had been fairly high (Heeks, 1995). It decreased by more than 20 per cent between 1982 and 1984, but then rose by over 40 per cent between 1984 and 1987, mainly due to import policy changes (GOI, 1987; IDC 1987; Shekhar, 1988). By then, around 80 per cent of the components, in value terms, for computers manufactured in India were imported. The remaining components were procured from domestic suppliers. However, after 1987, the Indian component industry showed remarkable progress and the import content of the computers manufactured in India fell to around 60 per cent in the early 1990s (Tandon *et al.*, 1991; Raman, 1993).

In the early 1980s, the Indian component industry was characterized by high costs, poor quality, outdated equipment and lack of R&D. Although the industry improved after 1987, the manufacture of many components, including the central processor, in a rapidly changing technological conditions, requires large scales of production and high investment costs. In a fiercely competitive international market for components, it may not be economically viable for India to undertake components production. In the computer industry, scale of production is an important factor determining competitiveness and the minimum efficient scale of production for microcomputers or basic PCs is around 50–100,000 computers per year (Cline, 1987; World Bank, 1987). However, in 1993–94, the biggest Indian company produced only about 20,000 micro-computers of different varieties, with not more than 8,000 units of a particular chip variety (*Dataquest*, 1994). Although there is a growing domestic capability in the manufacture of peripherals, the strength of Indian computer hardware producers lies not in the manufacture of components, but in the design and integration of PCs (*FTBR*, 8 February 1995).

The Indian computer market is small, but the potential is large. In 1993–94, only 180,000 PCs (1 per cent of the global sales of 18 million) were sold, but the market is projected to grow to one million PCs by the turn of the century. According to the International Data Corporation, the sales of 286-based systems are declining in India, while those of 386- and 486-based systems are increasing. The market share of local area network (LAN) servers is increasing even more impressively. In 1993–94, the Indian IT market grew by 33 per cent, whereas the LAN server market grew by 152 per cent. In 1995, growth in the IT industry was estimated to be around 40 per cent in value and 60–70 per cent in volume (*FTBR*, 8 February 1995).

The majority of Indian computer hardware companies are small, and import the components and assemble the computers in India. Such firms mainly deal with low-end PCs, with a very low scale of production, often working in the 'grey market' (using smuggled parts). Their competencies usually consist of low-tech activities such as sourcing of components from different suppliers both imported and indigenous, component insertion, flow soldering and limited functional testing. However, these limited technological competencies can form the base on which higher capabilities can be built (Heeks, 1995; *FTBR*, 8 February 1995).

In the 1980s, the large computer companies such as Hindustan Computers Ltd. (HCL), Delhi Cloth Merchants Data Processing (DCMDP), Operations Research Group (ORG) and Wipro Information Technologies Ltd. (WITL), which were leading in the micro- and mini-computer markets undertook design innovation production. They designed the overall layout for the circuit boards and peripherals, procured components such as processors from both foreign and domestic suppliers, and produced and tested the final units. These computers used locally produced operating systems, systems and application software (Heeks, 1995; Grieco, 1982; Subramanian, 1992).

However, due to the liberalization of imports in the mid-1980s, these design innovators could not compete with the kit assemblers in the market for low-end PCs and some of them lost their design capabilities. In some companies the R&D staff were shifted to develop more powerful computers based on the Intel 80286 and 386 and Motorola chips that came out into the market around this time. These design innovators, because of their technology and knowledge base were accepted as 'beta-test' centres for new Intel and Motorola chips, enabling them to design the machines based on the new chips before these chips were sold on the open market (Heeks, 1995).

The large companies had been able to build up design and systems integration capabilities, partly because of the government procurement policies. In 1985, the government adopted the more powerful UNIX operating system rather than the MS-DOS system for computerization of its banking industry. This policy decision opened up a large market for UNIX-based hardware built with mainly Motorola and Intel 80286 chips and encouraged R&D investment, which, in turn, resulted in the hardware innovations of the late 1980s and early 1990s (Heeks, 1995). Even after the import liberalization, many design innovators such as HCL, WITL and DCMDP were able to produce and market computers conceived, designed and developed entirely based on their in-house R&D (Jaikumar and Hutnik, 1988). Each of the large companies assigned more than a hundred personnel and about US$ 10 million to R&D. Their R&D pattern had been that of working simultaneously on ten or more new designs for main circuit boards, secondary boards and peripherals (Hutnik, 1988).

HCL, WITL and DCMDP produced the world's first Intel 486-based computer; multiprocessing board super-minicomputer; Reduced Instruction Set Chip (RISC)-based multiprocessing minicomputer; and Motorola-based multiprocessing UNIX minicomputer. They also started exporting their designs and machines to the industrialized countries, including the USA. Due to the difficulties of achieving scale economies and decreasing prices, it became difficult to be competitive in the export markets and many of India's IT firms found software exports to be more lucrative. However, liberal access to inputs has allowed the Indian firm, PCL, to export motherboards to the US company Dell since 1993 as part of a US$ 50 million contract. However, after 1992, the design skills began to ebb away with the growth in demand for, and availability of, foreign brands. Many companies became technical support units or entered into collaboration with TNCs. After the tie-up with Hewlett Packard (HP), HCL's R&D personnel were assigned to work on HP's research projects and WITL tried to do contract R&D work for TNCs. After 1992, these companies designed and marketed their own products, such as the HCL Meteor and WITL's

Synergy hardware range, but faced increasing pressure from competing products marketed by TNCs, with some of whom these firms had a tie-up (HP or Sun or Acer, respectively) (Heeks, 1995).

R&D strength only remained in still protected areas. For example, thanks partly to the US Government's earlier block on export of the Cray super-computer, at least four Indian parallel processing supercomputers had been designed and built by the mid-1990s: ECIL's Anupam system, C-DAC's Param (in collaboration with Tata Unisys), the National Aeronautical Laboratory's Flosolver (in collaboration with Wipro), and the Centre for Development of Telecommunications' Chipps-16. The export of four 'Param' supercomputers from the DOE's Centre for Development of Advanced Computing (C-DAC) shows that there are opportunities for export of specialist hardware from India based on local innovation. However, with large Indian companies being more interested in software exports, any large-scale hardware exports will have to follow the PCL-Dell model of international subcontracting. Given the barriers of scale economies, brand name, marketing channels, finance, skills and quality, collaboration with a TNC is the only way to begin large-scale exports (Heeks, 1995).

The software industry

The growth of India's software exports has a significance for the technology capability of a developing country. With the hardware technologies changing rapidly, it becomes difficult for developing countries like India to catch up with the industrialized countries. However, developing countries may have a competitive advantage over developed countries in software development due to the availability of skilled and educated manpower in some of these countries (Schware, 1987). Although the literature refers to software development as a labour-intensive process, the skills required are knowledge-intensive and are different from those used in assembling the hardware type of technologies. There is a substantial requirement of technical and knowledge inputs, and cognitive skills in software development. It is this kind of manpower that is in short supply in developing countries, and therefore, not all developing countries may be in a position to develop software both for domestic use and export (Reddy, 1991).

According to a study made by the Harvard Business School in 1994, 'software is one of the few industries in India closest to achieving a sustainable competitive advantage'. TNCs, such as IBM, perceive the Indian software industry to be advanced enough to be recognized for its ability to innovate and adapt to new circumstances (*FTBR*, 8 February 1995). The know-how and expertise of companies like Tata Consultancy Services (TCS) and Computer Maintenance Corporation (CMC) have greatly helped India in its early efforts to become a player in the global software industry.

Until recently, Indian software exports consisted mainly of 'body shopping', in which software engineers were sent abroad to work on a contract-basis at a client's premises. However, with the restrictions placed on the issue of visas to visiting Indian software professionals, the on-site software development has decreased sharply from 92 per cent of total software exports in 1987–88 to 58 per cent in 1994. Indian software firms are increasing off-shore software development. Around half of the 100 satellite data lines in India are used by software exporting companies to connect them with clients in Europe and the USA. Indian software development activities are not only cost-effective compared with those in the industrialized countries (salaries being less than a fifth of those in the USA), but have acquired a solid reputation. For instance, TCS, the largest software company in India with 4,000 professionals, was able to establish a facility for Swissair in Bombay to process one million flight coupons a month with just 100 people, while Swissair previously used to do this in Zurich with twice as many. In 1995, HCL America, an Indian company, was awarded the Datamation Quest award for contract programming. An Indian-designed software package 'Executive Desk' was launched in the USA and Europe in January 1995 (*FTBR*, 8 February 1995). 'Ramco Marshal', an enterprise-management system aimed at large- and medium-sized companies, designed by Ramco Industries, an Indian company, has become popular in the USA and other markets abroad.

To utilize the local software capabilities, several Western computer companies, including IBM, Motorola, Hewlett Packard, and Digital Equipment, have set up software development centres in India. The Software Engineering Institute (SEI), funded by the US military at the Carnegie Mellon University, USA, constructed a Capability Maturity Model (CMM) to evaluate the capabilities of different software companies. The companies are accorded various levels of the CMM, ranging from Level One to Level Five, depending on the quality standards achieved by them. Since 1994, it has rated 200 firms for excellence. Only two companies have achieved the highest Level Five, so far. One of them is the Motorola's software unit in Bangalore, the Motorola India Electronics Pvt. Ltd., and the other is the Laurel-NASA, based in USA, which is developing a space shuttle (*FTBR*, 8 February 1995; *Business Line*, 30 January 1996a).

A survey of 62 large US corporate users by Mehta Corp., a Massachusetts-based consulting group, found that 37 per cent of the companies have used or would consider using foreign vendors for software development. Among the foreign suppliers, India comes top as the most favourite supply source, with 82 per cent of them favouring India, followed by 59 per cent Ireland, 53 per cent Taiwan, 41 per cent Singapore and 29 per cent others (*News Week*, 18 January 1993, p. 33).

While the large companies have established their reputation for good quality work in India and abroad, many small companies have entered the market in the last few years lured by the export prospects and growing domestic market, as well as the relatively low barriers to initial entry in terms of capital requirements. Over three-quarters of the Indian software companies have fewer than twenty-five professionals. However, the structure of the sector is highly concentrated, with the top three companies selling more than US$ 10 million each. About 95 per cent of the firms had a sales turnover of lower than US$ 100,000 each. Nevertheless, the number of companies with sales exceeding US$ 1 million is growing: from fifteen companies in 1990 to forty-four in 1992; and twenty-seven of them exported over US$ 1 million each in 1992 (Hanna, 1994).

The demand for electrical and electronics engineering personnel is well established in India. Among them, the demand for telecommunications specialists has been increasing steadily, along with the expansion of satellite, telephone and TV transmission capacity in the country. The demand for tele-communications services by private sector firms is expanding, particularly for international services. The core of the informatics labour force is its software personnel. In India the demand for software personnel is larger than the supply, resulting in high turnovers of personnel. The main gaps appear to be in personnel for employment in computer software and computer application firms. To overcome this gap, the computer applications (user) firms will have to do much more in-house training (Hanna, 1994).

A small but growing number of domestic software firms possess some advanced technical capabilities that rival international competitors. But so far there has been little technology transfer from the large companies to the small and medium firms, as the large firms are reluctant to subcontract to other software houses. This has created barriers to specialization in software tech-nologies. Even the large hardware firms are not inclined to subcontract software design to the relatively smaller software companies. Strong links between large and small software firms could result in substantial benefits, and a case in point is the adoption of Computer-Aided Software Engineering (CASE). A large Indian software company is marketing a CASE package in the USA that was designed and developed in India. Its application results in substantial increases in the productivity of software engineers but in India very few companies have adopted CASE tools. The increased use of CASE by US software companies is likely to increase the productivity and quality gap between US and Indian software engineers, undermining India's current comparative advantage in this part of the market (Hanna, 1994).

The innovation system in Singapore

One of the main characteristic features of Singapore's development policies has been its emphasis on education and training for human resource develop-ment and the development of the industrial infrastructure. TNCs are attracted to invest in Singapore mainly because of the availability of low-cost engineers, technicians and workers. Singapore's S&T development is largely due to the TNCs that brought sophisticated technologies and know-how to the country, than to indigenous R&D efforts. In the 1970s, the Economic Development Board (EDB) organized apprenticeship programmes in specially established government-industry training centres with industrialized countries such as Japan, Germany and France. By 1991, there were five institutes in operation with a total of 2,500 students. The main objective of these institutes was to provide engineering, technology and craft education for the manufacturing industry. In 1991, Singapore produced 22,000 engineers and craftsmen. This annual supply of about 38 technically trained people per 100,000 population is one of the highest per capita in the world (Hobday, 1995).

Even though there have been some variations in Singapore's S&T policies from time to time, they mainly exhibit the following features: (a) reliance on FDI as the main means for technology transfer; (b) flexible and responsive human resources development; (c) infrastructure development to support application and diffusion of technologies; (d) rapid diffusion of technology in the government; and (e) gradual increase in indigenous R&D. While the reliance on TNCs served the economic purposes in the 1980s, the government realizes the importance of indigenous R&D efforts to sustain the growth in the 1990s and beyond. To enhance the capabilities of the national system of innovation, Singapore's Government devised a new National Technology Plan (NTP) in 1991 to promote R&D over the next five years. The National Science and Technology Board (NSTB) was established to co-ordinate the implementation of the plan. The key technology areas identified by the NTP include biotechnology, medical sciences, food and agrotechnology, microelectronics, electronics systems, information technology, manufacturing technology, materials technology, energy, water, environment and resources (Wong, 1995).

NSTB's mission is to develop Singapore's capabilities in science and technology to support selected industrial and service sectors, to enhance Singapore's competitiveness. NSTB actively assists both local companies and TNCs in Singapore to help them build up their R&D capabilities. NSTB provides comprehensive support services to individuals and start-up firms in all stages involved in bringing an idea from concept to commercialization. These include concept, prototyping and patenting stages, networking, seed funding as well as access to incubation space, technical advice and business consultancy.[4]

In 1995, R&D expenditure in the higher education sector, consisting of two universities and four polytechnics, was S$ 193.4 million, an increase of 7.7 per cent over the previous year. The government-established research institutes spent S$ 181.4 million, registering an increase of 54.8 per cent from 1994. This huge increase is partly due to the inclusion of four research centres, which were under the higher education sector in 1994. The government sector spent S$ 110.4 million in 1995, registering a decline of 22.3 per cent over the previous year. The private sector, however, accounts for the largest R&D expenditure, both in absolute terms and as a proportion of total R&D expenditure. In 1995, the private sector incurred an expenditure of S$ 881.4 million, which accounts for 64.5 per cent of the total gross expenditure on R&D (GERD) and an increase of 19.7 per cent over the previous year. The average R&D expenditure per company increased from S$ 1.72 million in 1994 to S$ 2.0 million in 1995, registering an increase of 16.3 per cent (NSTB, 1996, p. ix).

In 1995, Singapore spent a gross total of S$ 1,366.55 million on R&D, of which pure basic science research accounted for 4.5 per cent, strategic basic research 9.9 per cent, applied research 42.1 per cent and experimental development 43.4 per cent of the total (ibid., p. ix). This indicates that the innovation system in Singapore is highly geared towards development work, with little emphasis on research.

The data in Table 3.8 indicate that Singapore's R&D activities are highly focused in selected areas. It shows Singapore's strength in engineering and computer sciences. Nearly 60 per cent of the total R&D expenditure is incurred in the engineering field. In the case of private sector, this figure further increases to 67 per cent of the total R&D spending by the private sector. Private sector's R&D expenditures were the largest in electrical and electronics (S$ 284.19 million) and mechanical (S$ 143.81 million) engineering fields. Within the engineering sector, the public research institutes have exclusively focused on electrical and electronics field. The data also show the relative weakness of Singapore's innovation system in the science fields, particularly biomedical sciences.

The research institutes established by the government mainly targeted high-technology fields. Many of them are under NSTB's supervision. NSTB supervises fourteen research institutes and centres. They provide R&D infrastructure and the resources of manpower, skills, knowledge, products and

Table 3.8 Singapore's R&D expenditure by area of research in S$ million (%)

Area of research	Private sector	Higher education	Govt. sector	Public research institutes	Total
agricultural sciences	6.29 (0.7)	10.41 (5.4)	4.43 (4.0)	5.00 (2.8)	26.51 (1.9)
computer and related sciences	152.71 (17.3)	12.59 (6.5)	6.17 (5.6)	45.87 (25.3)	217.34 (15.9)
engineering	590.77 (67.0)	75.24 (38.9)	66.71 (60.4)	74.57 (41.1)	807.29 (59.1)
biomedical sciences	2.55 (0.1)	34.77 (18.0)	0.32 (0.3)	0.00	37.63 (2.8)
natural sciences	82.38 (9.3)	41.11 (21.3)	4.67 (4.2)	43.63 (24.0)	171.79 (12.6)
other areas	46.68 (5.3)	19.23 (9.9)	28.12 (25.5)	12.00 (6.6)	106.00 (7.8)
Total	881.38 (100)	193.36 (100)	110.41 (100)	181.42 (100)	1,366.56 (100)

Source: NSTB (1996, p. 13)

processes, which the industry can draw upon. Each institute or centre concentrates on specific technology areas to train and build up manpower, and to develop and refine enabling technologies and capabilities.

In the early 1990s, with a special focus on the electronics industry, the government established specialized technology institutes, such as the Institute of Manufacturing Technology, the Information Technology Institute and the Institute of Systems Science. These institutes have been involved in software training, electronics engineering, advanced mechanical engineering and research. The Magnetics Technology Institute carried out engineering and research work for the disk drive industry. The Institute of Microelectronics was established in 1992 to support the semiconductor industry with silicon processing technology, component reliability, failure analysis, computer-aided circuit design and systems applications. The institute's objective is to enable the large chip producers to carry out complex development work locally in the long run. To encourage links between these research institutes and the activities of TNCs, and to obtain advice on projects and strategic direction, the managers of TNCs were appointed to the advisory boards of these institutes (EDB, 1992; Hobday, 1995).

In an effort to use high technology to strengthen its economy, the government is also encouraging basic research at the National University of Singapore. The university accounts for about one-third of Singapore's R&D and has built up a solid reputation in materials technology, microelectronics and information technology. The Institute of Molecular and Cell Biology (IMCB) was established in 1987, with an investment of S$13.8 million and an annual budget of about S$17.5 million. It employs more than 200 scientists, many of them recruited from the leading laboratories in the West. It has so far published more than 200 scientific papers with impressive citation figures. Amylin Pharmaceuticals of the USA purchased the rights to the first product of IMCB, a transgenic rat model for Type II diabetes, to test a hormone called amylin as a potential treatment. IMCB has also been active in research on tyrosine phosphates (cancer research) and sequencing the genomes of several fish species, which could serve as a reference for the human genom project. Glaxo of the UK, convinced of the capabilities and infrastructure of the institute, established a S$ 31 million trust fund for a drug screening centre in the institute, and another S$ 30 million for a neurobiology laboratory focusing on genes that are expressed only in the brain (*Science*, 15 October 1993, p. 353).

Such successes made the government expand its research base by establishing the Bioscience Centre and the Food Biotechnology Centre. The Bioprocessing Technology Unit, established in 1990, seeks to improve purification, synthesis, and fermentation methods for commercial production. The establishment of IMCB was part of a broader strategy to target biotechnology, a field suitable for the island country as it requires few natural resources, is high value added and can make strategic use of the country's global business networks. To develop this industry, the EDB established the Singapore Bio-Investments Pte Ltd, and by 1991 had invested S$ 41 million in twelve local biotech start-ups, involved in health care, food and agricultural products. The company also invests in companies abroad that may in the long run become strategic partners (*Science*, 15 October 1993, p. 353).

However, Singapore's innovation system has several weaknesses. In contrast to its large pool of technicians and production engineers, Singapore lags behind industrialized countries in the supply of research engineers and scientists. In 1990, Singapore had only 28 research engineers and scientists per 10,000 workers, in comparison to 87 in Japan, 77 in the USA, 44 in Switzerland, 43 in Taiwan and 33 in South Korea. R&D expenditure as a percentage of GNP is also lower compared with industrialized countries as well as Taiwan and South Korea. To correct this imbalance, Singapore is rebuilding its science and technology infrastructure. In accordance with the NTP of 1991, the National Science and Technology Board is to spend S$ 2 billion over a five-year period to increase the number of researchers from 28 to 40 per 10,000 workers and to raise its R&D expenditure as a percentage of GNP from 1 to 2 per cent by 1995. Apart from the emphasis on R&D promotion, Singapore has been following several other strategies to upgrade the country's technological capabilities. Such strategies include promotion of creative and design skills; international acquisition of technology-based companies; strategic partnership with key TNCs and overseas research institutes; and attracting S&T talents from abroad (Wong, 1995; Hobday, 1995).

By 1995, Singapore had managed to increase the number of research scientists and engineers (RSE) per 10,000 labour force to 47.7. However, the R&D expenditure as a percentage of GNP remained at 1.13 per cent (NSTB, 1996, p. viii). As Singapore is a small country, its dependence on foreign research personnel is substantial. Foreign citizens, with no permanent citizenship in Singapore, constituted 16 per cent of the total R&D manpower in Singapore in 1995. Table 3.9 gives data on R&D manpower by citizenship.

Table 3.9 Singapore's R&D manpower by citizenship, 1995

Occupation	Singaporeans and permanent residents	Foreign citizens	Total
Researchers at RSE			
– PhD	1,433	454	1,887
– Masters	1,632	416	2,048
– Bachelors	3,434	971	4,405
– Non-degree	1,688	92	1,760
Total	8,167	1,933	10,100
Technicians	1,602	77	1,679
Supporting staff	1,171	75	1,246
Total	10,940	2,085	13,025

Source: NSTB (1996, p. 19)

4 New trends in the globalization of corporate R&D

Selected empirical evidence

This chapter provides some empirical evidence of new trends in globalization of corporate R&D, i.e. performance of strategic R&D in developing countries by TNCs.

Evidence from previous studies

Table 4.1 gives the results of Ministry of International Trade and Industry's (MITI) survey of globalization of R&D by Japanese companies in 1990. The data show the dominant functions of overseas laboratories of Japanese firms to be supporting local production and sales, developing products for the local markets and technology monitoring. However, the data also show that Japanese R&D laboratories in other Asian countries are playing a significant role in developing products for the global markets as well as in basic research. Out of forty-four that mentioned developing products for the international markets as the main function of their overseas laboratories, fourteen are located in Asia, twenty in North America and eight in Europe. Out of twenty-five respondents whose overseas laboratories' main function is to carry out basic research, ten have their laboratories in other Asian countries, while thirteen are located in North America and one in Europe.

The results of the survey above, when compared with the other surveys of TNCs conducted in the past, indicate the changing pattern of international corporate R&D activities in developing countries. During 1977–78, Behrman and Fischer (1980) surveyed thirty-one American and seventeen European TNCs. They found that although several TNCs had located R&D in advanced developing countries (especially in Brazil, India and Mexico), their functions were limited to adaptation, local technical services and in very few cases product development for the local markets. A survey of overseas R&D activities of seven US multinationals by Ronstadt (1977) showed that almost all of them had located their R&D in other industrialized countries. Only two firms had located R&D in India, a developing country. The function of these units was to adapt the transferred technology to the local environment. In the few cases where such R&D was located outside the industrialized world, the host country had the potential for a large market with unique characteristics.

Table 4.1 Main functions of overseas R&D units of Japanese firms, 1990

Function	N. America	Asia	Europe	Others	Total
Gather information and analyse	75	73	19	16	183
Maintain links with local universities and industries	11	3	3	3	20
Support local sales	65	66	24	19	174
Support local production	51	116	11	24	202
Design products and concepts	19	18	4	5	46
Adaptation of imported products	23	31	5	5	64
Develop products to be produced and sold in the host country	52	78	18	29	177
Develop products in pioneering fields of the host country	32	21	10	2	65
Develop products for international markets	20	14	8	2	44
Basic research	13	10	1	1	25
Others	7	17	1	7	32
Total	368	447	104	113	1032

Source: The 4th Survey of Statistics on Overseas Investment. The Ministry of International Trade and Industry (MITI), Japan, 1990. As given in Odagiri and Yasuda (1993)

Yamada (1990) discussed the strategies of Japanese TNCs that are involved in R&D abroad, especially in developing Asian countries. Japanese firms have started following a policy that has been referred to as 'glocalization', indicating that while the basic management strategy is determined on a global basis, complete attention is paid to localization. Localization includes such things as transfer of technology, development of local suppliers, strengthening local design and development activities, etc.

Among the Japanese companies, there is now an increasing trend towards 'international specialization by region'. The corporate strategy of Japanese companies divides the world into four regions, the United States, Europe, Asia and Japan, in which product development, production and sales are carried out in a co-ordinated manner for each region through regional management subsidiaries. Matsushita Electric has extended the 'four region' concept to the technological domain and has established overseas research centres in North America and Taiwan. This will be an important strategic consideration in the glocalization of Japanese companies. Aiwa established an R&D centre in 1988 in Singapore to develop new products such as a radio cassette unit with a compact disk player for global markets. Aiwa is also planning to set up an Asian regional management centre in Singapore. Matsushita and NEC have established integrated circuit design facilities in Singapore. TNCs like Sony are establishing a co-ordinated regional group structure in Singapore, independent of Japan and encompassing R&D, component purchasing, production, marketing, financing and personnel (Yamada, 1990).

Another trend that has been emerging among Japanese companies is to transfer the entire 'technology for low-end products', i.e. R&D, production and marketing, to firms in developing countries, so that the Japanese operations can concentrate on high-end products. Hitachi, for instance, has formed an alliance with Goldstar of South Korea, under which Hitachi is providing 1M DRAM technology to Goldstar. Many other Japanese companies have started to set up R&D centres in Asian countries for designing new integrated circuits (ICs): Taiyo Yuden has begun to design hybrid ICs in South Korea; Seiko Epson has started to design application-specific integrated circuits (ASICs) in Taiwan; Fujitsu has begun to design ASICs both in Taiwan and Singapore; Toshiba is transferring all prototyping, development and production of low-end video cassette recorders to Samsung Electronics in South Korea, so that it can concentrate its own resources on high-end market models (Yamada, 1990). Table 4.2, gives the evolution of R&D activities in East Asia by the Japan-based TNCs and the driving forces behind it.

The information Technology Strategic Alliances (ITSA) database registers publicly announced inter-firm alliances in information technologies (IT) worldwide. The release of 95.0 of ITSA registered 27,280 agreements (23,802 complete records) announced during 1984–94. These included 2,683 alliances (2,361 complete records) with at least one partner from a developing country or economies in transition. According to these data, the alliances involving non-OECD country firms not only kept pace with the rapid rates of growth in

Table 4.2 The evolution of Japan-based TNCs' R&D in East Asia

Industry	Information collection base	Development/ design base	R&D base
electrical appliances	early 1970s	mid-1980s	since 1988
– driving forces	market needs, data and standards	support of local manufacturing and politics	new tech concepts
automobiles	early 1970s	mid-1980s	mid-1990s
– driving forces	regulations, data and market needs	support local manufacturing and demand	regional markets and global sourcing
pharmaceuticals	mid-1970s	mid-1980s	since 1987
– driving forces	standards, technical information and data	establish standard R&D system	utilize local technicians
software	late 1980s	early 1990s	mid-1990s
– driving forces	local skills assessment	shortage of personnel in Japan	harness local talents

Source: *Nihon Keizai Shimbun*, 2 May 1991, p. 27 as adapted from Simon (1995, p. 24)

the total alliances world-wide but also gained considerable ground. Alliances involving at least one firm from a non-OECD country increased from 6 per cent in 1988 to 12.8 per cent of total alliance records in 1994 (Vonortas and Safioleas, 1997, p. 659).

Computers dominated the international alliances world-wide. But, in the case of developing countries, alliances in telecommunications surpassed those in computers in 1990. The majority of alliances by developing country firms involved either the creation or exchange of technological knowledge. Contractual agreements and joint ventures have been the dominant mode of alliances involving firms from developing countries. Equity investments, agreements for co-operative R&D, and licensing followed the order respectively. Mergers and acquisitions occupied the last place (ibid.).

Registered R&D alliances doubled during 1989–90 and doubled again during 1993–94 indicating an increasing number of developing country firms that are capable not only of adapting importing technologies but also of participating in the creation of new technologies. The rapid growth of alliances with developing country firm participation is largely due to growing alliances with explicit technological content. Purely marketing and distribution agreements did not exceed one quarter of the total since 1988. In fact, during 1984–94, 'a larger percentage of alliances with developing country firm participation had explicit technological content (75%) than the overall sample of reported IT alliances (worldwide) in the database (69%)' (ibid., p. 661).

Among developing countries, the firms based in East Asia had been particularly active in forming alliances. Alliances involving Asian firms (excluding the Asian republics of the former Soviet Union) accounted for 61.6 per cent of the total for non-OECD countries. Alliances involving firms from Eastern Europe and the former Soviet Union accounted for 21.2 per cent, Latin American firms accounted for 15.5 per cent, and the African firms accounted for only 0.2 per cent of the total for non-OECD countries. The countries of the former Soviet Union, together, accounted for more alliances than any other country, followed closely behind by China. Hong Kong and South Korea came third and fourth, respectively. Five other countries that registered more than 100 alliances are Taiwan, Mexico, Singapore, India, and Israel (ibid., p. 664).

RPI database on global corporate R&D in developing countries

A database on global corporate R&D activities outside the industrialized world has been developed at the Research Policy Institute (RPI), Lund University, Sweden. The database contains information on TNCs strategic R&D activities in developing countries and transition economies. Following the classification by Ronstadt (1977) and Reddy and Sigurdson (1994), the database contains data on TNCs' R&D activities aimed at developing products for the regional markets (regional technology unit-RTU) or developing products and processes for the global markets (global technology units-GTU) or basic research for long-term corporate use (corporate technology unit-CTU). R&D activities related to adaptation of products and processes to suit the local conditions (technology transfer unit-TTU) and product development exclusively for the local market (indigenous technology unit-ITU) are excluded from the purview of the database. The database lists own R&D affiliates of TNCs, joint venture R&D, subcontract R&D, university collaboration and technology alliances, when the source of technology is the developing country firm or when the alliance is two-way collaborative R&D (one-way technology flow to a developing country firm type of alliances are excluded).

Like most other databases, the sources of RPI database include national and international business journals, company brochures, press releases by companies, etc. The database is by no means exhaustive in its coverage. There will certainly be several more strategic R&D activities located in developing countries by TNCs that are not captured in this database. However, this database provides sufficient data to carry out an analysis of the trends in globalization of corporate R&D.

Table 4.3 provides data on TNCs' strategic R&D in developing Asia, host country and technology field wise. At the end of March 1999, a total of 286 strategic R&D activities were registered in developing Asia. In terms of technology fields, software R&D accounted for 36.7 per cent of the total, followed by R&D in telecom and network technologies with 17.1 per cent of the total. IC design and semiconductor technologies, and electronics have also registered

Table 4.3 TNCs' strategic R&D activities in developing Asia – host country and technology field wise (%)

	Hong Kong	Indonesia	Taiwan	South Korea	China	Malaysia	Singapore	India	Total
Biotechnology-food and plant genetics					7.1	6.3	2.8	3.6	3.5
Pharmaceuticals							4.2	8.7	6.6
Chemicals						6.3	4.2	4.1	3.8
Electronics			50.0	50.0	21.4	62.5	19.6	3.1	12.2
IC design and semiconductors	100.0	100.0	33.3	33.3	14.3	6.3	30.4	7.1	12.6
Software R&D					28.6	6.3	10.8	48.5	36.7
Telecom & networks					21.4	6.3	10.8	20.4	17.1
Computers			16.7	16.7		6.3	10.8	4.6	5.9
Engineering					7.1		6.5		1.4
Total	100 (1)	100 (1)	100 (6)	100 (6)	100 (14)	100 (16)	100 (46)	100 (196)	100 (286)

Note: Figures in parentheses are number of R&D facilities/units/activities registered

substantial R&D activities at 12.6 per cent and 12.2 per cent of the total, respectively. Conventional technologies, such as engineering, have registered little activity.

India (196) and Singapore (46) attracted the largest number of TNCs' R&D activities, followed by Malaysia (16) and China (14). In India, software has been the largest R&D activity, with 48.5 per cent of the country's total, followed by telecom and network technologies, with 20.4 per cent. In Singapore, IC design and semiconductor field registered the largest number of R&D activities, with 30.4 per cent of the country's total, followed by electronics, with 19.6 per cent. TNCs' R&D activities in Malaysia, Taiwan and South Korea are mainly concentrated in electronics. The data indicate that India has also become a location for TNCs' R&D in pharmaceuticals, chemicals and biotechnology (food and plant genetics) sectors. The data reflect broader technology-base of India across the range of technology fields, in comparison with other Asian developing countries.

Table 4.4 gives data on the form of TNCs' R&D activities in different host countries. Some 59.0 per cent of the total R&D activities in developing Asia have been in the form of own R&D affiliates, following far behind by joint venture R&D (18.2 per cent), technology alliances (10.5 per cent), university collaboration (7.0 per cent) and subcontract R&D (5.2 per cent). All forms of R&D are represented only in case of one host country, India. Technology alliances have been prominent in case of South Korea and Taiwan. This is largely because firms from South Korea and Taiwan have already gained international reputation for their technological capabilities, and therefore, TNCs do not hesitate to establish technology alliances with these companies. Such alliances are also growing in India, particularly in software field, where Indian companies earned international reputation. In case of India, what is interesting is the

Table 4.4 TNCs' R&D activities in developing Asia – host country and form of R&D

	Subcontract R&D	Own affiliate	Joint venture	Technology alliance	University collaboration	Total	
Hong Kong		100.0				100	(1)
Indonesia		100.0				100	(1)
Taiwan		50.0		50.0		100	(6)
South Korea		33.3		66.7		100	(6)
China		57.1	21.4		21.4	100	(14)
Malaysia		87.5	12.5			100	(16)
Singapore		95.7	2.2		2.2	100	(46)
India	7.7	49.0	23.5	11.7	8.2	100	(196)
Total	5.2	59.0	18.2	10.5	7.0	100	
	(15)	(169)	(52)	(30)	(20)	(286)	

Note: Figures in parentheses are number of R&D facilities/activities/units registered

collaboration between the Indian academic establishments and the TNCs, where significant CTU type of research is being carried out. University collaboration is also prominent in the case of China, but at a much smaller base of total R&D activities. Some of these collaborations may also be the result of Chinese government policy emphasis on location of R&D and technology transfer.

Table 4.5 gives data on the type of R&D performed in developing Asia by TNCs. Product and process development for the global market (GTU) accounts for 77.6 per cent of the total R&D activities, followed by RTU and CTU. In case of individual countries, these figures vary. Location of basic research to develop generic technologies (CTU) in developing countries is a significant development. China and Singapore have registered significant proportion of RTU type of R&D at 28.6 per cent and 26.0 per cent respectively of total R&D activities in those countries. CTU type has also been important (21.4 per cent) in case of China on a small base of fourteen in total R&D activities. The data indicate greater attraction of India's innovation environment as a location for CTU type of R&D activities.

Table 4.6 provides data from the home country perspective. US-based TNCs have been leading in investing R&D activities in developing Asia. Out of a total of 286 R&D activities registered in the database, US firms accounted for 157. The USA is followed by Japan with 45 activities, The Netherlands (16) and Germany (14). It is interesting to note the location of R&D by firms from developing countries in other developing countries. Firms from South Korea, Singapore, Malaysia and Thailand (included in others category in Table 4.6) have started using India as a base for their R&D activities, especially in software field.

For US-based TNCs, software (40.8 per cent) and telecom and network technologies (21.0) account for the largest proportion of their total R&D activities. However, US-based firms are the only ones performing R&D across

Table 4.5 TNCs' R&D activities in developing Asia – host country and type of R&D

	RTU	GTU	CTU	Total	
Hong Kong		100.0		100	(1)
Indonesia		100.0		100	(1)
Taiwan		100.0		100	(6)
South Korea		100.0		100	(6)
China	28.6	50.0	21.4	100	(14)
Malaysia	12.5	87.5		100	(16)
Singapore	26.0	71.7	2.2	100	(46)
India	8.2	78.6	13.3	100	(196)
Total	11.9	77.6	10.5	100	(286)
	(34)	(222)	(30)		

Note: Figures in parentheses are number of R&D facilities/activities/units registered

Table 4.6 TNCs' strategic R&D activities in developing Asia – home country and technology field wise (%)

	Food and plant genetics	Pharma-ceuticals	Chemicals	Electronics	IC design and semi-conductors	Software	Telecom and networks	Computers	Engineering	Total
USA	3.2	3.8	3.8	5.7	10.2	40.8	21.0	10.2	1.3	100 (157)
Japan	2.2	2.2		37.8	24.4	26.7	6.7			100 (45)
UK		40.0		10.0	10.0	10.0	20.0		10.0	100 (10)
Germany	7.1	7.1	7.1	14.3	21.4	42.9	7.1			100 (14)
Switzerland	14.3	28.6	28.6		14.3	14.3				100 (7)
South Korea		14.3				42.9	28.6	14.3		100 (7)
Sweden		28.6				14.3	42.9		14.3	100 (7)
France				14.3	28.6	42.9	14.3			100 (7)
The Netherlands	18.8		12.5	18.8	12.5	31.3	6.3			100 (16)
Others		12.5		12.5		56.3	18.8			100 (16)
Total	3.5 (10)	6.6 (19)	3.8 (11)	12.2 (35)	12.6 (36)	36.7 (105)	17.1 (49)	5.9 (17)	1.4 (4)	100 (286)

Note: Figures in parentheses are number of R&D facilities/units/activities registered

all technology fields in developing Asia. For Japan-based TNCs, electronics with 37.8 per cent has been the largest sector of R&D, followed by software and IC design and semiconductor technologies. Pharmaceutical and chemical fields have been the most important for Switzerland-based TNCs.

Table 4.7 provides data on form of R&D preferred by firms from different home countries. For almost all countries establishing own R&D affiliate seem to be the most preferred option in developing countries, accounting for 59.0 per cent of all R&D activities. Switzerland and France have the largest proportion of their R&D (87.5 per cent) in the form of own R&D affiliates, but at a base of only seven R&D activities each. In terms of absolute number US and Japanese companies have been involved in significant number of technology alliances with firms from developing countries. US-based TNCs have also been actively seeking collaboration with universities in developing Asia, especially in India, for their R&D in generic technologies (CTU).

Table 4.8 gives data on home country and type of R&D performed. The data indicate that the US-based TNCs have registered the largest number of CTU type of R&D in developing Asia. Sweden and Switzerland have the largest proportion (28.6 per cent) of their respective total R&D activities in the form of CTU, but at a smaller base of seven R&D activities each.

From the empirical evidence available on the emerging trends in the globalization of corporate R&D, it is also observed that different elements of new technologies prefer different types of technology environments among developing countries. These preferences in turn determine the direction of the flow of R&D-related investments, as shown in Figure 4.1.

Table 4.7 TNCs' R&D activities in developing Asia – home country and form of R&D

	Subcontract R&D	Own affiliate	Joint venture	Technology alliance	University collaboration	Total	
USA	3.2	61.2	17.2	10.8	7.6	100	(157)
Japan	8.9	60.0	20.0	11.1		100	(45)
UK	10.0	30.0	30.0	10.0	20.0	100	(10)
Germany	7.1	71.4	14.3	7.1		100	(14)
Switzerland		85.7		14.3		100	(7)
South Korea	14.3	28.6	28.6	28.6		100	(7)
Sweden		57.1		14.3	28.6	100	(7)
France		85.7		14.3		100	(7)
The Netherlands	12.5	62.5	18.8		6.3	100	(16)
Others	6.3	31.3	37.5	6.3	18.8	100	(16)
Total	5.2	59.0	18.2	10.5	7.0	100	
	(15)	(169)	(52)	(30)	(20)	(286)	

Note: Figures in parentheses are number of R&D facilities/activities/units registered

Table 4.8 TNCs' R&D activities in developing Asia – home country and type of R&D

	RTU	GTU	CTU	Total	
USA	9.6	80.3	10.2	100	(157)
Japan	11.1	86.7	2.2	100	(45)
UK	10.0	70.0	20.0	100	(10)
Germany		92.9	7.1	100	(14)
Switzerland	28.6	42.9	28.6	100	(7)
South Korea	28.6	71.4		100	(7)
Sweden	28.6	42.9	28.6	100	(7)
France	28.6	57.1	14.3	100	(7)
The Netherlands	12.5	68.8	18.8	100	(16)
Others	18.8	68.8	12.5	100	(16)
Total	11.9	77.6	10.5	100	
	(34)	(222)	(30)	(286)	

Note: Figures in parentheses are number of R&D facilities/activities/units registered

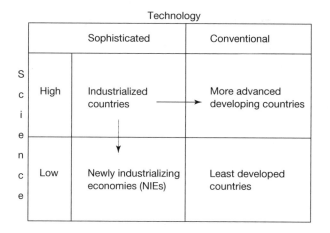

Figure 4.1 Direction of the flow of corporate R&D investments
Source: Reddy (1993, p. 98)

R&D into direct product design and development or embodied technologies (e.g. hardware technologies) are observed to prefer newly industrializing economies (NIEs – Hong Kong, Singapore, South Korea and Taiwan), that have a sophisticated technology base, but relatively not such a strong basic science base. On the other hand, R&D into generic technologies or disembodied knowledge seems to prefer the more advanced developing countries (e.g. Brazil and India), that have a relatively high basic science base, but do not have a sophisticated technology base. For a long time, these countries followed import substitution policies and built up broad but general capabilities in research-oriented upstream activities, which seem to be more suitable for R&D into generic and disembodied technologies. On the other hand, the NIEs followed export-led strategies and built up specialized capabilities in application-oriented downstream activities (especially superior production engineering) and this expertise seems to be more suitable for direct product design and development (Reddy, 1993).

Among the scientists and engineers engaged in research and experimental development, South Korea in 1983 had 16,371 people in engineering and technology fields, whereas there were 4,706 in natural sciences and 3,589 in agricultural sciences. By 1992, these figures had changed to 56,559 in engineering and technology, 11,950 in natural sciences and 5,364 in agricultural sciences. Figures for Singapore in 1987 were 2,007 for engineering and technology fields and 863 in the natural sciences and 55 in agricultural sciences (UNESCO, 1992, pp. 5–24; 1994, pp. 5–21). In other words, in 1983, South Korea had a ratio of two engineers engaged in R&D for every one scientist engaged in R&D, the ratio in 1992 changed to 3.3 engineers to one scientist. The ratio of engineers to scientists engaged in R&D for Singapore was 2.2 to 1. These figures suggest that South Korea and Singapore had a relatively greater concentration in building up a strong engineering capability than a science base.

On the other hand, among the scientists and engineers engaged in research and experimental development, India in 1988 had 20,599 in natural sciences, 16,306 in agricultural sciences and 32,068 in engineering and technology fields. The figures for Brazil in 1985 were 11,768 in natural sciences, 7,607 in agricultural sciences and 7,765 in engineering and technology fields (UNESCO, 1992, pp. 5–24). In other words, the ratio of scientists to engineers engaged in R&D in India was 1.2 to 1. The ratio for Brazil was 2.5 to 1. These figures suggest that India and Brazil had relatively more concentration in building capabilities in the sciences than in engineering fields.

Selected company-specific illustrations

This chapter includes information only on R&D centres of TNCs in developing countries dealing in product and process development for regional or global products and basic research, i.e. RTU, GTU and CTU types of units only. It does not include R&D units that are involved only in adaptation or product development for the local market, i.e. TTU and ITU types. However, it may be pointed out here that there are several cases of even TTU and ITU types of R&D units contributing to TNCs' global activities. For instance, Johnson & Johnson, a US-based TNC in the health-care products business, introduced a product in the USA, which had been developed in its R&D unit (TTU–ITU type) in Brazil (Behrman and Fischer, 1980). Similarly in 1988, ABB, in a reverse transfer of technology, introduced the SF6 Circuit Breaker technology, developed in its R&D unit in India (TTU–ITU type), in its activities in Europe.

VeryFone is a US-based TNC, manufacturing and marketing Transaction Automation Solutions, including all the associated hardware, software and networking. Its systems are sold in more than ninety countries. The company has globalized its engineering resources to minimize development bottlenecks and accelerate the delivery of new products. The company believes that dispersion of engineering resources around the world, close to different markets, provides a diversity of perspectives that leads to breakthrough products. To implement such a strategy, VeryFone established a system development centre and manufacturing facilities in Taipei, Taiwan, to leverage local product design and manufacturing resources. In addition, the company established system development centres in Bangalore, India, to take advantage of the wealth of high-quality engineering resources available in India, and in Paris, France, to gain access to chip-card and other technologies prevalent in Europe. Two other system development centres are located in the USA, in Auburn, California and Clear Water, Florida. Apart from these system development centres, VeryFone has also established application development centres in the USA, Germany, France, the UK, India and Singapore. Its manufacturing bases are located in the USA, Taiwan and China.

Motorola Semiconductors Hong Kong Ltd., a wholly owned subsidiary of Motorola Inc., was established in 1967 and is presently the headquarters of the company's Asia-Pacific Semiconductor Products Group. From a chip assembly and testing centre in the 1970s, the affiliate has been continuously expanded and upgraded. In 1986, chip design facilities were set up. In 1990, the Silicon Harbour Centre was established with an investment of about US$ 400 million, and the activities were expanded to include a new complex of chip assembly facilities, design activities, marketing and headquarters. Design facilities were upgraded to incorporate high density memories, ASICs, bipolar-MOS circuits and other complex chips. Out of 300 engineers that the affiliate employs, 90 are involved in design activities. Design and development activities include gate arrays and full custom chips for the consumer goods market. The centre mainly caters for the local firms and large TNC buyers. However, these chips become components in products manufactured for the global markets. Systems development is largely carried out in the USA, but some applied systems development work is being undertaken by the affiliate, e.g. for liquid crystal display drivers and action matrix TV displays (Hobday, 1995).

AT&T Consumer Products Private Ltd. (ACP), Singapore was established in 1986 with an investment of Singapore $ 100 million to make standard corded residential telephones, mainly for the US market. It was AT&T's first manufacturing facility outside the USA. By 1990, ACP had become AT&T's global centre for top-of-the-range cordless telephones. It has also designed and developed the new digital phones in-house. ACP's R&D unit is organized as a division of AT&T Bell Laboratories. It provides design support to ACP and the OEM suppliers in the region and is also responsible for developing new products (Hobday, 1995).

The Netherlands-based AKZO Chemicals assigned an R&D task on a contract basis to the National Chemical Laboratories (NCL) in India to devise a key ingredient for refining petroleum. NCL successfully developed the substance, Zeolite (*UNDP-World Development*, September 1991).

SGS-Thomson Microelectronics established a design and software development centre in India in March 1992 to utilize the highly skilled technical manpower in India. The centre presently employs more than 100 people, with a plan to double the number of people employed by the end of 1995. The centre has facilities for design and software development for R&D, full custom chip design, library development and application laboratory. The centre's various activities are carried out in six groups:

1   Central R&D – this group is responsible for developing new circuits and libraries, with the main focus on digital and analogue libraries, mixed analogue design, memories, VHDL modelling, synthesis, etc.;
2   Memory products group – this group is responsible for the complete development of SRAMs, EPROM, EEPROM, FLASH memories and Zeropower products, including design, characterization and transfer to production;
3   Programmable products group – this group is responsible for developing libraries on the latest embedded arrays and RAM generators for in-house and external customers world-wide. The group also develops software tools and test chips for validation and testing of circuits and libraries;
4   Asia Pacific Design Centre – design, layout and debugging of full custom ICs for telecom, consumer and computer peripheral applications. The chips include Monochip phone, PWM controller and Printer IC;
5   Application Laboratory – responsible for the design of complete system solutions in areas of multimedia, data communication, consumer products, computer peripherals, power, etc.;
6   Management Information System – all the in-house business applications are developed by this group.

An example of the success of the centre is the diffusion of the first 0.5 micron silicon at the crolles facility in early 1993. The full library was developed in the Indian design centre for this process.

Siemens Communications Software Ltd. was established in Bangalore, India, in April 1994. It currently has 110 employees engaged in R&D activities and is expected to employ 400 Indian professionals by the 1996 and 1,000 by the turn of this century. It is one of the fourteen R&D centres of the company world-wide, whose locations include Brazil, Canada, Germany, Italy, Portugal, Taiwan, South Africa, the UK and the USA. The entire R&D activities at the Indian centre relate to development of telecommunications software products for the global markets. R&D activities in these centres world-wide are in line with and integrated into the R&D activities of the international Telecommunications Network Division of Siemens AG, Germany. A dedicated 64KB digital satellite link connects the Bangalore centre to Siemens AG, Germany and other regional software development centres world-wide.

The Hoechst Centre for Basic Research was established in 1972, in Bombay, India. The centre is engaged in the search for biologically active substances from plants and microbial sources as leads for potential drugs or plant protection agents. The Indian centre forms a part of Hoechst's world-wide research and is the only 'lead discovery group' in target-oriented natural product research. India's vast natural resources and its long tradition of natural medicine made it a choice location for natural product research. The centre employs 200 scientists including over 50 PhDs. The centre's R&D activities cater to the domestic requirements as well as global market requirements. The centre works in close collaboration with the company's research laboratories in Germany and other countries. Over the years, it has discovered many lead compounds as potential drugs, some of which are being used world-wide as biochemical tools providing insight into cellular mechanisms. It has isolated 230 compounds of interest from micro-organisms and plant material, of which more than fifty have been found to be new. The focal points of research at the centre have been: (a) anti-infective – new effective anti-infectives against resistant bacteria, gram-negative pathogens, viral diseases; (b) cardiovascular – understanding of the related pathology aids to find new therapeutic approaches; (c) vaso-therapeutics – the search for safer and effective anti-inflammatory agents and immunomodulators; (d) metabolic disorders – new biochemical test models based on enzyme studies; (e) plant protection – biodegradable plant protection agents; and (f) animal health – veterinary drugs.

Hughes Software Systems (HSS), India, is a subsidiary of Hughes Network Systems, a unit of Hughes Aircraft Company and GM Hughes Electronics, USA. HSS specializes in the design and development of real-time embedded software for voice, data and video communication and other engineering applications for the global markets. HSS develops its own products and carries out turnkey projects. It is also involved in joint product development with the customers. HSS has been executing turnkey software development projects in the areas of integrated data communication networking, digital cellular communication, digital satellite communication, networking and integrated network management. The applications include development of software for VSATs, packet switches, routers, internetworking and wireless communication. Its design and development activities include real-time embedded systems, internetworking, routers, ISDN, system software and tools, switching systems, satellite, X.25, frame relay, ATM, protocols, software engineering, LAN/WAN, network management, signalling, GUI. HSS India has a state-of-the-art-computing infrastructure with individual workstations and common servers, and is linked up to the USA via a 64kbps-satellite link.

Wipro Infotech Group is part of the Wipro Corporation, an Indian conglomerate that is involved in services, technology and consumer products. Wipro Infotech Group offers its R&D competence to TNCs on a subcontract and collaboration basis. Wipro has core competencies in hardware design & ASIC, operating systems and networking technology. Its collaborative R&D projects with TNCs are characterized by replication of R&D environment similar to that of TNCs at Wipro, and sharing of sensitive technology. The distance factor is overcome through data and video links between the TNC and Wipro. This type of arrangement results in benefits similar to that of a joint venture, without the legal and equity problems. Wipro has also established an R&D centre in Silicon Valley, USA, to work with partners in evolving technologies. TNCs that have collaborative R&D ventures with Wipro include AT&T, Intel, Tandem and Stratacom. The Wipro group also has collaborations with British Telecom, General Electric and Acer of Taiwan.

Daimler-Benz Research Centre India (DBRCI) was established in 1996 as a wholly-owned company of Daimler-Benz AG. Its objectives are: (a) to be a part of the Daimler-Benz's global R&D network; (b) to become a link between the country's famed universities, software industry and research establishments; and (c) to benefit from the cost advantages of performing R&D in India and to cater to the needs of Daimler-Benz's business units in Asia. The core expertise of DBRCI lies in fundamental and applied research in areas that include communication technology based applications, avionics software (e.g. navigation and landing systems), software and hardware interfacing design and implementation and platform conversion. Presently, the centre has been working on fourteen projects, which include the interface design of avionics landing systems and the Smart GPS sensor project (an intelligent traffic guidance system and development of software). In its avionics project, the centre is collaborating with the Indian Institute of Science. The decision to locate in India was driven by the conviction that Daimler-Benz was investing in one of the world's leading high-tech regions. Daimler-Benz was attracted to India because of India's large pool of English-speaking high quality software professionals and the low costs of R&D.

5 International corporate R&D in India

Case studies and survey

The first section of this chapter presents three detailed case studies[1] of TNCs' R&D activities in India. In the second section the results of a questionnaire survey of thirty-two R&D units of TNCs in India are presented.

Astra Research Centre India (ARCI)[2]

Astra AB, founded in 1913, is one of the largest pharmaceutical companies in Scandinavia. Astra is highly research oriented and has its research laboratories in Södertälje (Astra Research Centre and Astra Pain Control), Gothenburg (AB Hässel) and Lund (Astra-Draco) in Sweden. Outside Sweden, it operates a Neuroscience Research Unit in London, Clinical Research Unit in Edinburgh and Astra Research Centre India in Bangalore. Recently two more R&D laboratories have been established abroad – one each in Canada and Australia. Astra's R&D budget exceeds US$ 130 million per year, amounting to about 20 per cent of the sales of Astra's products world-wide.

A new type of organization

Astra Research Centre India (ARCI) in Bangalore was established by Astra in 1985, although it was formally inaugurated in January 1987. As per the recommendation of the Government of India, at the time, the research centre was registered as a non-profit organization. ARCI is a unique organization in its structure and management. Although this centre is entirely funded (both capital and projects expenditure) and for all practical purposes, wholly owned by AB Astra, in legal terminology it is a society sponsored by AB Astra. Officially the centre views its relationship with AB Astra as a strategic collaboration and the companies, including Astra, utilizing any invention or know-how will pay a royalty fee to the centre. Such income gained will be used to expand the research activities at the centre and to enable it to become self-sufficient. AB Astra gets the first right of refusal to commercialize the innovations generated by the centre. The annual budget of ARCI accounts for approximately 2 per cent of Astra's total annual R&D budget. Every year the budget proposal from ARCI is reviewed by the corporate research committee of Astra. In 1995, Astra

AB has formed Astra Biochemicals Pvt. Ltd. in India. During 1995–96 the newly formed company acquired rights to all research work of ARCI.

Objectives of ARCI

- The pursuit of scientific research leading to the discovery of new diagnostic procedures, novel therapeutic products, and targets for rational drug design, for diseases afflicting large populations in both developing and developed countries.
- To achieve the above objective, by employing the powerful tools of molecular biology, immunology, cell biology, molecular dynamics and molecular graphics in highly focused and time-targeted projects.
- To closely interact with the research groups of Astra, Indian Institute of Science, and universities in India and abroad, through collaborative efforts, extramural support to projects of mutual interest, and sponsoring scientific meetings on relevant topics (Ramachandran, 1991).

In 1997, ARCI reprioritized its objectives. The charter of ARCI is now as follows:

- to sponsor biomedical research on infectious diseases with the objective of developing novel diagnostics and therapeutics;
- to maintain a library with specialization in biomedical sciences including medicinal chemistry and molecular modelling;
- to conduct workshops, symposia and seminars for the promotion of biomedical research.

Driving forces

The driving forces behind Astra are:

- Astra's awareness that India had much to offer in terms of scientific competence and talent, particularly in molecular biology, biochemistry and biophysics.
- Astra's corporate policy to pursue scientific research through collaboration with academic scientists in programs geared to the discovery of innovative drugs to combat diseases.

The primary driving force behind the establishment of ARCI is to recruit scientific personnel who meet the standards, requirements and needs of Astra. In terms of availability of scientific talents, Astra does not consider India as a developing country. In its opinion, scientists educated in India have made significant contributions both within and outside the country to the advancement of chemical and biological sciences. Indian scientists have occupied responsible leadership positions in major biotechnology R&D establishments throughout the world. Hence, it was considered that a centre for creative applied research in India would be able to attract and retain Indian scientists. From the corporate perspective of Astra, one of the driving forces to establish such a research centre outside the home country has been the shortage of R&D personnel in the field of biotechnology in Sweden. Although not officially admitted as a driving force, by establishing ARCI, Astra is also able to exploit the lower costs of R&D in India.

The organizational structure of ARCI is to be seen as a strategic collaboration with Astra. In recent years, corporate R&D units in industrialized countries have been participating in strategic collaboration, pooling of resources and expertise, to achieve cost-effectiveness. This practice is more prevalent in the case of biotechnology-based products, where developmental costs are very high (Ramachandran, 1991).

Astra's sponsorship of ARCI and its commitment to academic research may also be seen as an effort to ensure that new technologies are not bogged down by the expertise of in-house R&D. New ideas and knowledge may often emerge outside the conventional organization and location. Market motives did not play any role in the establishment of ARCI. The centre is not linked to Astra's Indian or Asian market strategy in any way. This is also clear from the absence of formal links between the centre and the Indian drug manufacturing company Astra-IDL, in which Astra owns 25 per cent of the equity.

Management of ARCI

ARCI's activities are supervised by a governing board, consisting of members nominated by Astra and the Government of India in equal numbers. In addition, the director of ARCI, appointed by Astra is an ex-officio member of the board. The governing board is presently headed by a Nobel Prize recipient in Medicine and includes several eminent scientists both from India and abroad. Working under the director are a deputy director and a pool of scientific staff and a small group of administrative staff. There are presently fifty scientific staff, with twenty-three of them holding doctoral degrees and the rest MSc, MPhil and MTech degrees. Only three have BSc degrees.

Several of the staff are Indian scientists who have returned from abroad. ARCI has been able to attract talented Indian scientists, including those with a number of years of experience abroad, to join the centre by providing all the facilities and a conducive environment similar to those in laboratories in industrialized countries. Many Indian scientists who are settled abroad, are also showing interest in spending a sabbatical year or two at ARCI. In this way ARCI is contributing to reversal of the brain drain.

Astra has more than 2,500 people engaged in R&D world-wide. From a world-wide perspective, the number of people employed at ARCI is not significant, but, according to Astra, the number of people employed at a centre is not a measure of its importance, because the resources required vary significantly between different stages of drug research and development.

Research projects

On the basis of the type of R&D performed, ARCI can be categorized as a global technology unit/corporate technology unit (GTU/CTU). R&D being carried out at ARCI relates to the products to be marketed world-wide by Astra. In addition, ARCI also carries out substantial mission-oriented basic research. The initial task at ARCI was to build the R&D standard up to international level in terms of laboratory equipment and personnel. Since drug R&D is a long-term process, to begin with, it was decided to develop products with a short-term time frame, such as enzymes of use in biotechnology and thereafter diagnostics. Many of these biochemicals were not available in India and were being imported from the USA and Europe in dry-ice shipments.

One of the major barriers to notable breakthroughs in India in the field of recombinant DNA technology has been the non-availability of reagents and the difficulties involved in obtaining dry-ice shipments (Sampath, 1990). During the initial years ARCI successfully developed the know-how for the preparation of several crucial reagents used in molecular biology research. The design and development of diagnostic procedures, using DNA probes and immunological methods, for the diagnosis of some infectious diseases were also successfully carried out. In addition, basic research on molecular biology, protein structure, gene coding etc., was also pursued. Successful development of such products of a standard to meet global market requirements helped in building up ARCI to the international level.

Since its inception, ARCI has filed patent applications for fifteen items and all of them have been approved. All the patents filed in India are also filed in Sweden. Applications for international patents, including the USA and Sweden, are being filed by Astra, the parent company. Having built up the organization to an international level, the centre is now entrusted with the tasks of drug discovery. Appraisal is underway to design a novel class of anti-bacterial agents.

In the decisions regarding the selection of long-term projects, the following criteria are applied: (a) the medical need; (b) the biological target suitable for drug design; (c) time needed to identify a candidate drug; (d) competition from other drug companies; and (e) estimate of financial resources required. These aspects are discussed in a forum consisting of scientists from different disciplines, university professors, medical experts, finance managers and marketing experts (Ramachandran, 1991). While allocating the R&D tasks in long-term projects, Astra takes into consideration the expertise available in its different research units including ARCI. For instance, ARCI has the full responsibility for drug R&D on malaria, tuberculosis and other infectious diseases. The main reason for allocating this task to ARCI is that Astra has a good research laboratory in a region where these diseases are prevalent. Because of the proven competence and performance of ARCI, Astra now has plans for its expansion.

ARCI's global and local R&D network

Figure 5.1 shows ARCI's integration into Astra's global corporate R&D structure and its external links, both locally and globally. It also indicates the extension of Astra's global research network with the establishment of ARCI. Through ARCI's local external network and network links abroad, Astra is gaining access to a wide network of scientists. Although, in legal terminology, it is a society sponsored by Astra, ARCI for all practical functioning is a wholly-owned R&D unit of Astra. Officially ARCI views its relationship with Astra as one of strategic collaboration, which gives the centre an opportunity to work with the research units of Astra as an equal partner and facilitates complementarity of collaborators' research efforts. As with other R&D laboratories of Astra, upgrading of equipment at ARCI has been taking place on a continuous basis. There are several joint R&D projects in which Astra's laboratories in Sweden and ARCI are collaborating, and intense project work with participants from R&D laboratories in Sweden and ARCI has been taking place. ARCI's researchers participate in project groups on an equal footing with the Swedish members, because of Astra's high opinion of their competence.

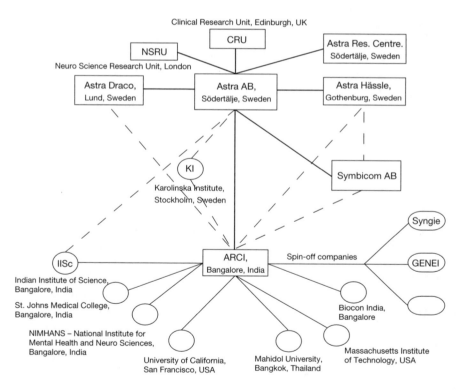

Figure 5.1 ARCI's global and local R&D network

ARCI and Astra-Draco have, for instance, collaborated in a research project on eosinophilcationic protein found in the lungs. This protein has anti-parasitic properties, but in large quantities can damage the lungs of asthma patients. Astra-Draco focused on the development of a protein inhibitor to be used in asthmatic therapy, while ARCI concentrated its efforts on the isolation of anti-parasitic qualities. Astra's laboratory in Gothenburg, Symbicom in Lund and ARCI are collaborating on a project, with each of them attempting to develop a different solution to the same problem. Astra's R&D structure provides ARCI with expertise in pharmacology and toxicology, whereas ARCI provides them with expertise in molecular biology. To avoid rivalries between different laboratories of Astra, each laboratory, including ARCI, is given the responsibility for defined therapeutic areas.

In addition to the joint R&D projects, the Indian centre also caters to specialized needs of Astra's units world-wide. ARCI has participated in a number of Astra's projects as experts in biotechnology. This expertise is utilized in the initial stages of most projects and has usually been limited in time to the first 2–3 years of a project out of its total duration of 15–20 years. Now, with ARCI getting the mandate for drug research and development, the proportion of joint R&D activities with the other laboratories of Astra will decrease. This is also a sign of Astra recognizing the competence of ARCI to pursue independent R&D.

Astra has a fellowship scheme for contacts among its R&D personnel in different units including ARCI. This provides for exchange of personnel between different units. Several scientists from other units of Astra have utilized the scheme to work at ARCI for short periods. ARCI's staff are also encouraged to present papers and attend conferences both abroad and in India.

ARCI's links with the innovation system in the host country

One of the objectives of ARCI is to collaborate with research groups in the Indian Institute of Science (IISc) and universities in India and abroad. Astra has a strong commitment to scientific research through collaboration with academic scientists in mission-oriented research projects. In pursuance of this policy, Astra has endowed two chairs of 'Astra Professorship' at the IISc. In its research projects, ARCI has so far received the co-operation of scientists at the IISc, the National Institute of Mental Health and Neurosciences (NIMHANS) and St. John's Medical College, all located in Bangalore. Through extra-mural grants, ARCI supports projects of mutual interest in all these institutes.

The centre's research on malaria was initiated by a professor of molecular biology at IISc, who worked together with ARCI's scientists on drug metabolism and drug resistance to pathogens. In a continuing relationship, IISc is also carrying out research on deriving the structure of ecoli enterotoxin, for ARCI (Shetty, 1991). The governing board of ARCI has among its members, the director and another professor of biochemistry from IISc; a professor of developmental biology from the Tata Institute of Fundamental Research

(TIFR); the director of the National Institute of Immunology; and the director of the National Institute of Virology. This facilitates access to expertise available in other research institutes.

Although ARCI is not an academic institution, it offers training on specific experimental procedures to researchers and students from local universities. So far, several post-graduate and post-doctoral researchers have availed themselves of this opportunity to be trained for periods of two to three weeks. ARCI also has a small post-doctoral programme for fresh doctoral degree holders in chemistry, biophysics, biochemistry, microbiology, molecular biology, cell biology and other related medical sciences. ARCI provides the post-doctoral fellows with a stipendium for a period of two years and allows them to join an integrated team to work on an ongoing project. For the established scientists ARCI offers facilities to spend a sabbatical year or two at the centre. ARCI regularly organizes seminars and symposia on relevant topics. For instance, the World Health Organisation (WHO) and Rockefeller Foundation held their annual meeting on tropical diseases research at the centre (Sampath, 1990).

One of the main reasons for India not reaping the benefit of its scientific capacity has been the lack of application-orientation of its R&D. Scientists in India largely pursued research to prove the principles and did not progress beyond this. ARCI, through its R&D activities, is contributing to the diffusion of application knowledge among the scientific community in India.

ARCI's network abroad

ARCI has also developed a network of external collaborators abroad. There are several projects at ARCI which are being conducted in co-operation with research institutes abroad. Presently there is a 'tripartite' research effort to develop a drug for malaria, between ARCI, University of California, San Francisco, USA and Mahidol University, Thailand. ARCI is also involved in a long-term research project on 'thioredoxin' with the Karolinska Institute in Sweden, with the latter supplying the peptides to ARCI for further research. In another project, ARCI is collaborating with the Massachusetts Institute of Technology (MIT), USA. The know-how is being developed at ARCI, while the manufacturing and the downstream processing will be done at MIT. This is a unique case of a developing country research institute sponsoring research in a developed country.

ARCI has been able to establish such links with the universities abroad, because both the director and the deputy director are well-known scientists abroad and have a good rapport with the research community abroad. The other Indian researchers recruited from abroad also tend to maintain their links with their former employers abroad. In addition, some of the students and young researchers who were trained by ARCI went to universities abroad, in turn expanding ARCI's R&D network.

ARCI also has among the members of its governing board, a professor of biochemical engineering from MIT; a professor from the National Institute for Medical Research, UK, and a professor of medical microbiology from the University of Gothenburg, Sweden. This gives ARCI access to international scientific expertise and advice.

Technology transfer and emergence of new class of entrepreneurs

ARCI has a policy of licensing and transferring the know-how for by-products generated in its R&D activities to the local firms in the host country. So far, ARCI's research results have led to the establishment of three spin-off companies locally. The products being in the high-tech area, the licensing is granted to the type of people who understand the complexities of these technologies well. Such people usually tend to be scientists, who are interested in commercializing them, leading to the emergence of a new class of entrepreneurs, 'scientific entre-preneurs'. For instance, the know-how for producing the basic tools of DNA recombinant technology has been transferred to a new local company called GENEI (Gene India), which is formed by two Indian scientists.

Genei was founded by a non-resident Indian scientist and another scientist who formerly worked in the Tata Institute of Fundamental Research (TIFR). The idea for the establishment of Genei arose when the non-resident Indian scientist, who is settled abroad, was on a consultancy assignment at ARCI. The financial support for the new firm was provided by the Technology Development and Information Corporation of India (TDICI), a venture capital company. Genei manufactures over 100 products that include restricting and modifying enzymes, DNA molecular weight markers and nucleic acids. Prior to ARCI's technology these products were being imported. Genei now exports some of these products to the USA. The major domestic customers for Genei are the universities pursuing basic research. Its future strategy is to branch out into three different business lines based on the production of reagents for basic research: (a) fostering the application potential of bio-tech tools in agriculture, veterinary and pharmaceutical usage; (b) the supply of basic tools for university research, at low-prices, to foster biotechnology research in India; and (c) other areas of possible entry are disease resistant rice, high-yielding strains of cows and prawn culture. Genei plans to enter the application sector by 2000 (Shetty, 1991).

The significance of the emergence of Genei, based on ARCI's technology and export of some of Genei's products, is that from being a net importer India has now become a net exporter of these products. ARCI's knowledge of the manufacture of certain biochemical inputs used for drug development has led to another spin-off company called 'Syngie'. The deal is now finalized with another local company for transferring and licensing the know-how to manu-facture some of the diagnostic procedures developed at ARCI. From ARCI's perspective such transfer of know-how to the local firms, apart from generating royalties, reduces its dependence on imports and provides a stable supply of inputs. These spin-off companies can now deliver ARCI's requirements on a just-in-time basis.

Problems faced by ARCI

Having been located in a developing country, ARCI had to face a few unique problems. First of all the basic tools of DNA recombinant technology were unavailable in India and had to be imported from abroad. This was delaying the progress of biotechnology research in India. Hence, the first two years of ARCI's time had to be spent on developing the know-how to produce these tools.

Second, it took a long time for ARCI to find a suitable manufacturer for the transfer of its know-how for the diagnostic kits. One of the major problems faced by the technology transfer team of ARCI is the lack of technology and expertise among the local recipients to develop marketable products on a mass scale (for by-products).

Third, in this fast-changing technology environment, ARCI found that it lagged behind in some areas. Set to develop compounds that would inhibit renin, a protein involved in blood pressure regulation, the ARCI team discovered that it was lagging behind globally. Cost-effectiveness being the dominant principle of the projects, this project had to be dropped. This was the only project in progress that has been dropped so far at ARCI. However, ARCI has filed a patent application for a further intermediate stage.

Finally, another problem being faced by ARCI is the lack of patent protection in India. In DNA recombinant technologies, the novelty is the product. The process of discovery is complicated, but once the product is obtained, its propagation can be achieved by many ways. In pharmaceuticals, the Indian patent laws protect only the process, but not the product. However, India's signing of the World Trade Organisation (WTO) agreement, along with the provisions of intellectual property rights (IPR), would remove this problem.

Conclusion

The ARCI case study shows that, given the opportunity and facilities, scientists in developing countries can also contribute to global technology developments. Joint projects facilitate formal and informal integration of different R&D units, complementarity of research and internal diffusion of knowledge. The case of ARCI indicates that biotechnology companies are seeking to locate R&D in places where scientists are available and research institutes are in close proximity. Because of the science base of biotechnology, in this type of research the links between universities and industry are stronger. Through its transfer of application knowledge and introduction of time- and cost-orientation to research, ARCI is inculcating a 'commercial culture' among the scientific community in India, which will go a long way to bringing the benefits of science to the society.

One of the main contributions of ARCI to the host country has been that it has introduced corporate R&D culture in a developing country like India and has become a model for others. This is evident from the number of domestic companies as well as TNCs that have been visiting ARCI to study its operations and set up R&D units themselves. The main shortcoming of ARCI so far has been that it had no plans to commercialize the research results in India. It was presumed that Astra would commercialize them abroad. However, this short-coming has now been rectified with Astra establishing a wholly-owned subsidiary Astra Biochemicals Pvt. Ltd. in India. This will increase the benefits to the host country.

Texas Instruments (India) Pvt. Ltd. (TI-India)

Texas Instruments Inc. (TI) is a US-based high-tech transnational corporation (TNC) founded in 1930 with its headquarters in Dallas, Texas. TI's global presence is reflected in its manufacturing facilities in eighteen countries and marketing or engineering services in more than thirty countries, employing about 59,000 people world-wide. Texas Instruments designs, manufactures and markets a range of products and services that include – semiconductors; defence electronics systems; software productivity tools; printers; notebook computers; consumer electronic products; custom engineering and manufacturing services; electrical controls; and metallurgical materials.

Texas Instruments (India) (TI-India) was established in August 1986, as a strategic move to establish Texas Instruments Inc.'s (TI) presence in the Asia-Pacific region. TI-India was the first high-tech company to pursue a global technology unit type of R&D in India and was India's first software technology park. TI expects this region to have one of the highest growth rates in the electronic industry over the next 20–25 years. TI-India is incorporated under Indian law as a 100 per cent export-oriented unit and is a wholly-owned subsidiary of TI. It operates entirely from its office in Bangalore, which presently represents an investment of about US$ 15 million and employs 300 engineers, almost all of them Indians recruited in India. The income (turnover) for the twelve months ending March 1994 was US$ 4.2 million. The company also announced additional investment of US$ 10 million over the next four years ending 1998 (*DataQuest*, 16–31 August 1994, p. 91).

Driving forces

The primary driving forces behind the location of R&D in India are twofold: first, to gain access to R&D personnel of required quality. Second, to have a long-term strategic presence in the Asia-Pacific region. TI already has manufacturing sites in several countries of the region, and from being an export-oriented manufacturing site, the region is rapidly becoming a consumer of many of these products. An R&D presence in the region would enable TI to identify market requirements and cater to the customers' needs. TI-India, however, is treated as a global resource centre and its activities are not confined to the region.

Generally South-East and Far East Asian countries are the most preferred locations for manufacturing investments. But TI chose India for location of its

R&D due to the easy availability of R&D personnel of required quality, relative to other countries in the region. India was selected as the location for TI's activities because of its strong educational system in theoretical sciences and engineering both at the under-graduate and graduate levels. This educational system supplies a large pool of technical manpower, which has an excellent theoretical training. The quality of these personnel is considered by TI to be on par with the personnel available in industrialized countries. TI-India provides on-the-job training for practical application of this theory to technical problems. Other reasons for the selection of India include the favourable climate for foreign investments and the common use of English in education, commerce, government and industry. The Government of India encourages establishment of such high-tech activities in the country through several concessions, especially for 100 per cent export-oriented units. Although not officially stated, the low wages of engineers and other scientific personnel in India is one of the important criteria for locating R&D in India.

R&D in India is not motivated by the need to be in proximity to the manufacturing site. This is evident from the fact that TI does not have a manufacturing facility in India. Although TI has manufacturing or assembly sites in other countries in the Asia-Pacific region, TI's R&D operations in India do not cater exclusively to these sites. Instead, the unit caters to the needs of TI's manufacturing units and other customers world-wide, including those in the USA and Europe. The unit is also not linked to any marketing strategy in India. Although TI markets some products in India, it is a very small market.

Organization of R&D

The initial activity of TI-India was the development and support of proprietary Computer Aided Design (CAD) software systems used for integrated circuit (IC) design by TI's semiconductor design centres world-wide. This activity includes development of applications for simulation, testing, layout and verification of ICs. In mid-1988, TI-India received permission from the corporate headquarters in the USA and the Indian Government to expand its activities to include design of ICs, and development of software for applications other than CAD. As a result, in 1988 the Linear Design Centre was established at TI-India. Following the successful operation of these two divisions, IC design activities supporting TI's application specific products and application specific memory products were established in late 1990. In 1990, TI-India also started serving TI's commercial software business by establishing the Information Technology Group.

The company focused on differentiated products and developed customized ICs and software, which included digital signal processors (DSP), memories and mixed-signal ICs. Its computer-aided design (CAD) software for very large-scale integration (VLSI) design include schematic and layout design editors, VLSI simulation tools, rule checkers for IC design, etc. In recent years, TI-India is paying increasing attention to the area of methodology development. Some of its staff have been selected to chair world-wide teams in methodology development for DSPs and mixed-signal ICs (*DataQuest*, 16–31 August 1994, p. 91).

R&D activities in TI-India are presently organized into six groups pursuing different technological directions:

1   Applications Specific Memory Product Development – TI has established this centre at the Bangalore site to strengthen its product design resources world-wide and to meet the needs of the emerging markets for ASM products world-wide. This group is responsible for the complete product development of Memory ICs from specifications to volume production. This includes design, simulation, verification, test as well as interface with the wafer fab and assembly/test sites world-wide (from product conception to implementation). With manufacturing and assembly sites in the USA, Japan, Taiwan, Singapore and Europe, the group works closely with product development experts from around the world. This division works jointly with TI marketing organizations world-wide, to identify new memory application opportunities and then to design products that meet these identified customer requirements.

2   Application Specific Products (ASP) – this group is responsible for the design of solutions based on differentiated products. These products include digital signal processors (DSP), graphics signal processors, microcontrollers and microprocessors. In addition, this group provides ASIC capabilities on its 100 K BiCMOS and CMOS gate arrays and FPGAs, to provide customers a capability for rapid prototyping and design. In the process area, the group at TI-India is involved in the development of design methodology for DSP chip designs. It also develops application software needed for debugging and simulation of DSP programs running on TI chips.

3   Corporate Venture Projects (CVP) – the objective of establishing this group is to identify and develop new business opportunities for the TI. This group has been set up in India to develop the new business based on the revolutionary product, the Digital Micro-Mirror Device (DMD). The group is working in the areas of multi processor real-time embedded software and IC design to enable development of products using the DMD.

4   Design Automation Division (DAD) – this is part of world-wide DAD operations with other centres located at Dallas, USA, Bedford, UK, and Tokyo, Japan. This group provides CAD software solutions to TI's IC designers and other customers world-wide, and provides total system solutions, involving software development in-house as well as integrating leading edge CAD technologies from external vendors. Current focus is on the areas of specification capture, simulation, placement and routing, characterization and optimization, electrical rule verification, process and device modelling, and testability.

5   Information Technology Group – this group is involved in software re-engineering, using TI's Information Engineering Facility (IEF)

Computer-Aided Software Engineering (CASE) toolset. The group is part of the Application Development Services (ADS) organization. IEF CASE toolset offers system developers dramatic improvements in productivity, ranging from 2 : 1 to 10 : 1 based on customer experience. The group in India uses IEF to re-engineer existing application systems to meet customers' specifications and build new systems. This group develops mainframe transaction-based applications for TI and TI's customers world-wide using PCs in Bangalore and TI's IBM mainframe computer centre in Dallas, Texas.

6   Mixed Signal Products Design Centre (MSP) – this group is involved in the design of mixed signal integrated circuits for a world-wide market. It is part of TI's world-wide team of technologists striving for all round excellence in TI's mixed signal product strategies. Established in 1988, the group is involved in developing design methodologies for mixed signal designers world-wide. On the design front, the group is focusing on mixed signal ICs which is the state-of-the-art technology where complex digital processing and analogue interface are integrated on to the same chip. The group is concentrating on three mixed signal applications: graphics palettes (embedded ASICs), telecommunication and multimedia, and hard disk drives. These designs range from above 125 MHz devices to ultra-low power applications to suit the emerging market needs. The group also develops mixed signal libraries for its world-wide design community.

Global communication links

TI-India has the latest Apollo and Sun Workstations and a variety of TI computers that are interconnected by the local area network (LAN), which in turn is connected to TI's world-wide data communication network. TI's network is one of the largest, totally integrated, privately owned systems in the world. TI-India is connected to this global network on a real-time basis and is the first company in India to have a dedicated 64KB link, now upgraded to 128KB, enabling the company to send and receive the latest support information, latest design technology and applications information for TI's products and services. All the software, databases and designs developed by TI-India are exported to TI in the USA via this dedicated 128KB satellite link between Bangalore and TI's unit in Bedford, UK, for distribution and use by TI and TI's customers. The earth station at TI-India's premises in Bangalore is owned and operated by Videsh Sanchar Nigam Ltd., a Government of India enterprise. This gives TI-India access to TI's world-wide computer network for transmission of electronic mail as well as software programs and data.

TI-India's global intra-corporate links

Figure 5.2 shows the global and local linkages of TI-India. TI-India is one of the four R&D centres that TI has established to pursue high-tech R&D of this

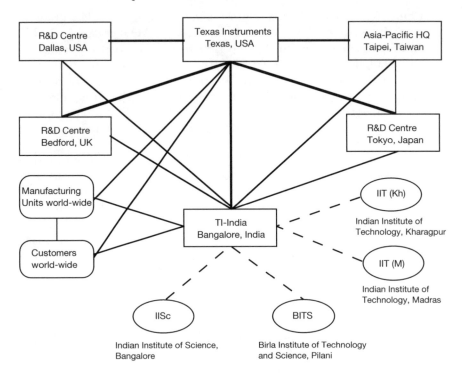

Figure 5.2 The global and local R&D network of TI-India

nature. The other centres are located in Dallas, USA, Tokyo, Japan, and Bedford, UK. Through the satellite link all the TI units world-wide, including the manufacturing units, are connected to one another in a global network. Through this communication link, TI-India draws upon the resources, data and expertise available in other units of TI and vice versa. It also has links with TI's manufacturing sites in Asia, Europe and the USA, so that the products designed and developed at TI-India can be transferred to the manufacturing sites smoothly. Through these links the R&D personnel are drawn into learning and solving the difficulties of larger-scale manufacturing of a newly developed product. Several of the R&D projects are joint projects with other R&D units of TI. Allocation of tasks is done on the basis of expertise and core competences of each of these units.

There is continuous exchange of personnel for short periods between different units of TI and TI-India is part of this global network. This facilitates not only widening of the knowledge of personnel, but also establishment of informal contacts between people working in different units of TI. TI-India also has links with TI's Asia-Pacific regional headquarters in Taipei, Taiwan.

Links with the innovation systems in the host country

In the initial four to five years of TI-India's operations, the links with the local technical universities were limited to the recruitment of personnel. TI-India recruits its personnel from the most reputed technical universities such as the IITs and IISc. After these initial years, the links were extended to include sponsorship of research and joint research in some of these universities. TI-India has links with the Indian Institute of Science (IISc), Bangalore and the Indian Institute of Technology, Kharagpur, in terms of research collaboration. In both these instances, the institutes concerned and TI-India together identified areas of mutual interests and agreed upon specific mission-oriented research projects that are funded by TI-India. In recent years, TI-India also forged research links with the Indian Institute of Technology, Madras, and Birla Institute of Technology and Science, Pilani.

However, there are no instances of TI-India subcontracting research to other companies in India. Because of the type of activities and the high technology tools (e.g. computers) with which TI-India performs these activities, there has been very limited need for links with local industries, whether in terms of supplies or in terms of logistic support. TI-India's R&D has so far not resulted in any spin-off companies in the host country.

TI-India's performance and progress

TI-India provides the opportunities and facilities for research and venture into new areas of work. It encourages its personnel to participate in international conferences and publish papers. So far, TI-India has made a significant contribution by presenting eighty international and national patents and its researchers have presented more than seventy papers at international conferences. The international patents are obtained directly by the parent company TI. TI-India has the distinction of having one of the lowest employee turnover rates in TI's operations world-wide and in the information technology industry in India. However, with more TNCs making R&D-related investments in high-tech areas in India, this may change in the future. TI has an internal evaluation of performance of its different units, using criteria such as the quality of work performed and the competence, based on which TI is continuously expanding its activities at TI-India by adding new groups.

The initial activity of developing proprietary CAD software systems for IC design by TI's semiconductor design centres world-wide within two years has been expanded to a range of high-tech R&D activities, including designing high-end ICs. Approximately 50 per cent of the resources at TI-India are now being used to design the high-end chips of 0.5 micron circuit elements. As of now, knowledge of the physics of chip design only allows designing and manufacturing chips of 0.5 micron. In other words, the operations at TI-India include some of the most complex and latest technological tasks.

In terms of R&D resources, TI-India accounts for one-third of the total resources that TI has world-wide in the fields of memory design and design automation. It is as a result of the competence the unit acquired that TI is doubling the capacity of its Indian operations. By the end of 1995, TI-India was expected to employ about 500 engineers in its R&D activities. TI is also building its own premises to locate all its activities under one roof.

Capability building through training of personnel

At TI-India, training of personnel is a major component. TI-India recruits new graduates who are only theoretically trained in the universities. First, therefore, they need to be trained in the methods of applying this knowledge to developing new products. Second, these new recruits from universities need to be exposed to the state-of-the-art technologies in the area and trained to absorb and use them. At TI-India, these training activities are given most importance. Apart from catering to the training needs of new recruits, TI-India considers training to be a continuous process in a rapidly changing technological world. For instance in 1993, the personnel at TI-India were trained for about ten working days on average. TI-India also encourages its personnel to acquire higher academic qualifications such as PhDs. Such people are given special leave and funding to acquire qualifications considered necessary to keep up to date in technology progress.

Conclusion

TI-India's activities are well integrated into TI's global operations. This gives opportunities for Indian R&D personnel to acquire expertise and gain access to the latest knowledge in the field. However, links with the national systems of innovation in the host country have become significant only in recent years. Hence, the diffusion of technologies to local S&T institutions has so far been limited. The nature of operations at TI-India, being one of design, the reliance on academic institutions which have expertise in basic sciences is limited. However, with increasing focus on developing methodologies at TI-India, links with local innovation systems are expected to increase. With a 15 per cent turn-over of R&D personnel at TI-India, some of them starting their own software enterprises, a wider diffusion of technology and knowledge into the host economy has already begun.

TI carries out its operations in accordance with its global strategies, seeking efficiency. If the host government creates an attractive environment both in terms of policies and infrastructural support, TI may be induced to manufacture some of the products designed and developed at TI-India in the host country. This would lead to increased benefits to the host economy by creating a network of suppliers and sub-contractors.

Biocon India Private Limited

Biocon India Pvt. Ltd. was formed in November 1978 as a joint venture between a dynamic woman scientist turned entrepreneur and a small biotechnology company from Ireland called Biocon Biochemicals Limited. The Irish company contributed 30 per cent of the equity and the Indian partner held 70 per cent of the equity. In 1989, Biocon Biochemical Ltd., Ireland and its subsidiaries were acquired by Quest International of The Netherlands, a wholly-owned subsidiary of Unilever p.l.c. and a leading manufacturer of flavours, fragrances and food ingredients. As a result of this acquisition by Quest International, Biocon India has now become an associate company of the Unilever conglomerate. But the equity base of Biocon India remains the same with the Indian partner holding the majority share.

Biocon India is mainly in the business of developing and manufacturing industrial enzymes. The company has grown from a modest manufacturer of Papain and Isinglass to a major producer of microbial enzymes. The company now employs 115 people. The company's domestic and international customers include brewing, distilling, processed foods and beverages, paper, pharmaceuticals, textiles, leather, poultry feed, effluent treatment, natural fibres and other related industries. A substantial portion of the resources of the company is devoted to R&D in order to generate new products, technologies and specialized applications. In order to commercialize the results of its R&D, a new company Biochemizyme India Pvt. Ltd. was formed in 1990 as a 100 per cent export-oriented unit. The new company manufactures a range of microbial enzymes using state-of-the-art solid substrate fermentation technology.

Prior to the joint venture, the Irish company had been importing raw materials from India. The Irish company felt that instead of importing raw materials, it would be better to process these raw materials in India to exploit the cost differentials and then import the manufactured products for marketing in Europe. At the time, Biocon Biochemicals was mainly interested in two products, namely, a plant enzyme called 'Papain' and a hydro colloid called 'Isinglass'. Several companies in Europe were sourcing the raw materials for these products from India and processing them in their plants in industrialized countries. Biocon Biochemicals felt that by processing them in India, it could gain a cost advantage over its competitors. The main markets for these products have been the Western countries.

Driving forces

The primary driving forces for the establishment of Biocon India had been the availability of raw materials and the low processing costs in India. After being in the field for some years, Biocon India built up expertise in the field of fermentation technology. As a result, gaining access to R&D personnel and expertise has been the primary driving force for Quest International to carry out joint R&D with Biocon India. The low cost of R&D in India has also been one of the important motives. Although some of these products are marketed in India by Biocon India, from Quest International's perspective local market-related motives did not play a role in locating R&D in India. Quest International utilizes the facilities at Biocon India to manufacture some of these products.

However, to be in proximity to manufacturing was not a motive for locating R&D in India. This is also evident from the fact that R&D results for some of the products are transferred to Quest International's manufacturing centres in other countries.

Corporate mission

Biocon India's corporate mission is:

- innovative research of commercial importance;
- outstanding product quality;
- customer satisfaction and market sensitivity;
- optimizing profitability in the business;
- novel products and technologies.

Research and development activities

As is clear from its corporate objectives, Biocon India is committed to carrying out innovative research to develop novel products and technologies. In keeping with the integral needs of biotechnology, Biocon India has built a strong R&D base with an initial focus on solid substrate fermentation. This in-house R&D base has now widened to include submerged fermentation, recombinant DNA technology and bio-reactor design.

R&D facilities at Biocon India in the area of microbial enzymes were established in 1984. A substantial amount of basic R&D work has been carried out to develop suitable technologies to produce enzymes through fermentation root. A plant enzyme is usually an extraction type and not a fermentation root type. This meant that considerable research effort had to be put in to develop this new method in terms of isolating and optimizing organisms, developing a process to obtain an enzyme expression and finally producing the enzyme. Biocon India has been very successful in its research projects, in terms of building up a track record of commercializing at least two new products every year.

Biocon India's strength has been in creating niche markets through innovative products and product applications. A number of novel enzyme applications introduced by Biocon India have qualified for patenting. A well-equipped technical services laboratory in conjunction with the R&D and quality assurance laboratories lends support to the marketing and customer servicing activities. Many of these applications have opened up significant export opportunities for the company, with exports now accounting for 50 per cent of the total sales turnover. R&D results obtained at Biocon India have not only resulted in new commercial projects, but also in royalty-earning technology transfer to the EEC. Biocon India envisages that with the growing emphasis on environmental protection, eco-friendly products such as enzymes will find an increasingly dominant place in the industrial world.

Global R&D network links

Although there was no formal agreement between them, the R&D was a sort of collaborative effort between Biocon India and Biocon Biochemicals, Ireland. Biocon Biochemicals did not have experience in this sort of R&D. However, there was successful collaboration between the two parties. R&D investments were made in India, because of the relatively better experience of Biocon India in this area of technology. In some cases, there was division of research activities between Biocon India and Biocon Biochemicals, i.e. joint research projects in which the majority of the work was done in India and part was carried out in Ireland. Most of the work carried out by Biocon Biochemicals in Ireland related to that of testing of the new enzymes. When a new enzyme was developed, the Irish company carried out the tests for its efficacy, suitability for plant-scale production, performance of the enzyme, etc. Such feedback from Biocon Biochemicals helped Biocon India significantly in its R&D projects. This type of division of work in joint R&D projects was based on the corresponding expertise of the partners.

By the time Biocon Biochemicals was acquired by Quest International of Unilever in 1989, Biocon India had built up substantial expertise in this field. Biocon India also became strong in production technologies of certain enzymes and has developed certain unique strains and process technologies through its in-house R&D programmes. Thus, Quest International, its new partner, entered into a formal agreement with Biocon India to manufacture certain enzymes exclusively for Quest International to be marketed by them world-wide.

In addition, Quest International also requested Biocon India to develop some new products exclusively for them through R&D and Biocon India agreed to do so for a payment (a form of subcontracting of R&D) and a formal contractual agreement was entered into by both parties. The driving forces behind this arrangement are twofold: first, Quest International did not have experience in this field and Biocon India had by then developed expertise in the field, which Quest International recognized; second, it is a cost-effective way of furthering technologies in which Quest International is interested. The cost-effectiveness arises from the low cost of scientific personnel in India. Biocon India does not feel that shortage of research personnel in industrialized countries is a major driving force behind Quest International's decision to subcontract R&D to them.

There are several R&D projects that Biocon India is carrying out for Quest International and this includes the whole range of activities from the laboratory stage through pilot plant to scale up. Although it is contract-based R&D, the set-up is not one where Quest International assigns a part of the R&D to Biocon India or sources specific R&D inputs. Instead, the total responsibility for product design and development is entrusted to Biocon India. Under the contractual conditions, Biocon India gets the exclusive rights to apply these new technologies or products in the Indian market, whereas Quest International gets the rights to world-wide markets. If the results of the research are patentable, the rights are jointly held both by Biocon India and Quest

International. Biocon India has specialist processing facilities, so some of the products developed through contractual R&D projects are also manufactured in India exclusively for Quest International to be marketed world-wide. In the case of products where the process facilities at Biocon are not suitable for undertaking large-scale manufacturing, Quest International manufactures them elsewhere in its manufacturing sites world-wide. In these cases Biocon India transfers the know-how to the manufacturing sites abroad. In both cases Biocon India receives royalties from Quest International. Since the complete expertise and responsibility lie with Biocon India, there has been no need for exchange of R&D personnel between Quest International and Biocon India.

Presently, out of the total R&D budget of Biocon India about 50 per cent comes from Quest International for its exclusive projects. The links with Quest International are helping Biocon India in several other ways also. For instance, Biocon India's knowledge of the complexity of patenting and its procedures was very limited, and the company's focus had always been on getting the product into the market as early as possible, instead of obtaining patent protection. But, now with the help of Quest International, it has been building up its knowledge on issues related to patenting. For the contractual R&D projects both national and international patents are jointly held by Biocon India and Unilever. The costs of joint patenting are, however, borne by Quest International alone, which has the responsibility to obtain the patents.

Biocon is further entering into a separate agreement with Unilever's corporate laboratory in Fladigan, The Netherlands, to carry out some collaborative and contract research for them. The association with the Unilever group is also helping Biocon India to acquire global market knowledge for Biocon's own products. While all the products developed exclusively for Quest International are global market-oriented, Biocon India's own R&D has a substantial focus on developing products for the local markets also.

Local external links

Figure 5.3 shows the global and local R&D network of Biocon India. Apart from the strong in-house R&D infrastructure, Biocon India has built up strong links with the national systems of innovation. It has several collaborative research projects with universities and research institutes in India. Biocon India has sponsored research projects in Astra Research Centre India, Bangalore, National Chemical Laboratories, Pune, and Central Institute for Food Technologies, Mysore. These research projects are of basic science nature for the results of which Biocon India works closely with these research institutes. With application-oriented R&D being the focus of Biocon India, by sponsoring basic research in universities and research institutes, the company benefits, first, from the expertise on pure science related matters available in these institutes; second, it avoids spending its own scientific resources on research not directly related to the product development; third, it is a cost-effective way of obtaining knowledge on basic science matters.

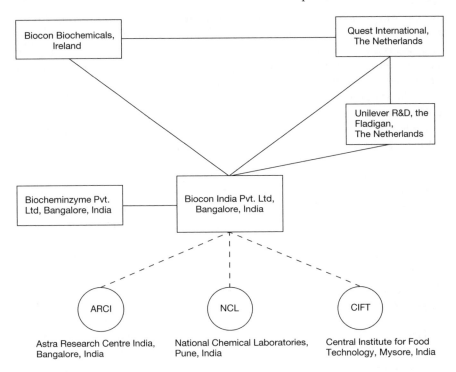

Figure 5.3 The global and local R&D network of Biocon India

Conclusion

Biocon India feels that international collaborative or contractual R&D activities are beneficial for the host country. First, such activities bring into the country an R&D culture that is essential for survival and growth of society and which has been sorely lacking in India. Second, TNCs are very experienced in R&D, so collaboration with them helps in upgrading the quality of research in the country and in gaining application knowledge. Third, such activities give access to global networks, which are very important in terms of widening the knowledge base as well as in learning to compete in the international environment. Finally, taking up R&D as a business proposition makes the R&D exercise more meaningful, as the culture of time and cost consciousness spreads and scientists become more aware of issues such as intellectual property rights.

Questionnaire survey[3]

To obtain a macro-level picture of international corporate R&D activities in the host country and to analyse the driving forces, a questionnaire survey was carried out in 1995. The survey was conducted among TNCs involved with new technologies as well as conventional technologies. The total number of companies contacted was fifty-five and responses were received from thirty-seven companies, amounting to a response rate of about 67 per cent. Among the responses received, only thirty-two could be utilized because of incomplete information from some companies. Out of the thirty-two responses utilized for analysis, sixteen were from the companies dealing with conventional technologies and the remaining sixteen were from companies dealing with new technologies. The conventional industries category includes: chemicals, pesticides, fertilizers, pharmaceuticals, engineering, hygiene and health care products, and branded consumer goods. The new technologies category includes: electronics (including information and communication technologies, and software), biotechnology and solar energy companies.

Table 5.1 shows the categorization of TNCs' R&D units in India on the basis of the type of R&D performed. The data show that the majority of the R&D units are performing TTU and ITU types of R&D, i.e. adaptation of products and processes to local conditions, and product development for the local market. This is more so in the case of conventional industries, where about 87.5 per cent of the firms are involved in these two types of activities. On the other hand, only 25 per cent of the new technologies firms are carrying out TTU and ITU types of R&D. All the GTU and CTU types of R&D units belong to new technologies firms, with 50 per cent of new technologies firms carrying out GTU and 12.5 per cent performing CTU types of R&D. This suggests that in new technologies there is less need for product or process adaptation to the local market. This is also evident from the fact that only 12.5 per cent of new technologies firms are involved in TTU type of R&D. Similarly, the development of products exclusively for the local market (ITU type) by new technologies firms is also less, except in the case of biotechnology companies developing new plant varieties based on the local soil and weather conditions. On the other hand, an overwhelming majority of new technologies firms are involved in developing products for the global markets, e.g. computers, communications equipment, etc. The data also show only a few R&D units as exclusively involved in research of long-term use, only 6.3 per cent.

Although R&D units are categorized into different types, they are not confined to performing only one type of R&D.[4] All of them perform other types of R&D also. In most cases, the R&D units were established to perform specific type of activities. However, over a time period the scope of their work was

Table 5.1 Questionnaire survey – different types of R&D units and number of firms

	TTU	*ITU*	*RTU*	*GTU*	*CTU*
Conventional industries	7	7	2	–	–
New industries	2	2	2	8	2
Total	9	9	4	8	2

increased to include more substantial R&D activities. In this survey, the categorization of R&D units is done on the basis of the largest activity performed by them. If a unit is stated to have spent 50 per cent or more of its resources on a particular type of R&D, then it is placed as belonging to that category. For example, if a unit stated that 50 per cent of its work involved adapting products and processes to local market conditions, then it was treated as a TTU.

Table 5.2, hence, presents the relative importance of each type of activity among the respondents in the survey. The data show that only ITU and GTU types of units stated that more than 75 per cent of their work involved only one type of R&D activity. However, their number is small. Only 9.4 per cent of all the firms stated that more than 75 per cent of their work was of ITU type, i.e. developing products for the local market, and this figure for conventional industries is 12.5 per cent. Overall, 34.4 per cent of all firms devote more than 50 per cent of their resources to developing products exclusively for the domestic market. This is not surprising, as India is a large market with unique characteristics.

It is also interesting to note that 43.8 per cent of the units stated that they did not carry out any adaptation type of activity. This figure for new technologies

Table 5.2 Questionnaire survey – relative importance of different types of R&D activities (%)

	TTU	ITU	RTU	GTU	CTU
No activity					
All firms	43.8	28.1	62.5	62.5	75.0
conventional	18.8	00.0	43.8	87.5	93.8
new	68.8	56.3	81.3	37.5	56.3
Below 25%					
All firms	6.3	6.3	25.0	9.4	12.5
conventional	6.3	12.5	43.8	12.5	6.3
new	6.3	0.0	6.3	6.3	18.8
25% to 49%					
All firms	21.9	31.3	0.0	0.0	6.3
conventional	31.3	37.5	0.0	0.0	0.0
new	12.5	25.0	0.0	0.0	12.5
50% to 74%					
All firms	28.1	25.0	12.5	6.3	6.3
conventional	43.8	37.5	12.5	0.0	0.0
new	12.5	12.5	12.5	12.5	12.5
75% to 100%					
All firms	0.0	9.4	0.0	21.9	0.0
conventional	0.0	12.5	0.0	00.0	0.0
new	0.0	6.3	0.0	43.8	0.0

firms is as high as 68.8 per cent, whereas for conventional industries the figure
is only 18.8 per cent. This once again suggests that the need for adaptation in
new technologies is less in comparison with the conventional technologies.
That new technologies products tend to be more global market-oriented is
also evident from the data. The majority of the new technologies firms also
reported zero activity of ITU and RTU types of functions. Some 43.8 per cent
of the conventional industries reported devoting some resources (below 25 per
cent) to developing products for the regional markets. This seems to stem
from the evolution of ITU functions into RTU, where some of the products
made for the domestic market are now exported to the countries in the region,
with some adaptations. With the liberalization of Indian and other regional
economies and the rationalization of TNCs' operations, allowing their
subsidiaries to export to the neighbouring countries, more ITUs may evolve
into RTUs.

GTU and CTU types of R&D activities are overwhelmingly concentrated
in new technologies firms. However, 12.5 per cent of the conventional industries
reported devoting some resources (below 25 per cent) to GTU type of activities.
This is because some of their products are exported world-wide, including
industrialized countries. As the data suggest, only a few companies perform
CTU type of activities and they are concentrated among the new technology
companies.

In terms of the size of the R&D units, the conventional industries have
smaller R&D units than new technologies companies. As the data in Table 5.3
indicate, 68.8 per cent of the conventional technologies companies have fewer
than fifty people devoted to R&D tasks and the corresponding figure for new
technologies firms is only 18.8 per cent. About 50 per cent of the new
technologies firms have more than 100 people employed in R&D activities.
About 18.8 per cent of the new technologies firms have more than 200 R&D
personnel in each of their units.

Table 5.3 Questionnaire survey – size of the R&D unit and percentage of firms

Average size	Conventional industries	New industries	Total
1 to 10	25.0	12.5	18.8
11 to 24	12.5	6.3	9.4
25 to 50	31.3	0.0	14.3
51 to 74	6.3	18.8	12.5
75 to 100	12.5	12.5	12.5
101 to 150	6.3	18.8	12.5
151 to 200	6.3	12.5	9.4
201 to 250	0.0	6.3	3.2
251 to 300	0.0	0.0	0.0
Above 300	0.0	12.5	6.3

In terms of the driving forces for the establishment of R&D units in India, the availability of personnel seems to be the main factor across all types of R&D activities and industries. As the data in Table 5.4 show, the weighted average rank of this motive is 4.12 across the industries and different types of R&D units. However, this factor has been relatively more important in the case of new technologies companies (4.31) than the conventional technologies firms (3.93). The next most important motive for the new technologies units is the low-costs of R&D, with a weighting of 3.25. On the other hand, the two most important motives for conventional industries are: to be in proximity to manufacturing facilities (4.56); and to be in proximity to the Indian market (4.06). The corresponding figures for these two factors in the case of new technologies firms are 2.13 and 2.81, respectively, suggesting that R&D in new technologies can be geographically uncoupled from manufacturing facilities.

The shortage of R&D personnel in industrialized countries as a driving force for location of R&D in India does not seem to be important with a weighting of only 1.69 across all industries. However, it assumes relatively greater importance in the case of new technologies firms with a weighting of 2.38. The company's image-building exercise as a reason for establishing R&D seems to be more important than the attractive government incentives, in both types of industries. Technology monitoring seems to be an important motive for locating R&D across all types of industries.

After classifying the R&D units on the basis of their main activity into TTUs, ITUs, RTUs, GTUs and CTUs, Table 5.5 presents the type of R&D units and the main motives for their location in India. For TTUs, being in proximity to

Table 5.4 Questionnaire survey – the mean weighting of motives for establishment of R&D

Motive	Conventional technologies	New technologies	Total
Availability of R&D personnel	3.93	4.31	4.12
Low-costs of R&D	2.88	3.25	3.06
Shortages of R&D personnel in industrialized countries	1.00	2.38	1.69
Proximity to manufacturing	4.56	2.13	3.34
Proximity to Indian market	4.06	2.81	3.44
Proximity to Asian market	2.06	2.38	2.22
Availability of raw materials	2.81	2.06	2.44
Government incentives	1.94	1.63	1.78
Company's image building	2.94	1.89	2.41
Technology monitoring	3.06	2.44	2.75

Note: Ascending order of weighting 0–5. The respondents were asked to rank the motives for locating R&D in India as they perceive on a scale of 0 to 5, with 0 as not a motive at all and 5 as the most important motive. Since there may be more than one equally important motive, the respondents were given the freedom to assign the same value to more than one motive.

manufacturing facilities has been the main driving force with a weighting of 4.78, followed by the motive to be in proximity to the Indian market, close behind with a weighting of 4.33. The same motives hold good for ITUs also with weightings of 4.33 and 4.22, respectively. For RTUs, the low-costs of R&D and proximity to the Indian market show equal weightings of 4.50, closely followed by the proximity to manufacturing with 4.25. On the other hand, proximity to the Asian market as a motive has a weighting of only 3.25. This discrepancy may be due to their reliance on the Indian market as the main base and then venturing into the regional market through adaptations. Moreover, the local operating conditions within the South-Asian sub-region tend to be more or less similar to that of India.

The main driving force for establishing GTUs is the availability of R&D personnel, with a weighting of 4.75. The next most important motive is the low costs of conducting R&D, mainly due to the lower wages of personnel, with a weighting of 3.25. Being in proximity to the market or manufacturing does not seem to be important for locations of GTUs. For CTUs also, the availability of personnel is the most important motive for location, with a weighting of 4.00. The next most important motive is stated to be the proximity to the region's market with a weighting of 3.00. This may be because some of the R&D, being carried out by the CTUs in the survey, involves developing potential biotechnology-based drugs and diagnostics for tropical or infectious diseases prevalent in the region. Therefore, proximity to the regional market may have been assigned a higher weighting. Availability of raw materials is also considered important for location of CTUs. All the CTUs in the survey are biotechnology-based units and some of them are working with tropical plant varieties, where availability of raw materials gains importance. The shortages of R&D personnel in industrialized countries as a driving force

Table 5.5 Questionnaire survey – type of R&D unit and major motives for its location

Motive	TTU	ITU	RTU	GTU	CTU
Availability of R&D personnel	4.00	3.78	4.00	4.75	4.00
Low-costs of R&D	2.78	2.67	4.50	3.25	2.50
Shortages of R&D personnel in industrialized countries	1.33	1.11	2.25	2.25	2.50
Proximity to manufacturing	4.78	4.33	4.25	0.75	1.00
Proximity to Indian market	4.33	4.22	4.50	1.25	2.50
Proximity to Asian market	2.56	1.67	3.25	1.75	3.00
Availability of raw materials	2.33	3.44	3.50	0.88	2.50
Government incentives	2.00	2.33	1.50	1.13	2.00
Company's image building	2.56	3.56	3.25	0.88	1.00
Technology monitoring	3.00	3.22	3.75	1.75	2.50

Note: as in Table 5.4

for location of R&D in India is of relative importance for RTU, GTU and CTU types of R&D functions. The government incentives seem to be most effective in attracting ITU and TTU types of R&D investments. The same holds true even for company's image building exercise.

Table 5.6 gives the data on the links of different types of R&D units both within the corporate structure and external agencies. All the units are linked to the TNCs' corporate R&D in their respective home countries. More than 80 per cent of the new technologies firms' R&D units are also linked to the parent's R&D units world-wide, whereas it holds true only for 50 per cent of the R&D units in the conventional technologies. The CTUs are the most integrated into the global corporate R&D network of the TNCs, with 100 per cent of them linked to parents' R&D units world-wide. The corresponding figures for other types of units are: GTUs (87.5 per cent), RTUs (75.0 per cent), ITUs (55.6 per cent) and TTUs (44.4 per cent), indicating the relative integration of these different functions within the corporate R&D structure. However, when viewed from the perspective of commercialization of R&D results within the host country, all the conventional industries are linked to manufacturing facilities in the host country, whereas only 50 per cent of the new technologies units are.

All the GTUs are linked to the parents' manufacturing facilities world-wide, whereas only 12.5 per cent of them are linked to manufacturing in India. This may be explained by the very nature of R&D performed by the GTUs. Global products tend to be manufactured in the most efficient locations in the TNCs' global structure, sometimes even outside the parent's own network, e.g. OEM supplies. This efficiency-seeking FDI most often involves location of R&D and production activities in different locations based on their national competitive advantages. TTUs, ITUs and RTUs, to a large extent, work on the basic technologies provided by the parent companies and are commercialized in their respective markets. Thus, their integration with the parents' world-wide manufacturing centres is limited. R&D units dealing with new technologies are better integrated with the global network of suppliers and customers of the parent. This is because most of the new technologies units are of GTU type.

In terms of external links, across all types of R&D units and technologies, there are only a few links with local industry. Part of the explanation may be that TNCs' R&D activities tend to be in high-tech areas, where it may be difficult to find domestic firms which can complement those activities in a developing host country. This also holds true in the case of conventional technologies, where the market in a developing host country is dominated by a handful of TNCs in oligopolistic competition, whose subsidiaries rely on technologies supplied by the parents. TNCs also protect their technologies and are wary of letting other companies know about their R&D activities, especially in an environment where intellectual property rights are not in accordance with international practices. Although 50 per cent of the CTUs show links with local industry, the sample size is too small to draw definite conclusions.

Table 5.6 Questionnaire survey – different types of R&D units and their corporate and external links (% of units)

Links with	TTU	ITU	RTU	GTU	CTU	Conventional technologies	New technologies
Parent's R&D in home country	100.0	100.0	100.0	100.0	100.0	100.0	100.0
Parent's R&D world-wide	44.4	55.6	75.0	87.5	100.0	50.0	81.3
Parent's manufacturing world-wide	11.1	00.0	00.0	100.0	00.0	00.0	56.3
Parent's manufacturing in India	100.0	100.0	100.0	12.5	50.0	100.0	50.0
Parents' customers world-wide	00.0	00.0	00.0	87.5	50.0	100.0	50.0
Parent's suppliers world-wide	22.2	11.1	50.0	12.5	00.0	12.5	25.0
Local industries	11.1	00.0	25.0	25.0	50.0	6.3	25.0
Local universities	44.4	44.4	75.0	50.0	100.0	62.5	43.8
Industries abroad	11.1	11.1	00.0	62.5	00.0	6.3	43.8
Universities abroad	00.0	11.1	00.0	37.5	100.0	6.3	31.3

On the other hand, links with the local university system seem to be much stronger. The conventional industries seem to rely more on the local academic system than the new technologies firms. Some 62.5 per cent of the conventional industries are reported as having links with the local universities, whereas this only applies to 43.8 per cent of the new technologies firms. Some 44.4 per cent of the TTUs and ITUs have also established links with local universities, a figure almost equivalent to 50 per cent of the GTUs. This appears to be contradictory to the conventional views.[5] Part of the explanation for this may lie in the fact that TTUs and ITUs are not confined to their specific activities alone. It is possible that they have these links in the course of performing other types of R&D activities. Another explanation could be that TTUs and ITUs, which are mostly in the conventional technologies, were established several years ago, prior to the liberalization of the Indian economy. At the time, due to import restrictions, these units had to carry out material substitution in products and therefore new processes also. These activities perhaps involved more than just tinkering with parent's technologies and had to rely on the local university system for support.

In establishing links with industry as well as universities abroad, new technologies R&D units are far ahead of those in conventional technologies. About 62.5 per cent of the GTUs have linkages with industries abroad, resulting mainly from the parents' global technological alliances with other TNCs. CTUs, due to the nature of R&D they are involved with, seem to interact more with the university system, both in the host country and abroad. Compared to this, GTUs are better integrated with the industry, as they are involved in direct product design and development. Given the limited nature of their R&D activities as well as the market orientation of their products, TTUs, ITUs and RTUs have limited linkages with both industry and universities abroad.

6 International corporate R&D in Singapore
Case studies

This chapter discusses four detailed case studies of international corporate R&D activities in Singapore.

Nestlé R&D Centre

Nestlé is a Switzerland-based transnational corporation (TNC), dealing with biotechnology and food technologies. Nestlé was established in 1867. Its original business was based on milk and dietetic foods for children, however, over the years it has expanded to include many products such as chocolate, instant beverages, culinary, refrigerated and frozen products, ice cream, mineral water and pet foods. While its core business emphasis is in the field of nutrition, Nestlé also has acquired interests in pharmaceutical specialities, with Alcon, and in the cosmetics industry, through its participation in L'Oréal.

Corporate R&D network

Nestlé's corporate R&D consists of a centralized research centre that carries out basic research on food science, health and nutrition, and a network of twenty-five development centres (DCs) that define product specifications and optimize the quality/price ratio of the products.

Nestlé Research Centre at Vers-chez-les-Blanc, Switzerland, was established with the following objectives:

- to evaluate future needs of the food industry and the consumer;
- to create new methodologies and discover new nutritional concepts which contribute to improving products and processes;
- to furnish scientific support to the whole Nestlé group.

The Nestlé Research Centre has a 450 research personnel. The centre's activities are organized into eight services: Food Sciences; Nutritional Sciences; Biological Sciences; Toxicological Sciences; Developmental Biology; Fundamental Sciences; Nutritional Evaluation and Control; and Administration and Central Services.

Through NESTEC, a wholly-owned affiliate based in Switzerland, Nestlé runs a decentralized network of DCs, spread over ten countries, which develop products and processes. Some of the DCs also have satellite research stations. The DCs are geographically spread out as follows: Switzerland (6 centres), Germany (2 centres), Spain (1 centre), France (4 centres), UK (2 centres), Italy (2 centres), USA (5 centres), and one centre each in Spain, Sweden, Singapore and Ecuador. A team of specialists at NESTEC headquarters in Switzerland has the overall responsibility for co-ordinating projects. They act as the links between the DCs and the Research Centre, the production and the marketing groups.

Nestlé's organization of development activity allows greater flexibility, gives a better knowledge of conditions in the local market place and permits close contact with local operating companies and production units. At the same time, it maintains the ability for each to draw upon the total experience of the whole network.

The DCs have two main objectives: (a) to develop new products, processes and methods of manufacture; and (b) to improve the existing products, taking into account the latest knowledge in technology, nutrition and socio-economic aspect. A typical DC will have both a national or regional responsibility for development and service, as well as global responsibility for one or more areas in which it has particular expertise. The scope of activities of a DC usually covers the whole range of food products manufactured by the Nestlé group. In certain important areas of technology, several DCs share the task between them. Many are situated near a production centre. This allows regular contact from the time of the original discovery until the point at which the process or product is put into production.

Generally, each DC has five separate but complementary departments: the experimental kitchen; the pilot plant; the workshop; the packaging laboratory; and the service laboratories. In addition, some DCs have an agronomic unit. The agronomic service unit investigates methods of growing the best quality crops at economic yields, in order that when commercialization occurs, advice and guidance can be given to the farmers producing these materials.

The Development Centre in Singapore

Nestlé R&D Centre (Pte) Ltd. Singapore, was incorporated in 1979. It is an integrated unit of Nestlé's global R&D network. The role of the Singapore-based R&D centre is to develop Asian-style convenient foods that are specifically suited to the various cuisines, preparation techniques and eating habits within the region. The centre's expertise in oriental cuisine also serves to support those Nestlé companies outside of Asia, which are pursuing Asian ethnic food categories.

Driving Forces

The major driving force for establishing a DC in Singapore is the dynamic economic growth of Asia. By having its presence in the region, Nestlé can be more sensitive to customers' needs in the region and thus become stronger in regional market for food products. In other words, market-related motive was the primary driving force. Singapore was chosen as Asia's first and only Nestlé R&D centre because of its unique geographical position, excellent infrastructure and its multi-cultural, multi-racial heritage. Singapore also has a skilled labour force, and an environment that facilitates conducting business in an efficient manner. Hence, several TNCs have chosen Singapore as a regional hub for their operations. Nestlé's activities are in line with the government policy of promoting Singapore as a location for high-tech activities, and Nestlé is often cited by the Prime Minister of Singapore as an illustration of what Singapore wants to be.

On a scale of 0 (least) to 5 (highest), Nestlé ranks the factors responsible for location of R&D in Singapore as follows: (a) proximity to regional and local markets (weighting 5); (b) availability of R&D personnel (3); (c) availability of raw materials (3); (d) government incentives (2); (e) proximity to manu-facturing (1); (f) low-costs of R&D (1); (g) company's image building (1); (h) technology monitoring (1); (i) shortage of R&D personnel in the home country (0).

R&D activities

The main activities of the centre include:

- Oriental Noodles – development of new and improved noodle products for markets in Asia and the world and the manufacturing processes;
- Bio-Flavours – development of flavours through fermentation and enzyme reactions;
- Seasonings and Cooking Aids – new concepts in seasonings and cooking aids for the Asia-Pacific markets through traditional food ingredients, spices and herbs;
- Rice and Cereal Products – development of rice and cereal products, such as instant rice-based porridge, for the Asian markets;
- Agriculture R&D – agricultural studies covering variety selection, cultural practices, harvest and post-harvest handling of strategic raw materials, including integrated pest management techniques that are environmentally friendly. The experiments are carried out in an experimental farm in Malaysia. Research findings are transferred to farmers in the region in collaboration with Nestlé operating companies. The current focus is on coffee.

Organization

The total staff strength in Singapore's R&D centre is ninety people, of which eight are expatriates. The scientists and engineers with advanced degrees account for one-third of the total staff and the rest are technicians and administrative staff. There are twelve people holding PhD degrees. The centre sends its researchers from Singapore to other DCs on assignments. The local recruits are trained for a couple of years at the centre, and then, depending on their performance, they may be deputed to other centres for training. The turnover of personnel is about 10 per cent, with the figure lower for professionals and higher for technicians. The centre on an average files for 6–8 patents a year and has so far obtained about 100 patents both in Singapore and internationally.

Global and local network of the R&D unit in Singapore

Figure 6.1 illustrates the global and local network of the R&D unit in Singapore. The centre is strongly integrated with the global internal R&D network of Nestlé, Nestec and other regional DCs. Resources and expertise from other centres within the Nestlé R&D network are readily accessed through various means of communication and collaboration. There is continuous exchange of personnel. Typically, the experts are deputed to Singapore for two to three years to apply technologies that are already in European or American markets in an Asian context. They transfer the expertise and train the local staff. Although not originally intended, because of the internationalization of Asian cuisine, Singapore centre's personnel are also deputed in a similar fashion to other centres. For instance, there are some sauces whose initial prototypes were developed in Singapore and transferred to the USA. Similarly, when the centre in Sweden introduced the frozen vegetable product, 'Taste of Asia', chefs from Sweden came to Singapore to learn the cuisine. Singapore centre's experts assisted in introducing Asian noodles production in Europe. The exchange of personnel takes place after informing the headquarters because of its implications for budgetary system, but who to send, etc. are negotiated directly between the R&D centres. Sometimes the centres ask the help of headquarters in identifying the key personnel available in the network.

Being part of such global technology network, the local staff can gain access to the knowledge related to food science and technology, as well the application knowledge related to product development. Due to the mobility of the personnel, there is scope for knowledge spill-over into the host country economy. The Singapore staff also contribute to the enrichment of the knowledge-base of Nestlé's R&D network, with their knowledge relating to local cuisine and customer habits.

The centre in Singapore provides R&D support to the seventeen markets of Nestlé in Asia, such as Nestlé Malaysia, Nestlé Japan, Nestlé Indonesia, Nestlé India, etc. As part of the centre in Singapore, there is an experimental agricultural farm located in Malaysia, helping to promote industries in key product areas such as coffee, cocoa, chillies, etc.

The links with the local external innovation system are very limited. The only link is with the National University of Singapore, which carried out the analysis of microstructure using its Scale Electronic Micros (SEM). It is not

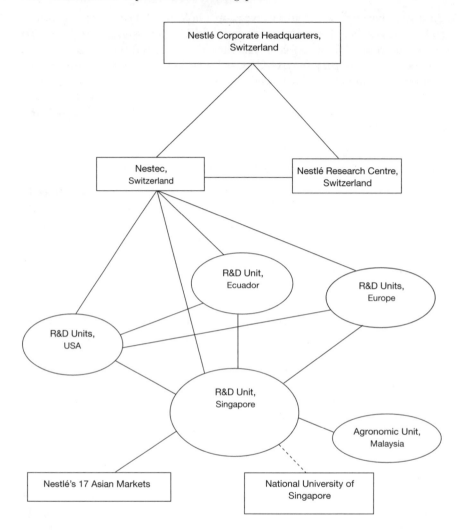

Figure 6.1 Nestlé R&D Singapore's global and local network

cost-effective for Nestlé to possess this sophisticated equipment for its limited needs so it depends on the university which has this equipment. The centre also makes use of consultants sometimes, mainly from abroad. Although not in recent years, there have been instances of researchers who left the centre to establish their own companies in Singapore.

Conclusion

In terms of strengths, Singapore has a well-educated and skilled labour force, coupled with an excellent infrastructure and pro-active government policies.

There business is conducted in an efficient manner. In terms of weaknesses, the labour market in Singapore is tight and it's often difficult to recruit people with the requisite qualifications. The centre is able to recruit people with degrees in basic science, but there is a problem in recruiting specialists in food science and technology locally. Food not being a major industry in Singapore, the subject is not taught in the universities. In its recruitment, Nestlé has to compete with petrochemical and pharmaceutical companies, which tend to be the first preference for new graduates. For recruitment of specialists in food science and technology Nestlé depends on Singaporeans educated abroad or outsiders. Singapore being an attractive place to live and work, it is easy to recruit specialists from abroad. However, expatriate staff are more expensive, so this process is used only selectively and only for those with experience and a good track record. Some outsiders are also recruited on the basis of local compensation. For its R&D project teams, the centre looks for a blend of people who have experience in food science and technologies as well as new graduates with no experience.

Fujitsu Singapore Pte. Ltd

Fujitsu Singapore Pte. Ltd (FSL), a wholly owned affiliate of Fujitsu Ltd., a Japan-based transnational corporation in the business of telecom and information technology, was established in 1973. Until 1997, the main business operations of FSL were mainly in the areas of telecommunications, information processing and international procurement. Since the rationalization of Fujitsu's operations in 1997, FSL has been focusing on telecommunication engineering. Other operations have been transferred to other Fujitsu group companies in Singapore.

Corporate mission

FSL's corporate mission is to be an excellent engineering centre of leading-edge telecommunications systems by conducting efficient software R&D, effective regional software R&D management and customer satisfying implementation support.

Principal R&D and other operations

FSL's operations are in the following three areas:

1   Telecommunications Software R&D – Telecommunications Software R&D group participates in developing Fujitsu's core network systems. The following are the major R&D projects currently being conducted:

    (a)   Asynchronous Transfer Mode (ATM) Switch;
    (b)   Integrated Services Digital Network (ISDN) Switch;
    (c)   Network Management System (NMS);

(d) Software Engineering Methodology and Tools;

(e) 21st Century Core Switch.

This group is the Asian Telecommunications Software R&D headquarters. The software R&D group co-ordinates software R&D activities in other Fujitsu's R&D centres in regional countries such as India, China and Hong Kong.

The main R&D activities of the centre are to develop new software products, both customized software products and standard generic software. Generic base is in turn used for customization of applications. The generic software developed in Singapore is also used by Fujitsu world-wide. The proportion of the generic version in the total software R&D will be around 60 per cent.

Total staff strength in R&D is 130 people, of which 80 are engineers (90 per cent university graduates). The centre was established in 1989. There are six Japanese expatriate staff.

2   Regional Telecommunications Support – Fujitsu's Fetex-150 switching system has many customers in the Asia region, with several ongoing system implementation projects. This team is responsible for the preparation of the switch for commissioning and creation of switch configuration database. The team also provides customer training and customer operation and maintenance support.

3   Asia Corporate Network Centre – Fujitsu has established a huge global corporate network of about 300 sites covering almost every part of the world. Fujitsu corporate network carries voice, data and videoconference traffic. The major Asia corporate network hub is located in FSL. Fujitsu's Asia corporate network centre in Singapore has international leased circuits linking all major Fujitsu establishments in the Asia region. The countries served by the Singapore hub include India, Thailand, Vietnam, Indonesia, Philippines, China, Hong Kong, Taiwan, etc. The Singapore network centre also has links to other major hubs in Japan, the USA and Europe for world-wide coverage.

Company organization

FSL has four major operation divisions:

1   The Switching Software Development Division (SSDD) is responsible for the software development of Fujitsu core switching products. The development activities include call application (CAP) software for Fetex-150 ISDN switching system, operation/administration/maintenance (OAM) software for ATM core switch, and both call application and OAM software for next generation switch.

2   The Network Software Development Division (NSDD) is responsible for the development of the Network Management System based on ITU-T's TMN model. The division is also responsible for the development of the Fetex-150 system control workstation (SCWS) software.

3   The Engineering Support Division (ENSD) is responsible for Fetex-150 switching system implementation support for Fujitsu regional markets. The responsibility includes exchange commissioning, exchange database generation, customer training, and customer operation and maintenance support.

4   Corporate Communications Network (Asia) Division is responsible for the operation of Fujitsu's main international corporate communication hub in Singapore.

The Regional Fujitsu's telecommunications software R&D activity is managed by the Fujitsu Asia Communication Technology Centre (FACT). The centre co-ordinates software R&D activities of Fujitsu Asia R&D facilities in Singapore, India, China and Hong Kong.

Fujitsu, Singapore, carries out R&D on telecom infrastructure for public network systems. So, unlike other products such as computers, this is mainly engineering operations. Telecom operators, including Singapore telecom, are the main customers in Singapore. The Singapore centre is the regional R&D headquarters, controlling R&D operations in India, China and Hong Kong.

Fujitsu has several patents in Japan and the USA. So far, the R&D work at Singapore has not contributed much in terms of patents.

Driving forces

Fujitsu develops complex systems software, which needs a large number of software engineers. There is shortage in the supply of software engineers in Japan. Companies compete with each other for recruitment of software engineers so this is one of the main driving force for Fujitsu's overseas R&D. Being close to markets is also very important as it permits faster response to customers' requirement. Hence, Singapore was chosen as the location to be close to the local and regional markets. By recruiting local people, the cultural barriers can be overcome, which in turn allows closer relationship with the customer/user. R&D costs in the region are lower than in Japan, but Singapore is not a low cost area. Hence, low R&D costs were not a driving force for location of R&D in Singapore. The manpower is not easily available in Singapore, but the people here are better exposed to the regional markets. The skill levels are high and they are multi-cultural. The government also encourages overseas education for its people, as well as the location of high-tech activities in Singapore.

On a scale of 0 (least) to 5 (highest), FSL ranks the factors responsible for location of R&D in Singapore as follows: (a) proximity to regional and local markets (weighting 5); (b) shortage of R&D personnel in the home country (4); (c) availability of R&D personnel (3); (d) proximity to manufacturing (3); (e) government incentives (3); (f) company's image building (2); (g) technology monitoring (2); (h) low-costs of R&D (1); and (i) availability of raw materials (0).

FSL's global and local R&D network

Figure 6.2 illustrates the global and local R&D network of FSL. FSL is integrated with the Fujitsu's corporate R&D network, although not globally. Fujitsu has eight groups working on telecom software in Japan. Fujitsu Singapore is linked to five of these groups in its R&D activities. Fujitsu also has software R&D units in Rolly, North Carolina, USA, and in the UK. FSL has no links with these units, but may need to establish links with the unit in the USA in the future.

There are also Fujitsu teams developing and outsourcing software in China, India and Hong Kong. The work of these teams is co-ordinated by Fujitsu Singapore, through its Fujitsu Asia Communication Technology Centre, which is a part of FSL. In India, Fujitsu is aligned with a software company called Network Program International, which develops dedicated software for Fujitsu. In China, Fujitsu has two joint venture companies: (a) Fujian Fujitsu Communications, a joint venture with the Ministry of Telecommunications and PTT, with Fujitsu holding 51 per cent of the equity; and (b) Jiangsuu Fujitsu Telecom Technologies, a joint venture with the Ministry of Electronics

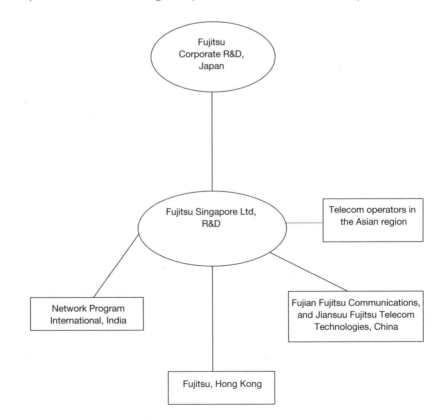

Figure 6.2 FSL's global and local R&D network

and Shanghai local government, with Fujitsu holding 51 per cent of the equity. In Hong Kong, Fujitsu operates a wholly-owned affiliate, Fujitsu Hong Kong.

There are no links with the local universities because they do not focus on telecom. Although there is group of researchers at the National University of Singapore, researching on wireless technology, at present, FSL is not working in the area of wireless systems. Therefore, there is no match. Similarly, there are no links with the local firms or locally-based transnational corporations in R&D activities, except with the local telecom operators, who are Fujitsu's customers. FSL's R&D teams join the telecommunication community in researching and developing network management solutions.

Knowledge is diffused through mobility of personnel, Fujitsu's training to its recruits and through its joint work with the local telecom operators. To its recruits FSL provides two months of classroom training and then on-the-job training. The turnover of personnel is around 15 per cent. The majority of the personnel leaving FSL get employed in other companies and a limited few start their own ventures. There is also knowledge exchange with Fujitsu's corporate R&D, giving FSL access to the latest technologies.

Conclusion

The strength of Singapore's knowledge base lies in its good quality engineering education. The engineers educated in Singapore have good skills and an ability to learn.

The weakness of the system is that there are not adequate supplies of personnel. A large number of companies are competing for the limited number of recruits, and, as a result, there is a high turnover of employees. It is difficult to keep professionals on a long-term basis and train them. The work at Fujitsu is technology-intensive, so other telecom companies find it attractive to recruit Fujitsu's personnel, since they are already well trained and need not be trained again. The shortage of people in Singapore requires Fujitsu to recruit non-telecom software engineers such as electrical and electronic engineers and train them in telecom.

Sony Semiconductor Engineering Centre

Sony, a Japan-based transnational corporation, established in 1946, is a leading company in the electronics and entertainment business. Sony's corporate objective is to harness the potential of digital technology to continue supplying hardware and software that provide enjoyment for customers around the world.

Sony Semiconductor is a wholly-owned affiliate of Sony Corporation. Sony Semiconductor, through its technology, supports the development of innovative products for which Sony Corporation has become famous – CDs, MDs, high definition television, digital VCRs, ISDN products, and multimedia.

Sony Semiconductor has concentrated on the most basic aspects of LSI design – process development and CAD technology development – in its operations division. LSI design for applied development and derivative device technology are handled by the production centres of Sony Kokubu and Sony Nagasaki. Other design centres, including those for the design of ASICs and micro-computers for the domestic market and for the development of microcomputer software, are headed up by Sony LSI Design.

Overseas, Sony operates design centres in the United States, Europe and Asia to design custom memories and LSI specifically for those regional markets. This type of organization of R&D gives Sony Semiconductor the flexibility to adapt to an ever-changing environment.

Sony Semiconductor Europe Design Centre is located in Basingstoke, UK. It deals with LSI design for European market and communication LSI; Sony Semiconductor Company of America Design Centre is located in San Jose, California, USA. It deals with LSI design for the American market, high-speed memory and MCU; Sony International (Singapore) Ltd Semiconductor Design Centre is located in Singapore. It deals with LSI design for Asian market and bipolar IC for audio-visual equipment.

Sony International (Singapore) Ltd (SONIS)

Sony entered Singapore in the early 1970s and since then has expanded its operations here rapidly. Presently, Sony has six companies operating in Singapore: (a) Regional Corporate Headquarters (HQ) for Asia-Pacific – Sony International (SONIS); (b) Two manufacturing plants – Sony Display Device and Sony Precision Engineering centre; (c) Regional sales and marketing headquarters for consumer products in Asia – Sony Marketing International (Singapore) Pte Ltd; (d) A logistics arm – Sony Logistics; and (e) a systems and software development company – Sony Systems Design International. Sony currently employs about 3,700 people in Singapore. Together, the six companies have a cumulative investment of over S$ 1 billion. To enhance its growing operations in the region, Sony has in recent years set up several design, research and development facilities in Singapore.

SONIS started as a Parts Centre in 1982, and rapidly expanded its operations. As Sony Corporation's regional HQ in Asia, SONIS now acts as the strategic planning and co-ordination centre, providing comprehensive support to Sony's manufacturing, sales and marketing companies in this region. These are in the areas of:

* Corporate support functions;
* Business functions;
* Marketing functions.

Sony Group companies in Asia with R&D facilities

Sony has set up R&D facilities within some of its operations in Asia better to meet the needs of customers as well as to respond more rapidly and flexibly to market demands in the region. To date, Sony has several R&D facilities located in Singapore, Malaysia, Korea, Taiwan and Indonesia.

While the three facilities in Singapore each focus on the development of core components such as optical data storage devices, semiconductors as well as multimedia and microchip software, those in Malaysia, Korea, Taiwan and Indonesia are more involved in the development and design of products manufactured in the respective companies:

- Singapore: 1. SPEC Components R&D Division – established in 1996, with an investment of US$ 50 million. R&D for key components and devices – optical pick-ups and mechanical units; Next generation optical data storage devices for IT and multimedia industries; 2. Design Centre Asia, SONIS – established in 1993, has only three design personnel. Industrial design (products); Package graphics design; and Interface computer graphics design; 3. Semiconductor Engineering Centre, SONIS – established in 1994, with an investment of US$ 1.8 million. IC design work with technical support for audio products and CD-ROM drives.
- Malaysia: 1. Sony Video (Malaysia), established in 1994, is engaged in video design; 2. Asia Design Centre, Sony TV Industries (Malaysia) – SBN – established in 1992, is engaged in design of derivative models and circuit blocks for new chassis; 3. Sony Electronics (Malaysia), established in 1989, is engaged in design of radio cassette, discman and hi-fi receiver.
- South Korea: 1. Sony Electronics Korea Corp., established in 1989, is engaged in design of compact disc radio cassette tape recorder, and car stereo.
- Taiwan: 1. Sony Video Taiwan, established in 1991, is engaged in design and development of video tape recorder, MiniDisc player, video-CD and duplicator (VHS).
- Indonesia: 1. Sony Electronics Indonesia, established in 1997, with a planned investment of US$ 2 million, is engaged in design of audio products.

SONIS Semiconductor Engineering Centre (SSEC): driving forces

SSEC was created in February 1995 as a division of SONIS. The centre was established to strengthen Sony's design assets and to help it adapt to the needs of markets and customers in the Asia region, and to enable it to provide greater differentiation in its products by being involved from the initial design stages in customers' product planning. The Singapore facility will add an Asian focus to design. SONIS currently provides bipolar design and development and applied technology support to Japanese, American, European and local producers of audio/visual equipment in the rapidly growing Asian market. The Singapore design centre will be in a better position to 'design in' its chips and serve the needs of this important international market. The primary driving force for establishing the new R&D unit was to be close to the local and regional markets. Another important factor responsible for locating R&D abroad has been the shortage of research personnel at home. The objective of the centre is to expand SONIS semiconductor business for customers in the region, especially from the emerging markets by promoting design-in activities with system solution.

On a scale of 0 (least) to 5 (highest), SSEC ranks the factors responsible for location of R&D in Singapore as follows: (a) proximity to regional and local markets (weighting 5); (b) shortage of R&D personnel in the home country (4); (c) availability of R&D personnel (3); (d) government incentives (3); (e) technology monitoring (3); (f) company's image building (2); (g) proximity to manufacturing (1); (h) low-costs of R&D (1); and (i) availability of raw materials (0).

Singapore was chosen as a location for R&D activity because it has good infrastructure, including a significant presence of Sony network, stable power supplies, and good engineering skills. In the near future, the unit will be increased in size steadily. Sony does not find it very difficult to recruit the right professionals, as Singapore universities offer courses in IC design. SSEC in Singapore has no PhDs among its staff, but one with a master's degree and the rest with bachelors of engineering degrees.

R&D activities and organization

Presently SSEC is engaged in two activities – Application Engineering and LSI Design. The centre presently employs sixteen members, including one Japanese manager and it plans to recruit more staff steadily over the years.

The Application Engineering focuses on Optical Disc System, CCD Camera System and TV System. Its activities include: providing support to local customers not only with hardware, but also software; enhancing engineering collaboration with the Optical Device Division and providing total system solution in optical disc system; training/seminar on optical disc system for customers in emerging markets, such as India, Indonesia, and Taiwan; demonstration on CCD Camera System for multimedia companies in Singapore, Australia and Taiwan.

LSI Design focuses on audio and visual IC design for local and regional markets and is presently designing only Analogue ICs. The centre already has eleven ICs designed by it in the market (RF Amp for CD-ROM, EVR for car audio, etc.) and five ICs are under development.

The Application Engineering group consists of six professionals and works on optical disc system, camera systems and other product systems. Its customers are in the Asian region, excluding Hong Kong, Taiwan and China. The customers are manufacturers of electronics, audio products, personal computers and TV products. The customers are offered both already designed product lines, as well as customized ICs. These customers, in turn, sell their final products world-wide.

SSEC's global and local network

Figure 6.3 illustrates the global and local network of SSEC. The links with the parent company's R&D unit are in the form of design verification meetings before finalizing a product, and in circuit testing. Sony Semiconductor has its corporate R&D unit in Astugi, Japan. Outside Japan, Sony Semiconductors also has IC design units in the USA and the UK. The Singapore unit does not have any links with them, as they deal with different product lines.

In terms of local links, there are no strong connections to local S&T institutions or companies. There is some tie-in with the Institute of Micro-electronics (IME), which carried out IC characterization for Sony. The institute has the necessary equipment for doing this task and Sony finds it expensive to have it in-house. Sometimes, the faculty of IME are also consulted on technical matters. Local diffusion of knowledge occurs through provision of solutions in applications engineering to local customers, some of whom used this solution. A few times some software is out-sourced from the local companies. Local

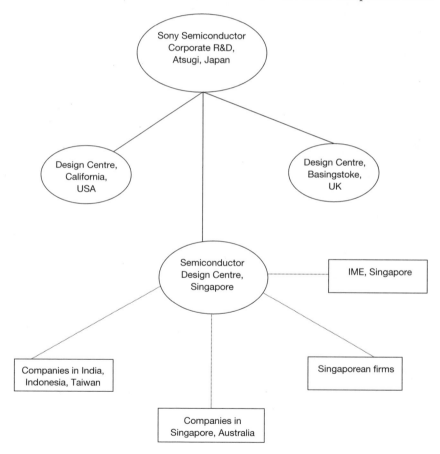

Figure 6.3 SSEC's global and local R&D network

PCB manufacturers also supplied some PCBs according to Sony's technical specification. The work carried out in the Singapore unit involves standardized technologies, where the product is matured, so not much external help is necessary. Singapore activities have not resulted in any patents so far. Within the Science Park Sony does not see much interaction among companies, in terms of agglomeration effects, except for the contact with the IME.

The Application Engineering group conducts training programmes on optical disc system for companies in India, Indonesia and Taiwan. It also provides demonstrations of CCD Camera System for Singaporean and other companies in the region. Newly recruited staff are sent to the IC design training courses conducted by the Economic Development Board.

Through its active participation in the Local Industry Upgrading Programme, it has helped the local supporting industries in quality upgrading and technology transfer. It is through its myriad of operations and involvement in community-related activities that Sony hopes to grow in tandem with Singapore in the years to come.

Conclusion

In terms of strengths, Singapore, with its good infrastructure, political stability and pool of highly skilled manpower, offers Sony a conducive place to operate in. The professionals in developing countries have the talent, but do lack exposure to the appropriate R&D environment. In due course of time such exposure will help the engineering talent in developing countries to contribute more to technical progress.

Parallax Research

Parallax Research is an entrepreneurial company started by a former employee of Hewlett Packard (HP). It provides technical consultancy, design and product development services, in areas that include: mechanical and electromechanical systems design; firmware and microelectronics systems; software application development; plastic tooling and injection moulding; international procurement; contract manufacturing; product qualification and certification; and complete turnkey product development. It carries out subcontract R&D activities for TNCs.

After the entrepreneur quit HP in 1993 and started the company as a one-man firm, he was also appointed as a consultant. Thus, Parallax Research started carrying out consultancy work for HP. The same year, Parallax was awarded a grant by the Economic Development Board (EDB) for the development of a multimedia information retrieval system (software), and was also awarded tenancy in the Singapore Institute of Standards and Industrial Research's Incubator Programme.

In 1994, the Wuthelam Group of Singapore invested in Parallax Research. This investment allowed Parallax to expand its operations and plug into a larger network of affiliated engineering service companies.

In October 1994, Parallax was awarded tenancy at the Innovation Centre of Nanyang Technological University. This affiliation gave access to design and research resources within the university. Parallax also became a part of the EDB's Local Industry Upgrading Programme. Through this programme, Parallax works closely with Hewlett Packard to support their R&D activities in Singapore. In November 1994, Parallax was awarded another grant from the EDB to develop core competency in a new technology area Serial InfraRed (SIR) technology.

The entrepreneur, having worked in HP, had a close relationship with that company, which helped in establishing the start-up. The entrepreneur had no partners but was motivated by his aptitude for innovating, his liking for a creative R&D environment, and new designs. Hence, the entrepreneur decided to take a chance on starting his own company. He wants to retain the creativity of the firm, and therefore does not want to grow into a large company. Presently, Parallax Research employs fifteen people, including eight engineers and seven support staff.

R&D activities

At the time of being selected for the incubator programme in 1993, Parallax was chosen for its idea in software development. The concept was to develop two new technologies:

1   Free text (multimedia product) – the concept was to take a multimedia object, e.g. a video clip, and describe it in 'pros on' and retrieve it using similar 'pros' and natural language description.
2   Integrated chip PLX 1000, developed exclusively for HP. Subsequently, PLX 7001 was also developed for HP. The product was a modulation and demodulation chip for infrared communications. Parallax took the responsibility for the total job, designed the chip, and got it fabricated and packaged by NEC of Japan. The product was handed over to HP, USA.

In 1994, an industry association called 'Infra Data Association', formed by a consortium of information technology companies, including HP, IBM and Sharp, embarked on a programme to standardize the protocol for the transmission of information using infrared, i.e. protocols for physical layout and software layout, etc. Parallax Research is a member of the consortium.

Parallax decided to go into new product development targeted on infrared technologies. Once again EDB became interested in the plans and granted S$ 250,000 to develop products based on infrared technologies. Parallax teamed up with the HP's optical communications division based in San Jose, USA. This division was in charge of developing and manufacturing optical modules for converting electrical signals to infrared and also vice versa. However, the division was lacking an 'interface chip'. HP subcontracted the work to Parallax on a turnkey basis to develop, design and manufacture the chip. The relationship between Parallax and HP was based on some guidelines. HP gave Parallax an idea of what they require, and Parallax wrote the specifications and the concept design. The design was also implemented by Parallax. There was continuous interaction between HP and Parallax. Parallax then linked up with NEC of Japan to fabricate the chip. After the manufactured products arrived from Japan, they were labelled as HP's product and handed over to HP for marketing world-wide.

The contract R&D projects undertaken by Parallax Research include:

- Development of a printer demonstration module for the Hewlett Packard Deskjet 3XX printer. The project involved both mechanical, electrical and firmware design. The project was executed completely on turnkey basis with design services, tooling, procurement, manufacturing and shipping of the product to HP sites world-wide.
- Hewlett Packard – PCPR Printer Language Development: Parallax Research consulted and developed firmware for the formatter of a Japanese inkjet printer based on the HP Deskjet 310 portable color printer. The formatt was developed for a large Japanese corporation. The product was successfully launched in July 1994.

Parallax's operations were split into two divisions: one focusing on developing new technologies, and the other focusing on consultancy activities to generate income for the company.

The consultancy division of Parallax, in some of its projects, had developed products for HP, Singapore, which had the global charter for calculator products, including the R&D. HP approached Parallax with a concept idea for a product to beam a calculator's output onto an overhead projector. Parallax carried out the complete work. Parallax also developed control units for Philips, Singapore, and designed a hearing-aid system for Siemens, Singapore, on subcontract R&D basis.

According to Parallax Research, TNCs generally subcontract R&D that is not part of their core product charter. Subcontracting is the most cost-effective way to accomplish the task, rather than using internal resources. This model of cost-effective product development is becoming increasingly popular.

In terms of consultancy, when Samsung of South Korea was developing a personal digital assistant, it approached Parallax to develop the infrared software protocol for the product. HP and Parallax co-operate closely in technical as well as marketing aspects. They also undertake joint marketing trips, offering HP's back-up products. When in Korea on a joint marketing trip, Samsung contacted Parallax through HP.

By now, Parallax has developed a number of infrared products under its own brand name also. One of the products is Lite Link, which is an infrared interface that allows transfer of data from notebook computer to PC. This product was developed in 1995. For this product Parallax collaborated with Microsoft, which wrote the device drivers for the product as part of Windows 95 operating system. The core of the product is the chip designed by Parallax.

The initial intention was to develop only this core building block, but it was later decided to develop the complete product as a low-cost high-end product. The product was manufactured locally by a contract manufacturing company. Another product developed was one which can connect a personal digital assistant or a notebook to a printer directly.

Parallax is a 100 per cent GTU. Some 80 per cent of its own products are sold in Europe. Parallax is a successful spin-off because it does not compete with HP but develops complementary products. The strategy of the company is to remain in such niche areas.

Infrared chips are not patented because of the consortium of companies involved. The patent for modulation is owned by HP. Parallax does not demand joint patenting in its subcontract deals. Parallax has one US design patent for Lite Link. Parallax is not interested in patenting, as because of its small size it cannot enforce its patent rights effectively.

Parallax Research's global and local R&D network

Figure 6.4 illustrates Parallax Research's global and local networks. In terms of local links, there is not much interaction with the local universities. However, in chip design activities, the Institute of Microelectronics has provided a lot of help. IME helped Parallax, when it started undertaking chip design by providing free advice on tools, vendors, etc. and direction. IME also carried out testing and characterization of the chips developed by Parallax.

Being part of the Innovation Centre of Nanyang University gives Parallax access to the university's design and research resources. Parallax Research has assigned consulting projects to the faculty of the university in the past. It also used industrial attachment students on a short-term basis.

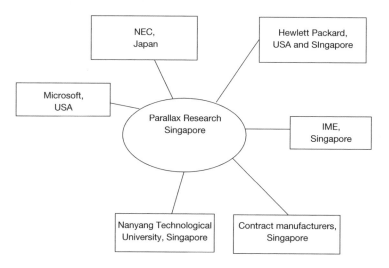

Figure 6.4 Parallax Research's global and local R&D network

Although Parallax wanted to establish a long-term relationship with one contract manufacturer, it was not possible because the contract manufacturers' product focus keeps changing depending on the business.

Conclusion

According to Parallax, the geographical position of Singapore offers the country a great advantage. The links with Malaysia and Indonesia create markets for mass volume manufacturing and the Singaporean government is very supportive of high-tech activities. However, Singapore does not have sufficient numbers of trained engineers. Most of the staff in Parallax are recruited either from overseas, such as India and China, or are overseas-educated Singaporeans.

7 Implications for innovation capability in host countries

Analysis of the host country studies

The database and the case studies presented in the earlier chapters clearly indicate that the scope of R&D activities carried out in developing countries has broadened in recent years. In the past, R&D activities performed in developing countries were limited to adaptation (TTU) and, at the most, product development for the local market (ITU). Behrman and Fischer (1980) in their survey found that of the 106 R&D units abroad belonging to the 31 US-based TNCs, about 28 per cent were involved in new product research and 59 per cent were carrying out limited functions of applied R&D. The former category was located entirely in Western Europe. Although some applied R&D activities were carried out in developing countries, their scope was limited to adaptation and local product development work. Developing countries were mainly locations of technical services. Animal and farm facilities for testing of veterinary products, pesticides and agricultural products were located mostly in tropical developing countries.[1]

By the mid-1980s, however, the global business environment had changed considerably. Companies needed to access science and technology resources from a geographically wider area than earlier. By this time, several developing countries had also built up technological capabilities that could support R&D activities. The performance of higher-order R&D in developing countries by TNCs is a recent phenomenon. The earliest date of establishment of GTU in India was 1985, while almost all the RTUs have evolved from the existing ITUs. Some 50 per cent of CTUs were established prior to mid-1980s and the other 50 per cent are newly created units. With the liberalization of the Indian economy and the rationalization of TNCs' operations in India, ITUs are expected to evolve into more RTUs and GTUs.

The case studies of TNCs' R&D activities have indicated that the primary driving force for locating R&D in India is technology-related, i.e. to gain access to R&D personnel of required quality and expertise. This factor as the main driving force has come out quite clearly even in the questionnaire survey results. Across all types of R&D units and technologies, the availability of R&D personnel is stated to be an important reason for locating R&D in India. This factor became the most important for location of higher-order R&D activities, especially for GTU and CTU types.[2] The case studies also suggest that some developing countries have achieved an international reputation in certain science and technology areas, for example, India in molecular biology, biotechnology and software technologies. TNCs are attempting to gain access to such knowledge and skills by making R&D investments in these countries.

The question that arises then is, why are the TNCs not making use of such skills available within the industrialized countries? TNCs, for an overwhelming proportion of their R&D, utilize the resources available within the industrialized countries but in recent years, due to rapidly shrinking product life cycles, TNCs have increased their R&D activities, in turn increasing the demand for R&D personnel. The supply of R&D personnel of the required specialization is not able to meet the current demands of TNCs.[3] The case studies suggest that there is a problem of lack of research personnel in the home countries of the TNCs.

The questionnaire survey, however, did not highlight this factor as a primary motive for the location of R&D in developing countries, such as India. Nevertheless, the RTU, GTU and CTU types of R&D units indicated that this factor was almost twice as important as a motive, compared to TTUs and ITUs. This factor was more than twice as important as a motive by the R&D units dealing with new technologies. In the discussions with managers in the corporate headquarters of TNCs, it became evident that in recent years gaining access to personnel has been the most important factor for locating R&D abroad.[4]

Another primary driving force, even though it may not be equally crucial, for the location of R&D in developing countries has been the cost-related factor. The total costs of carrying out R&D in developing countries, such as India, are much less compared to the industrialized countries,[5] mainly due to the lower wages of R&D personnel in developing countries. In general, wage costs account for the largest proportion of total costs in R&D activities. The survey indicates the importance of this factor, especially for higher-order R&D. For GTUs, it is the second most important factor.

In the discussions with the TNCs' headquarters, as a primary driving force the cost factor did not assume the same importance as gaining access to personnel. This is because sometimes, in developing countries, the cost advantages of lower wages of personnel may be eroded by the higher material and communications costs. For instance, some of the inputs may not be available locally and may need to be imported under special conditions and this adds to the total costs. Similarly, lack of infrastructure facilities may require TNCs to invest in captive facilities, adding to the total costs, e.g. shortages of power may require investing in back-up facilities or poor communication lines may require investing in a communication network.

However, the cost-related factor is also an important driving force for the location of R&D in India as the questionnaire survey revealed. Increasing global competition is mounting pressure on TNCs' profitability and survival.[6] At the same time, technology is assuming greater importance as a competitive factor. Therefore, one way of dealing with such pressures is to locate some activities, including R&D, in low-cost countries that have the capabilities to perform such activities.

However, in the case of Singapore, the primary driving force for location of R&D has been the need to be in proximity to the regional markets. However, the second most important driving force has been the availability of personnel. Part of the reason for this is that TNCs' R&D units in Singapore are closely linked to the production units located in the regional countries. R&D performed in these units is also mainly that of product design and development, i.e. engineering aspects.

Moreover, Singapore does not have large pools of research personnel with the required qualifications. However, Singapore's environment facilitates recruitment from neighbouring countries. The costs of performing R&D in Singapore may be lower than in the industrialized world, but not compared to other developing countries. However, the infrastructure available and the efficient business environment in Singapore make up for the higher costs.

The TNCs that are carrying out higher-order R&D activities in India and Singapore are mainly those dealing with new technologies, i.e. microelectronics and biotechnology. A few TNCs dealing with conventional technologies have established GTU and CTU types of R&D units. Even the RTU activities of TNCs dealing with conventional technologies have evolved in time from ITU type of activities.[7]

However, this does not imply that the TNCs dealing with conventional technologies are not at all involved in GTU or CTU types of R&D activities in India. There are several cases of such R&D conducted in India by TNCs in collaboration with national research institutes, mostly through non-equity arrangements.[8]

The question that arises now is: how is it that performance of higher-order R&D activities in new technologies can take place even in developing countries that are not as highly industrialized as the OECD countries? As Perez and Soete (1988) in their concept of 'life cycles of technology systems' explained, the emergence of a new techno-economic paradigm opens up windows of opportunity to latecomers for catching up with the leaders. In the development phases of a new technology system, Phase I involves original design and engineering. This implies that the scientific and technological knowledge required will be high, whereas the industrial skills and investment required will be low.[9] In other words, the countries that have an adequate supply of science and technology personnel, even though they lack considerable industrial experience in conventional technology systems, can become locations for innovation activities in new technology systems. This is evident from TNCs' R&D investments in non-OECD countries and some of the innovations occurring outside the industrialized world. Moreover, the proximity of new technologies to basic science permits theoretically trained personnel, with little industrial experience, to be employed in R&D tasks.[10]

In conventional technologies, in the initial phases of innovation, there is a need for continuous interaction between design, engineering, production, marketing and finance functions. Therefore, R&D, especially the activities related to new product design and development, tended to be located in the home countries of TNCs, where all these functions are also located. The need for location of R&D in conventional technologies close to the manufacturing and/or market still holds true as indicated by the survey in India. On the other hand, R&D in new technologies can be geographically delinked from manufacturing and market.[11] What this implies is that R&D in new technologies can be located in places where R&D personnel of required quality are available and there are academic centres of excellence, irrespective of the presence of TNCs' manufacturing facilities or market in that country.[12]

The products and processes in new technologies seem to have a higher level of standardization, compared to the conventional technologies and therefore, the products have global or regional market orientation. The adaptations required for local conditions also seem to be marginal or nil. Hence, as the survey in India showed, there are only a few TTUs and ITUs among TNCs dealing with the new technologies. All the GTUs and CTUs are established by the TNCs dealing with new technologies.

The case studies in India and Singapore indicate that the TNCs' R&D activities are establishing links with the local systems of innovation. Such ties are mainly with the local universities and research institutes. The links created by TNCs' R&D units in India are relatively stronger than those created in the case of Singapore. This mainly arises from the broader S&T base of India compared to Singapore's S&T system. In the case of Singapore, the interaction with the local research institutes seems to be limited to the utilization by TNCs of the testing equipment available at the institutes. On the other hand, the research institutes in India seem to be used by TNCs as collaborators in their R&D work, by assigning them substantial research work.

In both countries, the link with the domestic firms is to a large extent limited. However, in the case of ARCI, R&D activities have led to the emergence of spin-off companies in the host country. It indicates that there is diffusion of technology into the host country, leading to the introduction of new products and processes into the local economy. The case studies also show that these R&D activities are well integrated into the TNCs' global R&D networks. The joint projects involve carrying out specific tasks in a large R&D project, based on the expertise of personnel in the Indian or Singaporean unit, as well as utilizing the expertise available in other R&D units of TNCs. Such a complementary exchange of knowledge helps in building up core competencies in each of the R&D units in a TNC's network, including the Indian and Singaporean units.

The results of the survey in India show that R&D units of TNCs dealing with new technologies are better integrated into the TNCs' global R&D networks than the R&D units of TNCs dealing with conventional technologies. Some 81.3 per cent of the R&D units in new technologies are integrated with the parents' R&D units world-wide, compared to 50 per cent of the R&D units in conventional technologies. Conventional industries mainly depend on R&D support from the TNCs' home countries. TNCs dealing in new technologies are also integrated with the parents' manufacturing centres world-wide. GTUs, which belong to only new technologies TNCs, through their links with the parents' customers and suppliers world-wide and their links with the local systems of innovation, are contributing to the diffusion of knowledge relating to the global technology developments in the support industry, as well as the ability to cater to the global demands.

The RTU, GTU and CTU types of R&D activities have established stronger links with the local systems of innovation compared to traditional TTUs and ITUs, indicating greater diffusion of knowledge into the host country through higher-order R&D activities that have been carried out by TNCs in recent years. Many of the GTUs in India and Singapore were established fairly recently and are still exploring the ways to link up with the local systems of innovation. This implies that there is still scope for expanding and strengthening the local links through higher-order R&D units. On the other hand, almost all the TTUs and ITUs were established many years ago and have exhausted their scope for external local links for their R&D. GTUs and CTUs also have a better external network abroad, leading to an inflow of expert knowledge into the host economy.

The case studies and the database indicate that the TNCs' R&D activities are giving rise to the emergence of new types of organizations in developing host countries. The forms in which R&D is being carried out in developing countries by TNCs include:

- Own R&D centres – considered part of global in-house R&D facilities. Some of them are combined with manufacturing facilities and others are stand-alone R&D units (e.g. Texas Instruments R&D unit in India).
- Joint venture R&D (alliance) – with local firms to develop a new product for global or regional markets. Such joint ventures are in some cases combined with production and marketing arrangements and in other cases they are independent of these activities (e.g. alliances between Biocon India and Quest International).
- Sub-contracting of R&D – assigning a part or complete project to firms or research institutes on a payment basis (e.g. Hewlett Packard sub-contracting R&D to Parallax Research).
- Sponsorship of research – in research institutes in India, particularly in basic research or generic technologies for long-term corporate use (e.g. ARCI's link with the Indian Institute of Science).

ARCI, by licensing its technologies for by-products to local scientists, is contributing to the emergence of a new class of entrepreneurs, i.e. technocratic entrepreneurs. Since they were innovation-based products, scientists could gain access to venture capital funds that enabled them to become entrepreneurs.

The success of Biocon India in its R&D alliance with Quest International and the establishment of Parallax Research in Singapore by a former employee of Hewlett Packard are also indications of the emerging entrepreneurial zeal among scientists and engineers in developing countries. In discussions with researchers involved with TNCs' R&D activities, it became apparent that more and more scientists and engineers are showing an interest in becoming entrepreneurs themselves.

In recent years, a number of small high-tech firms have been established by technocrats in India, especially in software design and engineering. Similarly, in Singapore many contract manufacturing high-tech firms, started by technocrats, have emerged. The researchers felt that TNCs' R&D and TNCs' need for special talents are giving them an opportunity to take up challenging tasks based on their knowledge and at the same time to try their potential as entrepreneurs. Such opportunities were not available in India in the past.

Effects on innovation capability

The assessment of the implications of international corporate R&D activities for the host country is fraught with difficulties. The scope of this study was limited to, first of all, a study of the type of links established by the TNCs' R&D activities to the local systems of innovation and analysis of the potential for diffusion of technologies; and second, to study the type of spillovers from the international corporate R&D activities and their effect on the host economy.

As Dunning (1992) pointed out, there are two opposing views regarding the impact of TNCs' R&D on the host countries. One view considers inward R&D investments to be in general beneficial to economic growth, by providing technology and managerial skills, which in turn create indirect positive effects for the host country at a lower cost. These positive effects include technical support to local suppliers and customers, contract jobs from foreign R&D units to local R&D organizations, etc. The counter-view argues that R&D activities by foreign firms tend to tap into unique local R&D resources with little or no benefit to the host country. Concentrating on problems of little relevance to the local economy, they may be a little more than disguised 'brain drain', diverting scarce technical resources from more useful purposes.

However, in the context of developing countries, where scientific and technical resources are under-utilized, the counter-view may not hold much weight. The benefits are larger, while the costs involved may be marginal. In the case of developing host countries, the cost factor may be that such R&D activities may create islands of 'high-tech enclaves' with little diffusion of knowledge into the economy. However, knowledge and skills can not be isolated over the long term. The mobility of researchers, the need for local procurement of men and materials, etc. are bound to diffuse technologies throughout the economy. The study analyses these factors.

While analysing the implications for the host countries, it is important to consider the type of R&D being performed and its effects. This study showed that depending on the type of R&D being carried out, the effect on the innovation capability of the host country varies.[13] The strength and breadth of the ties with the local systems of innovation vary across the five types. The ties are limited in the case of TTUs, because it only involves adaptation of the parents' technology to local conditions and is better done within the manufacturing unit. However, the data indicated that they did have some links with the local innovation system in India. This is mainly because of the slightly higher level of technical activities undertaken by them, e.g. material substitution. The same is true of ITUs. Because of the policy environment in India in the past, which required material substitution in products due to import restrictions or sometimes to keep the costs lower, TTUs had to perform more than just tinkering with the parents' technology. This often blurred the distinction between TTUs and ITUs. ITUs were in general supposed to have stronger ties with the local S&T system because of their product development activities, even though they basically re-do the designs supplied by the parents. However, these stronger links are better reflected in the case of RTUs, which are basically ITUs gradually evolving into RTUs. GTUs and CTUs have stronger ties both to the local innovation system as well as the global research networks. Therefore, the scope for the diffusion of new knowledge to the local S&T system are higher through GTUs and CTUs, whereas TTUs, ITUs and RTUs mainly utilize the knowledge already available within the corporate system.

In the case of Singapore, the ITU type of R&D is not prevalent. The majority of the R&D units tend to be RTUs, because of the small size of the country and the TNCs' strategy of catering to the region with Singapore as the base. This establishes strong links between the manufacturing units in the regional countries and R&D units in Singapore.

However, this does not imply that TTUs, ITUs and RTUs do not have important implications for the host economy. Since the conversion of research results into manufacturing products occurs in the same place, it may lead to other benefits such as the development of supplier networks and technology transfer to domestic small and medium-sized enterprises. On the other hand, as GTUs and CTUs are delinked from the operations of production and marketing, their innovations are less likely to lead to production-related benefits in the host country.

On the face of it, TNCs' R&D activities appear to be using the talents already available in the host country rather than creating any new talents or knowledge. However, the case studies showed that TNCs are not only adding new innovation capacity by making greenfield investments in creating R&D facilities, but they are also bringing in new equipment and global knowledge networks. Through their links to the national systems of innovation in the host countries, these R&D activities are also contributing to the diffusion of new knowledge and technologies into the host economy.[14]

> The location of such multinational firm's plant will depend heavily, however, on the particular regional environment. Whereas the locational choice will often depend on the availability of local skills, infrastructure and access to knowledge, the firm *itself* will also contribute to the long-term growth in

the region, the availability of human resources, the access to knowledge, the local suppliers' know-how and networks. It is worth observing that these often scarce and geographically 'fixed' factors constitute precisely the 'externalities', increasing-return growth features of long-term development.

(OECD, 1991, p. 124)

As the case studies revealed, one of the most important positive spillovers has been that the international corporate R&D activities are infusing the scientific community in developing countries with a commercial culture. The sponsorship of research or subcontracting of R&D to the academic system also contributes to diffusion of such a culture. In other words, international corporate R&D activities are fine-tuning the innovation system in developing host countries to be competitive in generating knowledge. TNCs are also encouraging the scientists in developing host countries to venture beyond just proving the principles and to develop tangible products as a contribution to the benefit of the society. TNCs are also establishing 'Chairs' in local universities as well as adding new research equipment in university laboratories.[15] The case studies also showed that TNCs' R&D units are also involved in continuous development of their researchers through training programmes both within the country and abroad.

In the past, in a developing country like India, one of the main reasons for not reaping the benefits of its scientific capacity has been the lack of application to convert its knowledge into products. TNCs through their R&D activities are contributing to the diffusion of application skills to the researchers. In discussions with the researchers it became clear that TNCs impart training in application techniques to researchers for a few weeks before assigning them to R&D work. This aspect is also revealed in the case study of Texas Instruments. With the mobility of researchers from one company to another such skills are diffused throughout the economy. The discussions with TNCs in India revealed that the turnover of the researchers ranges between 10 to 15 per cent. Such turnover of personnel seem to be greater in the case of Singapore. If these personnel move to domestic firms, there will be significant diffusion of knowledge to the local firms.

Some TNCs are also collaborating in establishing technology institutions for imparting education. For instance, in India, Motorola is collaborating with the Pune Institute of Advanced Technologies (PIAT) in offering a post-graduate degree in advanced telecommunication engineering with software focus. The faculty will consist of both the staff at PIAT and the experts from Motorola. While such colleges make it easy for the TNCs to recruit the graduates of the required specialization, they also help in introducing such a specialized subject in the host country.[16]

One negative spillover of international corporate R&D activities in the host country has been that TNCs are able to recruit and retain the cream of the available talent, due to the higher salaries, advanced training and other career growth opportunities offered by them. The domestic firms, on the other hand, cannot match the TNCs in these aspects, so they have to make do with the rest of the talents. This, in turn, may affect the enhancement of technological capabilities in the domestic firms.

Other effects on the innovation capability of the host country include the diffusion of knowledge related to patents and other IPR. As the Biocon India case study reveals, Indian firms and scientists are realizing the importance of patenting and are acquiring the knowledge related to it with the collaboration of TNCs. With the TNCs' R&D investments in the country increasing, even the academic institutions realize the importance of teaching the IPR aspect to the students. The Indian Institute of Science (IISc) has started a course on IPR in its curriculum. The Indian pharmaceutical industry is gearing up for the implementation of the trade-related intellectual property rights (TRIPS) agreement, by increasing their R&D budgets and linking up with the TNCs.

Although not quantified, the R&D activities of TNCs and liberalization of the economy have also led to an increase in the R&D by domestic companies.[17] Domestic companies in India have also increased their dependence on the national research institutes. For example, Bharat Electronics and the Indian Institute of Science have started a joint venture R&D to develop high quality compound semiconductor films for device applications. This project aims to develop gallium wafers grown by a metal organic chemical vapour deposition process and this has application potential in defence, space and information industries.[18] Similarly, IISc and Metur Chemicals collaborated in making India self-sufficient in silicon manufacture.[19]

> A major consequence of multinational R&D activity world-wide is the creation within emerging economies of a substantial base of scientists and engineers experienced in the conduct of R&D within the environment of a private corporation. These people can become the nucleus for industrial research that may be initiated by domestic companies. Further, the establishment of R&D activity within multinational operations will be a competitive pressure up on domestic firms to do the same.
>
> (Fusfeld, 1995, p. 269)

Policy implications

The increasing science base of new technologies and growing competitive pressures to be innovative are necessitating multi-sourcing of corporate technologies. In their search for additional sources of technologies, TNCs have also started tapping S&T talents in some developing countries. In the overall phenomenon of the globalization of R&D, the emerging patterns are only of marginal significance. However, from the perspective of the developing host country, the implications assume greater significance. In the beginning such R&D activities may be directed by the needs of the TNCs' strategic interests, subordinating the national interests, but a rapid expansion of the local technology base and market in the host country may prompt extensive local production and expansion of R&D activities, thus shifting the relative balance in favour of the host country. However, such benefits are likely to accrue only to host countries with large domestic markets. Large developing countries, such as Brazil, China and India, have dual technology environments. On the one hand, there are high-tech S&T talents, which show complementarities with Western economies. On the other, a larger portion of the economy displays low S&T development. TNCs are attempting to exploit the former.

In order to increase the positive host country effects of such international corporate R&D, their interaction with local industry and S&T infrastructure through related production or marketing needs to be encouraged. To be able to reap positive benefits of such R&D, the national S&T infrastructure and the whole national system of innovation must have sufficient strength. The task for national policy-making bodies involves building up local S&T capabilities to assimilate and exploit foreign technology, to sustain frontier national research capabilities in some areas and to provide an environment conducive to technology-based innovation and entrepreneurship (Granstrand *et al.*, 1993).

Developing countries now have an opportunity to be part of international technology developments and provide meaningful employment to their scientific and technical personnel. Such international R&D activities will help stem the brain drain. The rapid growth in industrial R&D after the Second World War led to the migration of talented scientists and engineers from developing countries to the corporate laboratories in the industrialized countries, especially the USA. But today, there is a greater pressure on the TNCs to employ such people in their own countries, often through collaboration with the local institutions, but increasingly by establishing laboratories (Fusfeld, 1995, p. 269).

As noted earlier, in addition to the benefits of employment, international R&D activities will result in several other benefits. Hence, developing countries should create an attractive policy and R&D environment to attract such R&D investments. Such a policy environment includes favourable foreign direct investment policies; tax and other incentives; and non-discrimination between indigenous and foreign firms in their access to national scientific resources.

Most importantly, from the perspective of R&D investments, streamlining of patent and other intellectual property protection laws in accordance with the international practices is essential. The commercial value of new scientific knowledge generated in TNCs' R&D activities does not necessarily dictate greater confidentiality. Intellectual property law could be framed in such a way that, while affording protection to its owners, at the same time it facilitates the open and prompt publication of research (OECD, 1988).

Apart from the IPR-related legislative reform, a national infrastructure for implementing the IPR regime is necessary. Such infrastructure, 'according to patent law experts, includes a comprehensive information system to support patenting activities, a heightened professionalism among patent examiners, modernisation of India's main patent office, and increased awareness of the value of obtaining a patent' (*Science*, 26 January 1966, p. 443). Effective enforcement of the legislation is also necessary to create confidence among domestic as well as foreign innovators about the protection of their innovations in the country.

Dispersed R&D activities of TNCs require excellent communication and other infrastructural facilities. The countries seeking to attract R&D investments should establish such infrastructural facilities on a priority basis.

National research institutes should be given the freedom and motivation to collaborate with foreign firms and to undertake subcontract jobs from them. All over the world, academic institutions are forging closer links with industry. In some countries, academic institutions are even launching commercial ventures of their own or in collaboration with the corporate sector. In order to enhance the innovation capability and economic benefits through industry–university collaboration, the establishment of science or technology parks may assume importance. Such parks may attract both foreign and domestic firms to locate R&D, if the parks are situated in proximity to reputed academic establishments. Such parks may also lead to some locational advantages such as exchange of information between the firms located in the park, inter-firm technology collaborations and technology transfer, especially for by-products. To strengthen university–industry links, the senior managers from both domestic and foreign firms may be appointed to the management boards of universities. This will facilitate moulding university educational courses to suit the corporate requirements.

The most important reason for locating international corporate R&D activities in developing countries has been the availability of trained personnel. The host countries should ensure that this supply line does not dry up. For instance, in India, already there are reports of competition for recruitment of trained personnel between the domestic and foreign firms. This requires increasing the intake of students into science and engineering subjects, which in turn, may require building more colleges or universities. Since the quality standards of the graduates need to be maintained, if not enhanced, it may call for investment in establishing advanced equipment and sophisticated laboratories. With the technological specialization increasing, there may be demand from enterprises, both domestic and foreign, to develop new specialities in the universities. Development of such specialities may require initial financial support from the government.

The Third World scientists and engineers, who are working in industrialized countries, are playing a major role in TNCs' R&D activities in their home countries by entering into alliances with TNCs, by establishing firms or laboratories to undertake R&D activities on a contract basis. These expatriate scientists and engineers may be further encouraged to contribute to their home countries, by appointing them to the management boards of national research institutes, universities and public sector industries or as advisors to government ministries.

The emerging phenomenon seems to offer the developing countries, at least a few of them, some fresh opportunities. Just as international production activities benefited the NIEs, international R&D can be expected to benefit the developing host countries. Most important of all, international R&D would be an impetus to the R&D being performed by indigenous industry in some of the developing countries. If, by creating a proper investment climate, the developing host countries could persuade the TNCs to commercialize the research results in the country, the benefits would be even larger and faster.

From the perspective of developing countries, although inward R&D investments will bring in long-term benefits, inward manufacturing investments will bring faster and wider benefits. R&D investments will bring in international prestige as well as employment opportunities for the highly educated. However, in developing countries, such as India and Brazil, the vast majority of the population is unskilled and uneducated. For the economy to show substantial improvements in such large countries, the capabilities of this majority of the population need to be enhanced.

While not losing sight of the need for higher education, if the host governments can improve the skill and education levels of the mass of the people through vocational and primary education, it will stimulate inward FDI in manufacturing. The success of countries such as Malaysia, Thailand and the NIEs in achieving high growth rates reveals the importance of a workforce with a basic education that can be trained. One way of achieving such an objective is to privatize parts of the higher education and transfer the freed government financial resources to invest in basic educational facilities.

Moreover, the integrated international production activities of TNCs are leading to increased intra-firm trade. Such intra-firm trade gives a TNC's affiliate access to the marketing and distribution network of the TNC. This in turn will lead to specialized, but increased, international trade of the host country.

8 Conclusion

> Inevitably, the industrial research base of non-OECD countries will generate an increasing share of commercial technical advances in world markets . . . Technical institutions and universities in emerging economies will be upgraded as industrial demand increases for more sophisticated R&D programs and for more technical graduates with advanced degrees. More technical advances from non-OECD countries will stimulate more R&D by MNCs [multinational corporations] both at home and in host countries.
>
> (Fusfeld, 1995, p. 263)

In recent years, TNCs have been conducting higher-order R&D activities in developing countries. Although, in the past, there were cases of TNCs conducting R&D in developing countries, such R&D was mainly related to adaptation of products and processes to the local conditions and at most product development for local markets. It is only since the mid-1980s that TNCs have started carrying out higher-order R&D, such as developing products for regional/global markets or mission-oriented basic research for long-term corporate use, in developing countries.[1] It has been mainly only the TNCs dealing with new technologies that have been performing higher-order R&D in developing countries.

The primary driving forces for such a move by TNCs are both technology-related, i.e., gaining access to R&D personnel, as well as cost-related, i.e., exploiting the cost differentials between developing and industrialized countries. The case of Singapore showed that the need to be close to the regional markets is also an important driving force for location of R&D. TNCs dealing with conventional technologies have not yet started performing higher-order R&D on a large scale in developing countries. However, with the rationalization of their operations, some of their R&D units in developing countries that have been developing products for the local market (ITUs) are gradually evolving into units for developing products for the regional markets (RTUs).

This is mainly because of the increasing pressures of global competition. By the 1980s, the characteristic features of global competition in several industries had changed significantly, increasing the pressure on TNCs' profitability. Internationalization of marketing or assembly production activities is no longer sufficient to remain competitive. Globalization involves full-scale production, including component suppliers and product design and development, as well as international technology exchanges, such as strategic alliances and joint ventures (OECD, 1991, 1992).

However, it should be remembered that at the global level the proportion of R&D conducted in developing countries by TNCs is still only marginal. Over 90 per cent of TNCs' R&D activities are located within the industrialized world. It is often difficult to get an exact estimate of the R&D performed by TNCs outside their home countries. On average the globalized corporate R&D ranges between 10 to 15 per cent of total R&D conducted by TNCs, although the figure is rising steadily.[2] The figure, however, is greater for TNCs based in small industrialized countries.[3] Of this limited R&D conducted overseas, the share of developing countries would be only a small proportion. Their share again depends on whether it is measured on the basis of total R&D expenditures or R&D personnel or proportion of patents originating in developing countries.

This study, through empirical analysis, attempted to show that the characteristic features of R&D performed in some developing countries by TNCs are changing, making them locations for more substantial R&D investments and innovation,[4] i.e. something new that did not happen before is taking place, and why is it occurring? What are its implications for the host countries? Although when viewed from the perspective of all TNCs as a group or all developing countries as a block, such activities are marginal, when viewed from the host country perspective such development assumes greater significance. It may be pointed out here that in the 1970s, internationalization of production also started as a marginal activity, with labour-intensive assembly activities being relocated into low-cost countries, especially the NIEs. Starting with such low-tech activities of TNCs, the NIEs today have built up strong skills in production engineering and are now increasingly becoming locations for R&D activities.

Globalization of corporate R&D – driving forces

Demand-side forces

As discussed in the analytical framework, the globalization of corporate R&D can be said to be occurring in waves or phases. As TNCs gain more confidence in the capabilities of their affiliates abroad and the host countries, increasingly higher-order R&D is being assigned to them. Until the 1970s, the TNCs that were expanding abroad were mainly those dealing with conventional technologies, which required adaptations to each local market conditions. So, in the initial phases, TTUs, to carry out adaptation work and provide local technical services, were established abroad. In the mid-1970s, the need for increased sensitivity to local conditions became important for expanding the market shares abroad. So, along with the expansion of production facilities, some R&D activities were established abroad to develop products exclusively for the local markets (ITUs). However, most of such R&D was located within the industrialized countries. Only a few large developing countries, such as India, were locations for even these limited functions.[5] The TTUs and ITUs mainly depended on technologies transferred from the TNCs' home country and only modified them marginally. A good example of such ITU activities is Unilever's affiliate Hindustan Lever in India. Based on the detergent powder developed by the parent, the Indian affiliate developed a detergent cake for the Indian market. In India, where clothes are not washed in washing machines, but in flowing water, powder was not a good choice. Hence, due to this cultural habit, the cake had to be developed to gain a market share.

However, by the mid-1970s, the industries based on new technologies, especially microelectronics-based, had begun to expand rapidly. The emergence of a new techno-economic paradigm has transformed the characteristic features of global competition by impinging on the industrial production system. This change in the technological paradigm has eroded the competitiveness of firms and countries that were leaders in conventional technologies, and at the same time enabled some newcomers to take the lead (Ernst and O'Connor, 1989). This volatile competitive situation is evidenced by the threats posed to TNCs by the newly emerged high technology firms in the electronics and biotechnology sectors.[6] For instance, in the semiconductor business, during 1975–85, the US-based TNCs dominated the market for dynamic random access memories (DRAMs). After the mid-1980s, the Japanese TNCs surpassed the US companies in the global market share and hoped to maintain their lead for several decades. But, the newcomer to the field, Samsung of South Korea, snatched the lead by registering a phenomenal growth in a very short period. In 1989, Samsung was in ninth place in the global markets in memory chips, but by 1993, it had attained the number one position in the world (*Business Week*, 19 December 1994, p. 23).

Techno-economic and social developments, in recent decades, have created a more unified market in which consumer needs world-wide could be met with standardized products. This compelled TNCs to adopt global strategies to remain competitive (Levitt, 1983). The convergence of consumer needs and the rapid international diffusion of technologies have significantly influenced both the pace and the location of innovation. TNCs could no longer depend on their home countries alone to provide the ideal conditions for innovation. New needs could emerge anywhere in the world and the technological solutions to meet such needs might be located in another part of the world. These developments have increased the necessity for world-wide learning and the location of some strategic R&D activities away from home countries (Bartlett and Ghoshal, 1991). As a result, in the 1980s, several TNCs located some higher-order R&D activities abroad. IBM's basic research centre in Switzerland and global product development R&D in Germany are good examples of this phenomenon.

In the 1980s, with the global competition further intensifying, technology became one of the most critical factors of competitiveness. As a result, companies increased their R&D activities and in many cases, to reduce the risks as well as development time and to obtain complementary knowledge and skills, firms started joining hands with their earlier rivals in technological alliances.[7] However, all these activities were confined to the industrialized world. By the mid-1980s, the frenzy of innovation and technological activities had increased the demand for R&D personnel, surpassing supply in the industrialized world. The competition for recruitment of R&D personnel of required quality among firms was also pushing up the costs. As a corollary, companies started searching world-wide, including uncommon locations such as India, Israel and South Korea, to locate their R&D activities in order to gain access to R&D personnel.

Supply-side forces

Complementing the demand-side forces, some developing countries possessed supply-side factors. In their efforts to build up technological capacity for economic development, over the years many developing countries have built up large reserves of scientifically and technically trained manpower. However, such efforts, instead of resulting in rapid economic development, mostly resulted in increased unemployment among the educated or in a brain drain. The twin reasons for such a situation have been: (a) the mismatch between the requirements and human resources development planning; and (b) the low-level and slow pace of industrialization. Even the limited industrialization in such countries mainly took place through transfer of ready-made technologies by TNCs.

In some developing countries the scientifically and technically trained manpower was lying dormant due to its under-utilization by the indigenous industry. In most of these countries, either the industrialization did not take place at a corresponding level or the existing industry, because of their low-emphasis on R&D, had not been able to fully utilize the available trained manpower. These reserves of trained manpower are now available for utilization by TNCs for their R&D activities at much lower wages compared to their counterparts in industrialized countries.[8] TNCs, by locating R&D in such countries, can gain access to much needed talents as well as reduce their total R&D costs, without compromising their innovativeness.[9]

On the supply side, an added attraction for TNCs has been the interest among researchers from developing countries, who are educated and working in the USA and Europe, to return to their native countries and work on challenging tasks for TNCs.[10] Many researchers from developing countries have attained reputations in their respective fields of study in industrialized countries. Earlier, such people who were educated in industrialized countries stayed abroad, because of the lack of technologically challenging tasks in their home countries. Now with TNCs creating facilities similar to those available in industrialized countries, these researchers are showing an interest in returning to their home countries, leading to a reverse brain drain. These expatriate researchers are familiar with the operations of TNCs and the systems in industrialized countries.

In addition, some developing countries in Asia, especially the NIEs, and Latin America are already global manufacturing bases for many TNCs. This means that many manufacturers of end products are located in these countries, who in turn, become customers for TNCs dealing with intermediate products such as semiconductors and other electronics. To be in proximity to such customers and manufacturers, the supplier TNCs are locating R&D activities in these developing countries, especially in the Asian region. Moreover, with rapid economic growth rates, the Asian region is also increasingly consuming the final products, encouraging TNCs dealing with final products also to locate R&D in the region.[11]

According to Fusfeld (1994), the availability of educated, but under-utilized personnel in developing countries representing a combination of talent and low wages, has an important implication for industrial research.[12] These pools of scientists and engineers in non-OECD countries will continue to grow. There are three ways in which these personnel will influence future industrial research: (a) TNCs from industrialized countries will locate more R&D activities in developing countries with huge reservoirs of scientists and engineers; (b) TNCs will subcontract specific R&D projects and related technical services to firms or research institutes or universities or government agencies in developing countries; and (c) entrepreneurial activity and industrial growth in developing countries will lead to the evolution of a base of industrial research in domestic firms, with increased absorption of domestic scientists and engineers.

Facilitating forces

In the early 1970s, one of the main reasons for not locating substantial R&D abroad by TNCs was the difficulties involved in co-ordinating and supervising such activities (Mansfield, 1974). But, by the mid-1970s, the improvement of information and communication technologies (ICT) and the emergence of telematics had vastly facilitated the scope for international sourcing of knowledge. The new technologies have become not only the driving forces, but also the facilitating forces of globalization of R&D.

By the late 1970s, many TNCs dealing with new technologies had established world-wide organization of R&D and international sourcing of science and technology resources. ICT have facilitated the geographical dispersal of corporate R&D world-wide as well as ensuring the flow of technologies within the international group structures (OECD, 1992). ICT, especially with the introduction of digital technology, facilitates exchange of detailed designs, drawings and specifications without time delays. It permits accessing of central databases of TNCs' parents by affiliates around the world and obtaining customer requirements.

The developments in ICT are also showing their effects on research methods. Many of the experiments which earlier required expensive laboratories and building time-consuming prototypes, such as wind tunnels, can now be simulated on computers. Such inexpensive computer models open up opportunities for even developing countries to participate in global technology developments. ICT permits powerful simulations as well as scanning of scientific journals published world-wide at a faster pace. Such developments are breaking the geographical barriers and are offering access to basic science by even developing countries, which earlier only researchers in the industrialized countries could afford. Today, researchers located in Taiwan or South Korea can access the same computational models through their desk-top computers as their counterparts in the USA or Europe.[13]

Another feature of new technologies that enables globalization of their R&D has been their closeness to basic science. R&D functions in high-tech industries, such as pharmaceuticals, chemicals, microelectronics, biotechnology and new materials, have become more science-based and research-intensive (Freeman, 1982). The increasing role of scientific knowledge in major technological developments is also increasing the number of fields relevant to innovation and thereby the necessity for companies to depend on external sources, especially the academic system, for basic science-based knowledge inputs (Chesnais, 1988a). Some of the developing countries, although they are not highly industrialized, have internationally reputed academic establishments (Reddy, 1993). The proximity of new technologies to basic science are allowing TNCs to utilize the talents in such academic establishments in developing countries for their R&D requirements either by sponsoring research or subcontracting R&D or through research collaboration.[14]

Moreover, because of their basic science base even theoretically trained personnel, with little or no industrial experience, can be employed for R&D functions in new technologies. Such theoretically trained personnel are available in surplus in some developing countries, opening up opportunities for them to join the global R&D networks of TNCs. Unlike in conventional technologies, where 'learning by doing' plays a vital role in acquiring skills, the skills in new technologies can be acquired through formal training and education (Ernst and O'Connor, 1989).

Another characteristic feature of new technologies that has come out in the discussions with the TNCs' R&D personnel is that R&D in new technologies is divisible into sub-activities, which can later be integrated to result in final innovation. For instance, in the initial phases of establishing ARCI, the molecular biology portion of R&D was carried out at ARCI in India and the pharmacology and toxicology were carried out by Astra's R&D units in Sweden, with the final integration for product development taking place in Sweden. This divisibility of R&D functions in new technologies is what enables joint R&D projects and technology alliances, where each partner contributes the knowledge in which it has expertise. By implication, this also means that R&D in new technologies can be divided into 'core' and 'non-core or supplementary' activities. TNCs can save on costs by locating some of the non-core activities in low-cost countries, at the same time releasing resources in home countries for concentration on core activities.[15] Many of the higher-order R&D units in developing countries seem to initially concentrate on joint projects and as the confidence of TNCs in the capabilities of affiliates grows, higher responsibilities or even complete R&D are being entrusted to them.

In the past, especially in conventional technologies, the scale economies required for R&D were considered to be one of the main reasons for retaining substantial R&D in the home countries of TNCs. But, in recent years, in the new techno-economic paradigm the advantages of economies of scope have overcome the barriers of economies of scale. According to Mytelka (1993, pp. 702–3), contrary to earlier views, the critical mass can now be achieved in terms of the size of the 'system' needed to acquire the knowledge rather than the size of the firm itself. This applies to all activities in the value chain from conception of the idea to the marketing. This has allowed some TNCs to decentralize R&D, especially product development activities to affiliates in developing countries and they have entered into collaborative activities with academic establishments there. 'These changes in firm strategies have opened new windows of opportunity for innovation in developing countries.'

At the macro-level, one of the important facilitating factors for TNCs' R&D activities in developing countries has been the changes in government policies related to trade, foreign direct investment and particularly, the intellectual property rights (IPR) regime, in the host countries.

In the 1980s, following the economic and technological successes of the NIEs, many developing countries gave up their import-substitution policies and liberalized their trade and investment regimes. This liberalized environment enabled intra-firm and intra-industry trade and opened up opportunities for these countries to be integrated into TNCs' global R&D, production and marketing networks. With the successful conclusion of the General Agreement on Trade and Tariffs (GATT) negotiations and the establishment of the World Trade Organisation (WTO), these liberalized policies became internationally enforceable. Among the policies affected by GATT is the IPR legislation in developing countries, which now has to adhere to minimum international standards.

However, in the discussions with TNCs, the IPR legislation in the host country did not seem to be critical, except for the pharmaceutical industry, in locating R&D activities. Most of the R&D investments in India were made prior to its commitment to the WTO agreement.[16] The reasons for this seem to be twofold. First, the entire R&D for a product or process innovation did not take place in one location. Thus, each location had only the knowledge related to the portion related to it and such information without input and collaboration from units in other locations is not of much use for imitation. Second, in new technologies, the ability to copy and produce a product is not sufficient to be successful in business. The global marketing and distribution networks and the brand names, apart from technological-edge, have become equally important for entry into global markets. And these advantages rest with the TNCs, giving the global markets an oligopolistic characteristic.[17]

Another policy change in developing countries that has direct bearing on the location of TNCs' R&D activities has been the opening up of access to their national research institutes to foreign firms. Following a reduction in government financial support, the research institutes are now motivated to earn a portion of their budgets from enterprises, including foreign-owned ones.

Internal forces

To meet these external forces, TNCs have also carried out some internal changes within the corporate structure, which in turn acted as enabling factors for globalization. TNCs, including those dealing with conventional technologies, changed their earlier multi-domestic strategies and adopted methods to achieve global economies. TNCs rationalized their global operations, including their product lines, standardized parts design and specialized their manufacturing units. Such rationalization of internal operations of TNCs spurred globalization in a range of industries that included automobiles, office equipment, industrial bearings, construction equipment and machines tools (Bartlett and Ghoshal, 1991).

From the operational perspective of TNCs, the nature of demand and the increasing science base of new technologies are leading to homogenization of certain international markets and standardization of technologies for the global markets. At the same time, they are also generating wider variety and fragmentation in other markets (Granstrand *et al.*, 1992). This necessitates changing the traditional headquarters–subsidiary relationships into a global intra-organizational network-based management structure. The creation, exploitation and dissemination of new technology in a global organization require simultaneous achievement of efficiency, local responsiveness, and world-wide learning and know-how transfer. These management tasks will be the critical ones in the management of modern global corporations (Bartlett and Ghoshal, 1991).

According to Porter (1986a, 1986b), TNCs have been compelled to shift from a multidomestic approach, where each subsidiary was confined to servicing a local market, to a global strategy, where subsidiaries are assigned a specialized role to play in the developments planned and organized from the centre. This new role of subsidiaries may involve an increased emphasis on deriving distinctive new product variants as part of a regional or world product mandate, or if a unique 'global product' is envisaged, providing research input into its creation.

To achieve such results, companies have been developing more specific strategies, which Howells (1993) terms as 'global switching' and 'global focusing' for international innovation. In global switching, companies develop the ability to geographically 'switch' between sites in an integrated fashion on a global scale in terms of functional sequencing and link-ups. R&D or part of it, initial production scale-up, full production, component production, and market launch may be located in different countries, to exploit the different technical and other skills of various sites as well as the international compatibilities. Global focusing involves the spatial concentration of research, production and other key facilities specializing in a particular product or technology on a single or related set of sites in locations across the world.[18]

Product life cycle model and developing countries

The 'product life cycle' theory suggested by Vernon (1966) has had a profound influence on the studies concerning the internationalization of production activities. However, in recent years, especially in the light of globalization of R&D, the relevance of the model to the new global environment is increasingly being questioned.

The product life cycle model is based on the hypothesis that R&D activities are almost always carried out in the home country of the TNC. The reasons for this are: first, economies of scale are important in R&D activities and depending on their strength R&D may need to be concentrated in a single centre. Second, there are locational economies of integration involved in R&D activities. In the development of new products or processes, close interaction between R&D and manufacturing and customers is required. Third, innovation is perceived as a demand-led process, where the special demands of sophisticated consumers and skill-intensive downstream facilities in the home countries are seen as providing stimulus for innovation (Cantwell, 1995).

Based on the results of subsequent studies, the theory was criticized on the grounds that the changes in the behaviour of TNCs, due to internal pressures from well-established affiliates or external pressures from the host country governments, may lead to the compression of product cycle (Giddy, 1978), giving scope for near simultaneous occurrence of innovation in several major markets (Pearce, 1989).

In a later paper Vernon (1979) observed that there has been a considerable increase in the spread of the geographical network of TNCs' operations. As TNCs increasingly adopted a global approach, the spread of their operations increased, and the overall time lag between the introduction of a new product in the USA and its diffusion into other locations decreased dramatically. By the late 1970s, there had been a number of changes in Europe's macro environment, closing the gap between Europe and the USA. Moreover, the global standardization of a number of products, such as computers and pharmaceuticals, made the product cycle theory less applicable.

Using the US patent data for 100 years, which specifies the location of technological activity at the corporate level, Cantwell (1995) points out the weakness of the product life cycle's hypothesis concerning the location of R&D activities. Based on the data, he argues that even historically the model was not correct. The US electrical companies and European chemical companies had significantly internationalized their technological activity in the inter-war period. The data also indicate that, in recent years, the categories of industries internationalising their technological activities have further broadened, including a wider range of companies.

In the present context, the product life cycle theory is only relevant to the extent that the home countries of TNCs tend to be the location of a greater amount of technological activities, as the largest proportion of R&D expenditures are incurred there. However, the changes in the global environment have made it possible for the product cycle to start anywhere in the world in the corporate system. Today, the latest fashion or market need can emerge in other countries and the technologies to meet such demands may be located in some other country (Bartlett and Ghoshal, 1991). This implies that the initial phases of the product cycle can also be located in countries other than home base.

In today's business environment, products and processes designed at the corporate central laboratories in the home countries still have a substantial role to play, but innovations are also created by the affiliates abroad. TNCs are pooling the resources available at the corporate level and affiliates to find global solutions. Efficient manufacturing affiliates may be converted into 'international production centres' and the innovative R&D units of affiliates may be treated as 'world-wide centres of excellence' for a specific product or process development (Bartlett and Ghoshal, 1991).

Such technologically advanced activities are being located not only in industrialized countries, but also in several developing countries. The same factors that made Vernon concede the relevance of the model to the new global environment are applicable in the emerging developments also. Investment in science and technology education and industrial training gained through the activities of TNCs has resulted in a global workforce that can perform a range of technologically advanced activities once reserved for personnel in industrialized countries. The advances in telecommunication technologies are also permitting geographical delinking of R&D, manufacturing and marketing activities, effectively eroding the basis for keeping the initial phases of the product cycle in home countries.

In new technologies, the advantages of economies of scope have overcome the barriers of economies of scale arguments for decentralization of R&D. With the emergence of flexible manufacturing systems, the barriers of economies of scale are overcome even in the internationalization of production activities. The opportunities for developing countries to participate in international technology development and production activities arose mainly because of the onset of a new techno-economic paradigm.

In the field of electronics, cities such as Penang, Singapore and Taipei, which are situated far from the centres of technological breakthroughs and end-users in industrialized countries, have already emerged as global product-development centres. For instance, Motorola Inc.'s paging-device plant in Singapore employs seventy-five local engineers in a new building nicknamed the Motorola Innovation Centre. In this centre, the Scriptor pager was developed by the local industrial designers using locally developed software. Hewlett Packard's facilities in Penang, Malaysia, has been made into a global centre for many components used in the company's microwave products. The responsibility for computer hard disk drives is being shifted from Palo Alto to Penang. Hewlett Packard's plant in Singapore has become the global R&D and production centre for the company's portable ink-jet printers (*Business Week*, 19 December 1994a).

TNCs' higher-order R&D investments in developing countries negate the conventional views that some countries have the competence to perform only low-tech activities. Instead, the trend suggests that even in developing countries there are segments that can perform high-tech activities, given the resources. This does not imply that developing countries have achieved advanced technological capabilities equal to the industrialized countries. However, just as Vernon observed the developments in Europe that negated his product cycle theory, there are also changes taking place in some developing countries that make them conducive for the location of activities related to the initial phases of the product cycle. Typecasting all developing countries into one block or group obscures the progress achieved by some of them. Individual countries or sub-groups of developing countries differ widely from one another in several aspects.

Notes

1 The global business environment

1 This trend contradicts the earlier statement that product needs in different countries are becoming more similar. However, according to Porter (1986a), the market segmentation in recent years seems to be based less on national differences, and more on buyer differences that transcend country boundaries; differences such as demographics, user-industry, or income group. Many companies adopt global segmentation strategies in which they cater to a narrow segment of an industry world-wide, e.g. Daimler-Benz cars, Rolex watches, etc. (ibid., p. 44).
2 See De Meyer and Mizushima (1989) and also De Meyer (1993).
3 Even prior to such need for deliberate efforts towards globalization of R&D, partly through mergers and acquisitions, companies have already started performing some R&D outside their home countries, but mainly in other industrialized countries.
4 Ericsson recruits most of the engineering graduates from Stockholm's technical universities. But the supply of graduates, especially in software engineering, is not sufficient to meet its huge developmental requirements at home. So, it increasingly relies on its operations in the UK and the USA (Bartlett and Ghoshal, 1991, p. 90).

2 Globalization of corporate R&D: a conceptual framework

1 According to Terpstra (1977, p. 26) 'the last activity of the firm to be organized on an international basis – if it is at all – is R&D. Indeed, some multinationals do not conduct any R&D outside their home country.'
2 According to Levitt (1983, p. 93), global standardization is not limited to raw materials and high-tech products, but even products such as Coca-Cola and Pepsi Cola have successfully penetrated markets across 'multitudes of national, regional and ethnic taste buds trained to a variety of deeply ingrained local preferences of taste, flavour, consistency, effervescence, and aftertaste'.
3 The emergence of these generic technologies is often attributed to the onset of a new techno-economic paradigm, in turn associated with long-wave theory and the rise of the fifth Kondratieff wave (Kondratieff, 1935; Schumpeter, 1939).
4 Pearce (1991), Dörrenbächer and Wortmann (1991), Håkanson (1992) and Granstrand et al., (1992).
5 Also noted by Howells (1990).
6 Håkanson and Zander (1986), Pearce (1989), De Meyer and Mizushima (1989), Bartlett and Ghoshal (1991), Casson and Singh (1993).

7 The division of time periods should only be taken as approximate indications and not as precise cut-off dates.
8 Behrman and Fischer (1980).
9 See OECD (1988).
10 Mansfield *et al*. (1979).

3 The innovation environment in the developing world

1 Because of the labour intensity of R&D activities, the developing countries account for a higher proportion of personnel employed in such activities. For instance, in 1986, India employed 172,370 people in R&D activities and was ranked sixth as a global employer (UNESCO, 1987 and 1990, as given in Dunning 1992).
2 On the front page of a newly issued patent, the patent examiner lists any 'prior art' that led to, or borders, the new technology. These citations can be to the scientific literature, to other patents, or to other technologies. When an earlier patent is included as a citation on a new patent, it indicates that the earlier patented invention was important to the creation of the newly patented invention. When a previously patented invention receives many citations, that patent has probably led to many subsequent inventions and, more than likely, contained an important or seminal advance in its field.
3 Not all of them have faculties of science, engineering, medicine and agriculture.
4 NSTB (1985).

5 International corporate R&D in India: case studies and survey

1 A short paper based on these case studies was earlier published in Reddy (2000).
2 Also see Reddy and Sigurdson (1997) for an earlier version.
3 A short paper based on this survey was earlier published as Reddy (1997).
4 Ronstadt (1977) also in his study found that often the R&D functions performed by different types of units overlapped and also their functions evolved over time.
5 Westney (1988) stated that the links with the local S&T structure in the host country will be none at all in the case of TTUs, but some in the case of ITUs, stronger for GTUs and strongest for CTUs. Behrman and Fischer (1980) in their study of TTUs and ITUs found little diffusion of knowledge to the local economy through links. In the limited cases where such links were reported they were not of significance and were established as a matter of chance and confluence of interests, rather than the results of planning.

7 Implications for innovation capability in host countries

1 See Ronstadt (1977) also.
2 De Meyer and Mizushima (1989) also found the ability to build up a critical mass of local researchers as the most important criterion for selection of location, particularly for global technological research.
3 An OECD study (1988) found that the mismatch between the outputs of higher education and the needs of the industry are giving rise to shortages of research personnel throughout the OECD. In recent years, firms in the USA, Japan, the UK, Germany, Finland, The Netherlands, Sweden and other countries have reported

difficulties in recruiting research personnel in certain categories, especially in engineering fields related to electronics, automation and CAD/CAM. According to Håkanson (1990), for instance, two Sweden-based TNCs, ASEA and Ericsson, alone would require 150 per cent of all electronics engineers graduating in Sweden in a year. The problems are similar in other emerging areas such as biotechnology.

4 According to Granstrand *et al.* (1992), the availability of specialized biotech researchers is many times greater in India, with its conglomeration of knowledge activities in biotechnology and software, than in Sweden.

5 According to Granstrand *et al.* (1992), the total costs of R&D in India, with researchers having qualifications similar to those of their counterparts in Western countries, will be 1/10th of that in industrialized countries.

6 See OECD (1992) Chapter 10 Technology and Globalization, and Chapter 11 Technology and Competitiveness.

7 However, it should be noted here that some of the TNCs dealing with conventional technologies that are involved in ITU and RTU types of R&D activities have been exporting some of their products world-wide including OECD countries and former Eastern bloc countries. But the products involved are mainly based on technologies supplied by the parent firms rather than newly designed products. In that sense, even though they are involved in global exports, their R&D is not primarily oriented towards such markets.

8 For example, The Netherlands-based AKZO Chemicals, subcontracted R&D related to the development of a key ingredient for refining petroleum to the National Chemical Laboratories (NCL) in India. This product 'Zeolite' developed by NCL is being used by AKZO in its operations world-wide (*UNDP-World Development*, September 1991). Similarly the US-based Dupont entered into R&D collaboration with the Indian Institute for Chemical Technologies (IICT).

9 Perez and Soete (1988)'s life cycles of technology system involves four phases. (See the section on new technologies and catching up opportunities for latecomers for detailed discussion.)

10 According to Ernst and O'Connor (1989), the production systems in conventional technologies primarily require skills based on extensive 'learning by doing', whereas the skills required for new technologies can be more easily acquired through formal education and training systems.

11 Wortmann (1990) found that R&D activities of IBM, a new technology company, in Germany, are mainly related to global products and that the product manufacturing need not take place in the same country where R&D took place.

12 For example, one of the main features of ASICs is the decoupling of the semiconductor design technology from the manufacturing or fabrication technology. As a result of such decoupling, an independent design sector has emerged to service the downstream users of semiconductors. The emergence of electronic design automation (EDA) has removed the entry barriers into the design sector of integrated chips, opening up opportunities for the NIEs (Hobday, 1991).

13 See also Westney (1988).

14 To facilitate their R&D activities, TNCs are bringing in advanced design tools, process technology and quality control know-how to the developing host countries (*Business Week*, Special report, 30 November 1992b).

15 For example, Microsoft donated twenty-five PCs for a software training facility at Jiaotong College, Shanghai University, China, and Matsushita Electric provided machinery required for designing robots (*Business Week*, 19 December, 1994, p. 50).

16 A number of TNCs and local companies have sponsored the establishment of a training centre in Penang, Malaysia, to train local engineers in skills ranging from drafting and basic electronics to CAD and robotics (*Business Week*, Special report, 30 November 1992b).

17 See *Science* (1996) 26 January, pp. 442–3.

18 See *Business Line* (1996b).

19 See *Science* (1995a, p. 1419).

Conclusion

1 The TTU and ITU types of functions still predominate TNCs' R&D in developing countries. However, RTU, GTU and CTU types of functions are also spreading steadily.

2 During 1982–91 the R&D expenditures of parents of the US-based TNCs in the manufacturing sector increased by an annual average of 4.8 per cent in constant dollars from US\$ 36.5 billion to US\$ 50 billion. During the same period, the R&D expenditures of their affiliates abroad increased more rapidly at an annual average rate of 12.1 per cent from US\$ 3.5 billion to US\$ 7.2 billion, indicating that R&D has become more international. However, the total proportion of internationalized R&D by US-based TNCs remains small. In 1991, overseas R&D by US-based TNCs in the manufacturing sector accounted for 12.7 per cent of their total R&D expenditures, rising from 8.7 per cent in 1982 (OTA, 1994, pp. 85–6).

3 The shares of foreign R&D among Swedish, Swiss, British and Canadian firms range between 30 and 42 per cent (Cantwell, 1992; Patel and Pavitt, 1992).

4 While the adaptation (TTU) and local product development (ITU) continue to be the most prominent types of R&D being conducted in developing countries, the higher-order functions, such as product development for regional/global markets (RTU/GTU) and basic research (CTU) activities are also spreading rapidly.

5 See also Ronstadt (1977) and Behrman and Fischer (1980). In countries with small markets, research teams were sent from the headquarters on missions to provide technical support for adaptation, rather than establishing an R&D unit.

6 For example Nokia of Finland has become the second largest supplier of mobile telephones world-wide. Similarly, Samsung of South Korea became the first company in the world to develop a working prototype of the 256-megabit chip that will dominate the market by 2000 (*Business Week*, 19 December 1994, p. 23).

7 See also Hagedoorn and Schakenraad (1989) for the motives for technological alliances.

8 Some developing countries, such as India and Brazil, are characterised by dual segments. One small segment is technologically highly developed and exhibits complementary characteristics to the systems in the industrialized world and the other larger segment is highly under-developed and poor, making the whole country less developed. TNCs are attempting to utilize this advanced segment through R&D investments.

9 Also see *Business Week* (1994) The New Global Workforce – High-tech jobs all over the map. 19 December, pp. 42–7.

10 Astra Research Centre India was in fact established mainly because of the interest among the Indian researchers settled in the USA to return to India. For related detailed discussion see also *Science* (1993 pp. 346–67) and *Business Week* (1994) 'Technology and Manufacturing – High-tech Free Agents', 19 December, pp. 36–7.

11 See also Fusfeld (1995); *Business Week*, 30 November, 1992a, pp. 65–77; and *Business Week*, 19 December 1994, pp. 20–68 for related discussion and reports.

12 See also O'Reilly (1992) for more discussion on the implications of the availability of R&D personnel in non-OECD countries for industrial research.

13 For more details on developments in ICT and their implications for companies and countries see *Business Week* (1994) 'Technology & Manufacturing – In the Digital Derby, there is no inside lane', 19 December, pp. 20–6.

14 The cases presented earlier of AKZO Chemicals subcontracting R&D to National Chemical Laboratories, India, and the research collaboration between Glaxo and the Institute of Molecular and Cell Biology, Singapore, are good examples. Similarly, even the TNCs based in developing countries are also entering into research collaboration with universities abroad. The collaboration between United Microelectronics Corp. of Taiwan and Fudan University of China in VLSI chip designing is a good example of that.

15 Dörrenbächer and Wortmann (1991) note that in the generation of new technologies, the innovative potential in the overseas location does not necessarily have to be more advanced than the potential in the TNC's home country. Technology expertise can be complementary.

16 However, several pharmaceutical companies stated that they were waiting for the Indian government to amend the IPR legislation before making higher-order R&D investments in India. The Indian Patent Act of 1970 recognizes only the process and not the product in the pharmaceutical sector. Pending the amendment of the Act by the parliament, the Indian government has been giving a pipeline protection to the new drugs since 1995, through an ordinance.

17 See also Ernst and O'Connor (1989 and 1992).

18 The strategy of Japan-based TNCs is to categorize the global markets into four regions, the USA, Europe, Asia and Japan. The product development, production and sales are carried out in a co-ordinated manner for each region through regional management subsidiaries. Matsushita Electric has extended the 'four region' concept to the technological domain and has established R&D centres in North America and Taiwan. Similarly, Sony established a co-ordinated regional group structure in Singapore that is independent of Japan and encompassing R&D, component procurement, production, marketing, financing and personnel (Yamada, 1990).

Bibliography

Allen, T. J. (1977) *Managing the Flow of Technology*. Cambridge, MA: MIT Press.

Amsden, A. (1989) *Asia's Next Giant: South Korea and Late Industrialization*. New York: Oxford University Press.

Antonelli, C. (1984) *Cambiamento Tecnologico e Imprese Multinazionale: il Ruolo delle Reti Telematiche Nelle Strategie Globali*. Milano: Franco Angeli.

Bartlett, C. A. and Ghoshal, S. (1991) *Managing Across Borders: The Transnational Solution*. Boston, MA: Harvard Business School Press.

Behrman, J. N. and Fischer, W. A. (1980) *Overseas R&D Activities of Transnational Companies*. Cambridge, MA: Oelgeschlager, Gunn & Hain.

Berendsen, H., Grip, A. de. and Willems, E. (1995) 'The Future Labour Market for R&D Manpower in The Netherlands', *R&D Management*, Vol. 25, No. 3, pp. 299–307.

Bonin, B. and Perron, B. (1986) 'World Product Mandates and Firms Operating in Quebec', in H. Etemad and L. Séguin Dulude (eds) *Managing the Multinational Subsidiary*. London, Croom Helm. pp. 161–76.

Brainard, R. (1990) *Towards Technoglobalism: A Summary of the Tokyo TEP Conference*. Mimeo, Paris, Organisation for Economic Cooperation and Development.

Brash, D. T. (1966) *American Investment in Australian Industry*. Canberra, Australian National University Press.

Burstall, M. L., Dunning, J. H. and Lake, A. (1981) *Multinational Enterprises, Government and Technology: Pharmaceutical Industry*. Paris, Organisation for Economic Cooperation and Development.

Business Line (1996a) Internet edition, India, 30 January.

—— (1996b) 'BE, IISc to Develop Silicon Technology', 12 July, India.

Business Week (1992a) Special Report – 'Asia's High-Tech Quest: Can the Tigers Compete Worldwide?', 30 November, pp. 65–77.

—— (1992b) Special report, 'Hold that Tiger? Not for Long – High-Tech Teams are Benefiting Multinationals and Asia', 30 November.

—— (1994) '21st Century Capitalism – Part II: Technology and Manufacturing, The New Global Workforce, The Emerging Middle Class, and Where are We Going?' 19 December, pp. 20–68.

Cantwell, J. A. (1992) 'The Internationalisation of Technological Activity and its Implications for Competitiveness', in O. Granstrand, L. Håkanson and S. Sjölander (eds) *Technology Management and International Business: Internationalisation of R&D and Technology*. Chichester, John Wiley & Sons Ltd, pp. 75–95.

—— (1995) 'The Globalisation of Technology: What Remains of the Product Cycle Model?', *Cambridge Journal of Economics*, Vol. 19, No. 1, February, pp. 155–74.

—— (1998) 'The Globalization of Technology: What Remains of the Product-Cycle Model?', in A. Chandler, P. Hagstrom and O. Solvell (eds) *The Dynamic Firm*. New York, Oxford University Press, pp. 263–88.

Cantwell, J. and Janne, O. (1999) 'Technological Globalisation and Innovative Centres: The Role of Corporate Technological Leadership and Locational Hierarchy', *Research Policy*, Vol. 28, Nos. 2–3, pp. 119–44.

Casson, M. and Singh, S. (1993) 'Corporate Research and Development Strategies: The Influence of Firm, Industry and Country Factors on the Decentralisation of R&D', *R&D Management*, Vol. 23. No. 2, April, pp. 91–107.

Caves, R. E. (1971) 'International Corporation: The Industrial Economics of Foreign Investment', *Economica*, Vol. 38, February, pp. 1–27.

—— (1982) *Multinational Enterprise and Economic Analysis*. Cambridge, Cambridge University Press.

CEC (1989) *A Framework for Community RTD Actions in the 90s*. Discussion Document, Brussels, Commission of the European Communities.

Chatterji, D. and Manuel, T. A. (1993) 'Benefiting from External Sources of Technology', *Research. Technology Management*, Vol. 36, No. 6, November–December, pp. 21–6.

Chesnais, F. (1988/a) 'Multinational Enterprises and the International Diffusion of Technology', in G. Dosi, C. Freeman, R. Nelson, G. Silverberg and L. Soete (eds) *Technical Change and Economic Theory*. London and New York, Pinter Publishers, pp. 496–527.

—— (1988/b) 'Technical Cooperation Agreements between Firms', *STI Review* 4, pp. 51–119.

Cline, W. R. (1987) *Informatics and Development: Trade and Industrial Policy in Argentina, Brazil, and Mexico*. Washington, DC, Economics International Inc.

Communications International (1988) 'Part of a Larger Task', February, pp. 36–8.

Craemer, D. (1976) *Overseas Research and Development by United States Multinationals, 1966–1975: Estimates of Expenditures and a Statistical Profile*. New York, The Conference Board.

CSIR (1994) *Compilation and Analysis of Indian Patent Data*. Patents Unit, Technology Utilisation Division. New Delhi, Council of Scientific and Industrial Research (CSIR).

Dataquest (1994) 'The DQ Top 20', Vol. 2, 16–31 August, pp. 41–204.

De Meyer, A. (1993) 'Internationalizing R&D Improves a Firm's Technical Learning', *Research. Technology Management*, Vol. 36, No. 4. July–August, pp. 42–9.

De Meyer, A. and Mizushima, A. (1989) 'Global R&D Management', *R&D Management*, Vol. 19, No. 2, April, pp. 135–46.

Dollar, D. (1991) 'Convergence of South Korean Productivity on West German Levels – 1966–78', *World Development*, Vol. 19, Nos. 2/3, February–March. pp. 263–73.

Dörrenbächer, C. and Wortmann, M. (1991) 'The Internationalisation of Corporate Research and Development', *Intereconomics*, May–June, pp. 139–44.

Dowrick, S. and Gemmell, N. (1991) 'Industrialisation, Catching Up and Economic Growth: A Comparative Study Across the World's Capitalist Economies', *Economic Journal*, Vol. 101, March, pp. 263–75.

Doz, Y. (1987) 'International Industries: Fragmentation versus Globalization', in B. R. Guile and M. Brooks (eds) *Technology and Global Industry*. Washington, DC, National Academy Press.

Dunning, J. H. (1958) *American Investment in British Manufacturing Industry*. London, Allen and Unwin.

—— (1977) 'Trade, Location of Economic Activity and the Multinational Enterprise: A Search for an Eclectic Approach', in B. Ohlin, P. O. Hesselborn and P. M. Wijkman (eds) *The International Allocation of Economic Activity*. London, Macmillan, pp. 395–418.

—— (1980) 'Toward an Eclectic Theory of International Production: Some Empirical Tests', *Journal of International Business Studies*, Vol. 11, No. 1, Spring/Summer, pp. 9–31.

—— (1988) *Multinationals, Technology and Competitiveness*. London, Unwin Hyman.

—— (1992) 'Multinational Enterprises and the Globalisation of Innovatory Capacity', in O. Granstrand, L. Håkanson and S. Sjölander (eds) *Technology Management and International Business: Internationalisation of R&D and Technology*. Chichester: John Wiley & Sons Ltd, pp. 19–51.

DST (1984–85) *Research and Development Statistics 1984–85*. New Delhi, Department of Science and Technology, Government of India.

—— (1994) *Research and Development Statistics 1992–93*. New Delhi, Department of Science and Technology, Government of India.

EDB (1992) *Economic Development of Singapore: 1960 to 1991*. Singapore, Economic Development Board.

EPW (1995) 'Making Research Pay', *Economic and Political Weekly*, Vol. XXX, No. 26, July 1, p. 1539.

Ernst, D. and O'Connor, D. (1989) *Technology and Global Competition: The Challenge for Newly Industrialising Economies*. Development Centre Studies, Paris, Organisation for Economic Cooperation and Development.

—— (1992) *Competing in the Electronics Industry: The Experience of Newly Industrialising Economies*. Development Centre Studies, Paris, Organisation for Economic Cooperation and Development.

Finn, M. G. (1997) 'Stay Rates of Foreign Doctorate Recipients from U. S. Universities, 1995', Oak Ridge, TN: Oak Ridge Institute for Science and Education.

Forrest, J. E. and Martin, J. C. (1992) 'Strategic Alliances between Large and Small Research Intensive Organisations: Experiences in the Biotechnology Industry', *R&D Management*, Vol. 22, No. 1, pp. 41–53.

Freeman, C. (1982) *The Economics of Industrial Innovation*. 2nd edition, London, Frances Pinter Publishers.

—— (1994) 'Technological Revolutions and Catching-Up: ICT and the NICs', in

J. Fagerberg, B. Verspagen and N. V. Tunzelmann (eds) *The Dynamics of Technology, Trade and Growth*. Cheltenham, Edward Elgar.

Freeman, C. and Hagedoorn, J. (1994) 'Catching Up or Falling Behind: Patterns in International Interfirm Technology Partnering', *World Development*, Vol. 22, No. 5, May, pp. 771–80.

Freeman, C. and Perez, C. (1988) 'Structural Crises of Adjustment: Business Cycles and Investment Behaviour', in G. Dosi, C. Freeman, R. Nelson, G. Silverberg and L. Soete (eds) *Technical Change and Economic Theory*. London, Pinter Publishers. pp. 38–66.

Frobel, F., Heinrichs, J. and Kreye, O. (1980) *The New International Division of Labour: Structural Unemployment in Industrialized Countries and Industrialization in Developing Countries*. Cambridge, Cambridge University Press.

FTBR (1995) *India: Computers: India Joins the International Market*, 8 February. Financial Times Business Reports.

Fusfeld, H. I. (1986) *The Technical Enterprise, Present and Future Patterns*. Cambridge, MA, Ballinger.

—— (1994) *Industry's Future: Changing Patterns of Industrial Research*. Washington, DC, American Chemical Society.

—— (1995) 'New Global Sources of Industrial Research', *Technology in Society*, Vol. 17, No. 3, pp. 263–77.

Giddy, I. H. (1978) 'The Demise of the Product Cycle Model in International Business Theory', *Columbia Journal of World Business*, Vol. XIII, No. 1, pp. 90–7.

GOI (1987) *Studies on the Structure of the Industrial Economy: Report on Electronics*. Bureau of Industrial Costs and Prices, Ministry of Industry, New Delhi, Government of India.

Göransson, B. (1993) *Catching Up in Technology: Case Studies from the Telecommunications Equipment Industry*. London, Taylor Graham.

Granstrand, O., Håkanson, L. and Sjölander, S. (1992) 'Introduction and Overview', in O. Granstrand, L. Håkanson and S. Sjölander (eds) *Technology Management and International Business: Internationalisation of R&D and Technology*. Chichester, John Wiley & Sons, pp. 1–18.

—— (1993) 'Internationalisation of R&D – A Survey of Some Recent Research', *Research Policy*, Vol. 22, pp. 413–30.

Grieco, J. M. (1982) 'Between Dependency and Autonomy: India's Experience with the International Computer Industry', *International Organization*, Vol. 36, No. 3, Summer, pp. 609–32.

Hagedoorn, J. (1995) 'Strategic Technology Partnering During the 1980s: Trends, Networks and Corporate Patterns in Non-Core Technologies', *Research Policy*, Vol. 24, pp. 207–31.

Hagedoorn, J. and Schakenraad, J. (1989) 'Strategic Partnering and Technological Cooperation', in B Dankbar, B. Groenewegen and H. Schenk (eds) *Perspectives in Industrial Economics*. Dordrecht, Kluwer, pp. 3–37.

—— (1990) 'Inter-firm Partnerships and Cooperative Strategies in Core Technologies', in C. Freeman and L. Soete (eds) *New Explorations in the Economics of Technical Change*, London and New York, Pinter Publishers.

—— (1993) 'Strategic Technology Partnering and International Corporate Strategies', in K. Hughes (ed.) *European Competitiveness*. Cambridge, Cambridge University Press, pp. 60–86.

Håkanson, L. (1990) 'International Decentralisation of R&D – The Organisational Challenges', in C. A. Bartlett, Y. Doz and G. Hedlund (eds) *Managing the Global Firm*. Routledge, London and New York, pp. 257–77.

—— (1992) 'Locational Determinants of Foreign R&D in Swedish Multinationals', in O. Granstrand, L. Håkanson and S. Sjölander (eds) *Technology Management and International Business: Internationalisation of R&D and Technology*. Chichester, John Wiley & Sons Ltd, pp. 97–115.

Håkanson, L. and Zander, U. (1986) *Managing International Research and Development*. Stockholm, Mekanforbund.

Hamel, G. (1991) 'Competition for Competence and Inter-Partner Learning within International Strategic Alliances', *Strategic Management Journal*, Vol. 12, pp. 83–103.

Hanna, N. (1994) *Exploiting Information Technology for Development – A Case Study of India*. Discussion Paper No. 246. Washington, DC, The World Bank.

Heeks, R. (1995) 'Import Liberalisation and Development of Indian Computer Industry', *Economic and Political Weekly*, Vol. XXX, No. 34, August 26, pp. M82–93.

Hladik, K. (1985) *International Joint Ventures – an Economic Analysis of U.S.-Foreign Business Partnerships*. Lexington, MA, Lexington Books.

Hobday, M. (1991) 'Semiconductor Technology and the Newly Industrializing Countries: The Diffusion of ASICs (Application Specific Integrated Circuits)', *World Development*, Vol. 19, No. 4. April, pp. 375–97.

—— (1995) *Innovation in East Asia: The Challenge to Japan*. Cheltenham, Edward Elgar.

Hood, N. and Young, S. (1982) 'US Multinational R&D: Corporate Strategies and Policy Implications for the UK', *Multinational Business*, Vol. 2, pp. 10–23.

Horst, H. T. (1978) *A Home Abroad: A Study of Domestic and Foreign Operation of the American Food Processing Industry*. Cambridge, MA, Ballinger Publishing Co.

Howells, J. R. (1990) 'The Internationalisation of R&D and the Development of Global Research Networks', *Regional Studies*, Vol. 24, No. 6, pp. 495–512.

—— (1993) 'Emerging Global Strategies in Innovation Management', in M. Humbert (ed.) *The Impact of Globalisation on Europe's Firms and Industries*. London and New York, Pinter Publishers.

—— (1995) 'Going Global: The Use of ICT Networks in Research and Development', *Research Policy*, Vol. 24, pp. 169–84.

Hutnik, I. (1988) 'Design and Manufacture', *Computers Today*, January, pp. 54–63.

Hymer, S. (1972) 'United States Investment Abroad', in P. Drysdale (ed.) *Direct Foreign Investment in Asia and the Pacific*. Canberra, Australian National University Press.

—— (1976) *International Operations of National Firms: A Study of Direct Foreign Investment*. Cambridge, MA, MIT Press.

IDC (1987) *Directions '88, Vol. I and II*. New Delhi, International Data Corporation.

IDRC (1995) *In Person – Profiles of Researchers in Africa, Asia, and the Americas*. Ottawa, Canada, International Development Research Centre.

Jaikumar, V. M. and Hutnik, I. (1988) 'The State of Manufacturing – Made in India', *Computers Today*, January, pp. 36–53.

Jansson, H. (1982) *Interfirm Linkages in a Developing Economy: The Case of Swedish Firms in India*. Upsala, Acta Universitatis Upsaliensis, Studia Oeconomiae Negotiorum 14.

Kim, L. (1989) 'Korea's National System for Industrial Innovation'. Paper prepared for the National Technical System Conference at the University of Limburg in Maastricht, The Netherlands, 3–4 November.

Kindleberger, C. P. (1969) *American Business Abroad: Six Lectures on Direct Investment*. New Haven, CT, Yale University Press.

Kogut, B. (1988) 'Joint Ventures: Theoretical and Empirical Perspectives', *Strategic Management Journal*, Vol. 9, pp. 312–32.

Kondratieff, N. (1935) 'The Long Waves in Economic Life', *Review of Economics and Statistics*, Vol. 17, pp. 101–15.

Korea Business World (1989) December.

Kuemmerle, W. (1999) 'Foreign Direct Investment in Industrial Research in the Pharmaceutical and Electronics Industries – Results from a Survey of Multinational Firms', *Research Policy*, Vol. 28, Nos. 2–3, pp. 179–93.

Lall, S. (1979) 'The International Allocation of Research Activity by US Multinationals', *Oxford Bulletin of Economics and Statistics*, Vol. 41, No. 4, pp. 313–31.

LAREA/CEREM (1986) *Les Stratégies d'accords des Groupes Européens entre la Cohésion et l'éclatement*. Nanterre, Université de Paris-X.

Levitt, T. (1983) 'The Globalization of Markets', *Harvard Business Review*, May–June, pp. 92–102.

Liang, W. W. and Denny, W. M. (1995) 'Upgrading Hong Kong's Technology Base', in D. F. Simon (ed.) *The Emerging Technological Trajectory of the Pacific Rim*. New York, M. E. Sharpe Inc., pp. 256–74.

Liebenau, J. (1984) 'International R&D in Pharmaceutical Firms in the Early Twentieth Century', *Business History*, Vol. 26, pp. 329–46.

Lim, Y. (1992) 'Export-Led Industrialisation: The Key Policy for Successful Development?', Global Issues and Policy Analysis Branch, UNIDO. Paper prepared for Wilton Park Conference, London, 14–18 December.

Long, F. A. (1988) 'Science, Technology and Industrial Development in India', *Technology In Society*, Vol. 10, pp. 395–416.

Mansfield, E. (1974) 'Technology and Technical Changes', in J. H. Dunning (ed.) *Economic Analysis and the Multinational Enterprise*. London, George Allen and Unwin.

Mansfield, E., Teece, D. and Romeo, A. (1979) 'Overseas Research and Development by US-Based Firms', *Economica*, Vol. 46, pp. 187–96.

Martin, T. (1994) 'The World Economy in Charts', *Fortune*, 25 July.

Menzler-Hokkanen, I. (1995) 'Multinational Enterprises and Technology Transfer', *International Journal of Technology Management. Special Issue on the Management of International Intellectual Property*, Vol. 10, Nos. 2/3, pp. 293–310.

Michalet, C. A. and Delapierre, M. (1978) *The Impact of Multinational Enterprises on National Scientific and Technological Capacities in the Computer Industry*, Mimeo, Paris, Organisation for Economic Cooperation and Development.

MOST (1993) *Science and Technology in Korea*. Seoul, Ministry of Science and Technology.

Mowery, D. C. (1992) 'International Collaborative Ventures and US Firms' Technology Strategies', in O. Granstrand, L. Håkanson and S. Sjölander (eds) *Technology Management and International Business: Internationalisation of R&D and Technology*. Chichester, John Wiley & Sons Ltd, pp. 209–49.

Mowery, D. C., Oxley, J. E. and Silverman, B. S. (1998) 'Technological Overlap and Interfirm Cooperation: Implications for the Resource-Based View of the Firm', *Research Policy*, Vol. 27, pp. 507–23.

Mytelka, L. K. (1990) 'New Modes of International Competition: The Case of Strategic Partnering in R&D', *Science and Public Policy*, Vol. 17, No. 5, October. pp. 296–302.

—— (1991) *Strategic Partnerships and the World Economy*. London, Pinter.

—— (1993) 'Rethinking Development: A Role for Innovation in the Other "Two Thirds"', *Futures*, Vol. 25, No. 6, pp. 694–712.

NEDO (1973) *Innovative Activity in the Pharmaceutical Industry*. Pharmaceuticals Working Party, Chemicals Economic Development Committee, London, National Economic Development Office.

News Week (1993) 'Hacking for Hire', 18 January, pp. 32–3.

Niosi, J. (1995) *Flexible Innovation: Technological Alliance in Canadian Industry*. Montreal and Kingston, McGill-Queen's University Press.

—— (1999) 'Introduction – The Internationalization of Industrial R&D: From Technology Transfer to the Learning Organization', *Research Policy*, Vol. 28, Nos. 2–3, pp. 107–17.

NSB (1998) *Science and Engineering Indicators: 1998*. National Science Board, NSB 98–1, Arlington, VA: National Science Foundation.

NSF (1995) *Asia's New High-Tech Competitors*. Arlington, VA, National Science Foundation, NSF 95–309.

—— (1996) *Selected Data on Science and Engineering Doctoral Awards: 1995*. Arlington, VA, National Science Foundation, NSF 96–303.

NSTB (1991) *Science and Technology: Windows of Opportunity*. National Technology Plan. Singapore, National Science and Technology Board.

—— (1995) *Corporate Profile NSTB: The Singapore National Science and Technology Board: Building a Bridge to the Future*, Singapore, National Science and Technology Board.

—— (1996) *National Survey of R&D in Singapore: 1995*. Singapore, National Science and Technology Board.

O'Connor, D. (1995) 'Technology and Industrial Development in the Asian NIEs: Past Performance and Future Prospects', in D. F. Simon (ed.) *The Emerging Technological Trajectory of the Pacific Rim*. New York, M. E. Sharpe Inc.

Odagiri, H. and Yasuda, H. (1993) 'The Overseas R&D Activities of Japanese Firms'. Paper prepared for the conference on innovation in Japan, Oiso, Kanagawa, Japan, 18–20 September.

—— (1996) 'The Determinants of Overseas R&D by Japanese Firms: An Empirical Study at the Industry and Company Levels', *Research Policy*, Vol. 25, pp. 1059–79.

192 *Bibliography*

OECD (1988) *Science and Technology Policy Outlook 1988*. Paris, Organisation for Economic Cooperation and Development.

—— (1991) *Technology in a Changing World*. Paris, Organisation for Economic Cooperation and Development.

—— (1992) *Technology and the Economy: The Key Relationships*. Paris, Organisation for Economic Cooperation and Development.

—— (1994) *Science and Technology Policy: Review and Outlook*. Paris, Organisation for Economic Cooperation and Development.

O'Reilly, B. (1992) 'Your New Global Workforce', *Fortune*, 14 December.

OTA (1994) *Multinationals and the U.S. Technology Base: Final Report of the Multinationals Project*. U.S. Congress, Office of Technology Assessment. OTA-ITE-612, Washington, DC, U.S. Government Printing Office, September.

Patel, P. and Pavitt, K. (1992) 'Large Firms in the Production of the World's Technology: An Important Case of Non-Globalisation', in O. Granstrand, L. Håkanson and S. Sjölander (eds) *Technology Management and International Business: Internationalisation of R&D and Technology*. Chichester, John Wiley & Sons Ltd, pp. 53–74.

Pearce, R. D. (1989) *The Internationalisation of Research and Development by Multinational Enterprises*. London, Macmillan.

—— (1991) 'The Globalization of R&D by TNCs', *The CTC Reporter*, No. 31 (Spring), pp. 13–6.

—— (1999) 'Decentralised R&D and Strategic Competitiveness: Globalised Approaches to Generation and Use of Technology in Multinational Enterprises (MNEs)', *Research Policy*, Vol. 28, Nos. 2–3, pp. 151–78.

Perez, C. (1988) 'New Technologies and Development', in C. Freeman and B-Å. Lundvall (eds) *Small Countries Facing the Technological Revolution*. London, Frances Pinter.

Perez, C. and Soete, L. (1988) 'Catching up in Technology: Entry Barriers and Windows of Opportunity', in G. Dosi, C. Freeman, R. Nelson, G. Silverberg and L. Soete (eds) *Technical Change and Economic Theory*. London and New York, Pinter Publishers, pp. 458–79.

Petrella, R. (1992) 'Internationalisation, Multinationalisation and Globalisation of R&D: Toward a New Division of Labour in Science and Technology?', *Knowledge and Policy*, Vol. 5. No. 3, Fall, pp. 3–25.

Porter, M. E. (1980) *Competitive Strategy: Techniques for Analyzing Industries and Competitors*. New York and London, The Free Press.

—— (1986a) 'Introduction and Summary' and 'Competition in Global Industries: A Conceptual Framework', in M. E. Porter (ed.) *Competition in Global Industries*. Boston, MA, Harvard Business School Press, pp.1–11, 15–60.

—— (1986b) 'Changing Patterns of International Competition', *California Management Review*, Vol. XXVIII, No. 2, pp. 9–40.

—— (1990) 'The Competitive Advantage of Nations', *Harvard Business Review*, March–April, pp. 73–93.

Poynter, T. A. and Rugman, A. M. (1982) 'World Product Mandates: How Will Multinationals Respond?', *Business Quarterly*, Vol. 47, No. 3, pp. 54–61.

Ramachandran, J. (1991) 'Strongly Goal-Oriented Biomedical Research – Astra Research Centre India', *Current Science*, Vol. 60, Nos. 9 and 10, 25 May, pp. 533–6.

Raman, R. (1993) 'Grey Galore', *Dataquest*, May. pp. 90–2.

Reddy, P. (1991) *Technology Transfer Among Developing Countries: The Case of Technology Flow from India*. Research Policy Studies, Discussion Paper No. 188. Research Policy Institute, Sweden, Lund University.

—— (1993) 'Emerging Patterns of Internationalisation of Corporate R&D: Opportunities for Developing Countries?', in C. Brundenius and B. Göransson (eds) *New Technologies and Global Restructuring: The Third World at a Crossroads*. London, Taylor Graham.

—— (1994) *New Trends of Locating Corporate R&D in Developing and East European Countries by Transnational Corporations and Their Implications*. Vienna, United Nations Industrial Development Organisation (UNIDO), ITPD.13 (SPEC.).

—— (1997) 'New Trends in Globalization of Corporate R&D and Implications for Innovation Capability in Host Countries: A Survey from India', *World Development*, Vol. 25, No. 11, November, pp. 1821–37.

—— (2000) 'Emerging Patterns of Globalization of Corporate R&D and Implications for Innovation Capacity in Host Countries', in P. Conceicao, D. Gibson, M. V. Heitor, and S. Shariq (eds) *Science, Technology and Innovation Policy: Opportunities and Challenges for the 21st Century*. Westport, Connecticut and London, Quorum Books.

Reddy, A. S. P. and Sigurdson, J. (1994) 'Emerging Patterns of Globalisation of Corporate R&D and Scope for Innovation Capability Building in Developing Countries?', *Science and Public Policy*, Vol. 21, No. 5. October, pp. 283–94.

Reddy, P. and Sigurdson, J. (1997) 'Strategic Location of R&D and Emerging Patterns of Globalisation: The Case of Astra Research Centre India', *International Journal of Technology Management*, Vol. 14, Nos. 2/3/4, pp. 344–61.

Reuber, G. L. *et al.* (1973) *Private Foreign Investment in Development*. Oxford, Clarendon Press.

Ronstadt, R. (1977) *Research and Development Abroad by US Multinationals*. New York, Praeger Publishers.

—— (1984) 'R&D Abroad by US Multinationals', in R. Stobaugh and C. Wells, Jr. (eds) *Technology Crossing Borders*. Boston, MA, Harvard Business School Press, Boston.

Safarian, A. E. (1966) *Foreign Ownership of Canadian Industry*. Toronto, McGraw-Hill of Canada.

Sampath, K. (1990) 'Astra Research Centre India: A Unique Experiment in Strategic Collaboration', *BioSpectra*, November–December, pp. 13–16.

Schoenberger, E. (1988) 'Multinational Corporations and the New International Division of Labour: A Critical Appraisal', *Inst. Reg. Sci. Rev.* 11, pp. 105–19.

Schumpeter, J. A. (1939) *Business Cycles: A Theoretical, Historical and Statistical Analysis of the Capitalist Process*. London, McGraw-Hill.

Schware, R. (1987) 'Software Industry Development in the Third World: Policy Guidelines, Institutional Options and Constraints', *World Development*, Vol. 15, Nos. 10/11, pp. 1249–67.

Science (1993) 'Science in Asia', Vol. 262. 15 October, pp. 345–81.

—— (1995a) 'Joint Research – India Cracks Whip to End Addiction to State Funds', Vol. 267, 10 March, pp. 1419–20.

—— (1995b) 'Science in China: A Great Leap Forward', Vol. 270, 17 November, pp. 1131–54.

—— (1996) 'India – Industrial R&D Gets Boost Despite Lack of Patent Reform', Vol. 271, 26 January, pp. 442–3.

Shekhar, C. (1988) 'The Truth of the Matter', *Computers Today*, January, pp. 64–6.

Shetty, A. (1991) 'SCI-TECH: Astra Research Centre – Straining for Success', *The Economic Times, India*. 28 September, p. 9.

Sigurdson, J. (1990) 'The Internationalisation of R&D: An Interpretation of Forces and Responses', in J. Sigurdson (ed.) *Measuring The Dynamics of Technological Change*. London and New York, Pinter Publishers.

Sikka, P. (1990) 'Forty Years of Indian Science', *Science and Public Policy*, Vol. 17, No. 1, February, pp. 45–53.

Simon, D. F. (1995) 'Introduction', in D. F. Simon (ed.) *The Emerging Technological Trajectory of the Pacific Rim*. New York, M. E. Sharpe Inc., pp. xi–xx.

Singh, A. (1995) 'IITs Yesterday and Tomorrow', *Economic and Political Weekly*, Vol. XXX, No. 38, 23 September, pp. 2389–94.

Soete, L. (1983) 'Long Cycles and the International Diffusion of Technology'. Paper presented at the International Seminar on Innovation, Design and Long Waves in Economic Development, Royal College of Art, London.

—— (1985) 'International Diffusion of Technology, Industrial Development and Technological Leapfrogging', *World Development*, Vol. 13, No. 3, March, pp. 409–22.

Soete, L. and Dosi, G. (1983) *Technology and Employment in the Electronics Industry*. London, Frances Pinter.

Stubenitsky, F. (1970) *American Direct Investment in the Netherlands Industry*. Rotterdam, Rotterdam University Press.

Subramanian, C. R. (1992) *India and the Computer*. New Delhi, Oxford University Press.

Swinbanks, D. (1992) 'More Yen for Japan's University Research System', *Research. Technology. Management*, Vol. 35, pp. 3–4.

—— (1993) 'What Road Ahead for Korean Science and Technology?', *Nature*, Vol. 364, July, pp. 377–84.

Tandon, A. *et al.* (1991) 'Export or Perish?', *Dataquest*, September, pp. 63–76.

Teece, D. J. (1982) 'Towards an economic theory of the multiproduct firm', *Journal of Economic Behaviour and Organization*, Vol. 3, pp. 39–63.

—— (1992) 'Competition, Cooperation, and Innovation: Organizational Arrangements for Regimes of Rapid Technological Progress', *Journal of Economic Behaviour and Organization*, Vol. 18, pp. 1–25.

Terpstra, V. (1977) 'International Product Policy: The Role of Foreign R&D', *Columbia Journal of World Business*, Vol. 12, pp. 24–32.

Teubal, M. (1982) *Some Notes on the Accumulation of Intangibles by High Technology Firms*. Mimeo, as cited in L. Soete (1985), 'International Diffusion of Technology, Industrial Development and Technological Leapfrogging', *World Development*, Vol. 13, No. 3, March, pp. 409–22.

UNCTAD (1995) *World Investment Report 1995*. United Nations Conference on Trade and Development. New York and Geneva, United Nations.

—— (1998) *World Investment Report 1998*. United Nations Conference on Trade and Development. New York and Geneva, United Nations.

UNDP (1991) 'Looking South for Answers: The Developing World is Offering Solutions to Many Global Problems', *UNDP-World Development* Vol. 4, No. 5. September.

UNESCO (1987) *Statistical Year Book*. Paris, United Nations Education, Social and Cultural Organisation.

—— (1990) *Statistical Year Book*. Paris, United Nations Education, Social and Cultural Organisation.

—— (1992) *Statistical Year Book*. Paris, United Nations Education, Social and Cultural Organisation.

—— (1994) *Statistical Year Book*. Paris, United Nations Education, Social and Cultural Organization.

—— (1997) *Statistical Year Book*. Paris, United Nations Education, Social and Cultural Organisation.

US Tariff Commission (1973) *Implications of Multinational Firms for World Trade and Investment and for US Trade and Labor*. Washington, DC, Government Printing Office.

Vernon, R. (1966) 'International Investment and International Trade in the Product Cycle', *Quarterly Journal of Economics*, Vol. 88, pp. 190–207.

—— (1974) 'The Location of Industry' in J. H. Dunning (ed.) *Economic Analysis and the Multinational Enterprise*. London, Allen and Unwin, pp. 89–114.

—— (1979) 'The Product Cycle Hypothesis in a New International Environment', *Oxford Bulletin of Economics and Statistics*, Vol. 41, No. 4, pp. 255–67.

Vogel, E. F. (1991) *The Four Little Dragons: The Spread of Industrialization in East Asia*. Cambridge, MA, Harvard University Press.

Vonortas, N. S. (1989) 'Economic Interdependence Among Developed Market Economies and Multinational Enterprises', in H. I. Fusfeld (ed.) *Background Papers for Conference on Changing Global Patterns for Industrial R&D*. Troy, New York, Centre for Science and Technology Policy, Rensselaer Polytechnic Institute.

Vonortas, N. S. and Safioleas, S. P. (1997) 'Strategic Alliances in Information Technology and Developing Country Firms: Recent Evidence', *World Development*, Vol. 25, No. 5, pp. 657–80.

Westney, D. E. (1988) *International and External Linkages in the MNC: The Case of R&D Subsidiaries in Japan*. Working Paper Y No. 1973–88, Massachusetts, Sloan School of Management, MIT.

Williamson, O. E. (1981) 'The Modern Corporation: Origins, Evolution, Attributes', *Journal of Economic Literature*, Vol. XIX, pp. 1537–68.

Wong, P. K. (1995) 'Singapore's Technology Strategy', in D. F. Simon (ed.) *The Emerging Technological Trajectory of the Pacific Rim*. New York, M. E. Sharpe Inc., pp. 103–31.

World Bank (1987) *India: Development of the Electronics Industyr: A Sector Report*. No. 6781-IN, Washington, DC, World Bank.

Wortmann, M. (1990) 'Multinationals and the Internationalisation of R&D: New Developments in German Companies', *Research Policy*, Vol. 19, pp. 175–83.

Yamada, B. (1990) *Internationalisation Strategies of Japanese Electronics Companies: Implications for Asian Newly Industrialising Economies (NIEs)*. Paris, Organisation for Economic Cooperation and Development (OECD).

Yu, S. (1995) 'Korea's High-Technology Thrust', in D. F. Simon (ed.) *The Emerging Technological Trajectory of the Pacific Rim*. New York, M. E. Sharpe Inc., pp. 81–102.

Yuan, Z. (1995) 'Reform and Restructuring of China's Science and Technology System', in D. F. Simon (ed.) *The Emerging Technological Trajectory of the Pacific Rim*. New York, M. E. Sharpe Inc., pp. 213–38.

Zander, I. (1994) *The Tortoise Evolution of the Multinational Corporation: Foreign Technological Activity in Swedish Multinational Firms 1890–1990*. Stockholm, Institute of International Business, Stockholm School of Economics.

Index

DATE DUE